Blue Angels

BLUE ANGELS

YENKO/SC

GOODYEAR WIDE TREAD GT

COPO

CAMARO, CHEVELLE & NOVA

INCLUDES
CORVAIR & VEGA

MATT AVERY

CHEVROLET'S
Ultimate
MUSCLE CARS

CarTech®

CarTech®, Inc.
838 Lake Street South
Forest Lake, MN 55025
Phone: 651-277-1200 or 800-551-4754
Fax: 651-277-1203
www.cartechbooks.com

Edit by Paul Johnson
Layout by Monica Seiberlich

ISBN 978-1-61325-391-5
Item No. CT620

Library of Congress Cataloging-in-Publication Data
Names: Avery, Matthew, author.
Title: COPO Camaro, Chevelle, and Nova : Chevrolet's ultimate muscle cars / Matthew Avery.
Description: Forest Lake, MN : CarTech Books, [2018] | Includes index.
Identifiers: LCCN 2018006993 | ISBN 9781613253915
Subjects: LCSH: Chevrolet automobile–History. | Muscle cars–United States–History.
Classification: LCC TL215.C5 A94 2018 | DDC 629.222–dc23
LC record available at https://lccn.loc.gov/2018006993

Written, edited, and designed in the U.S.A.
Printed in China
10 9 8 7 6 5 4 3 2

CarTech books may be purchased at a discounted rate in bulk for resale, events, corporate gifts, or educational purposes. Special editions may also be created to specification.
For details, contact Special Sales at 838 Lake Street S., Forest Lake MN 55025 or by email at sales@cartechbooks.com.

Publisher's note:
Some of the vintage photos in this book are of lower quality. They have been included because of their importance to telling the story.

DISTRIBUTION BY:

Europe
PGUK
63 Hatton Garden
London EC1N 8LE, England
Phone: 020 7061 1980 • Fax: 020 7242 3725
www.pguk.co.uk

Australia
Renniks Publications Ltd.
3/37-39 Green Street
Banksmeadow, NSW 2109, Australia
Phone: 2 9695 7055 • Fax: 2 9695 7355
www.renniks.com

Canada
Login Canada
300 Saulteaux Crescent
Winnipeg, MB, R3J 3T2 Canada
Phone: 800 665 1148 • Fax: 800 665 0103
www.lb.ca

TABLE OF CONTENTS

DEDICATION

To my friend, mentor, guide, and coach, George Kiebala. You've pushed me to excellence in all that I do, and your love of cars, people, and life has truly been an inspiration. For all that you've done, thank you, George.

ACKNOWLEDGMENTS

Telling this story was a massive undertaking, only made possible through the collective effort of many different individuals contributing to its success. The greatest thanks go to my beautiful wife, Becca. Her enduring patience, support, and understanding have been integral throughout this long and arduous journey. She went above and beyond, attending many of the field assignments and on-location photoshoots, lending a hand and ensuring they went off without a hitch. Thank you, love.

I have to say a special thanks to my team of primary technical advisors. There would be no COPO story without Ed Cunneen, who was at the forefront of preserving these cars decades before anyone knew of their provenance or significance. Ed has worked tirelessly to save them and their stories, being so generous to me with his time, knowledge, and many years' worth of research and data, all of which was critical to the success of this project. Brian Henderson, of the Super Car Workshop, lent his top-notch insight, expertise, and real-world knowledge of the assembly of these cars. Many of the gorgeous vehicles profiled in this book were restored in Brian's shop and are certainly the benchmark by which all others are measured. Joe Barr, my lead Yenko historian, shared his world-class library and collection of memorabilia, granting me unparalleled access to his treasure trove of history. Phil Borris, my specialist for the 1970 ½ Camaro, gave great insight and documentation of these seldom spotlighted but very important vehicles. All of these experts deserve so much credit for lending long hours reviewing, consulting, and discussing, ensuring the extreme accuracy of my material.

Mark Pieloch, Ed Dedick, and Jerry Frye deserve a special thank you. Even after enduring one of the worst hurricanes to ever hit Florida's coast, the guys did all they could to make my visit to Mark's fantastic American Muscle Car Museum a priority, allowing me to keep on schedule. David Boland also deserves a special thanks. He, too, was quick to regroup from the hurricane, making my visit to see him and his collection a priority.

Thank you to: Dennis Albaugh and Andy Snetselaar, for granting access to Dennis's world-class collection of cars. To Stefano Bimbi of Nickey Performance, for helping talk through the organization of the project and connecting me to more than a few car owners. To Dru Diesner, who came through in the clutch on more than one occasion, lending his time and connections to help me, and the project, out. To all the wonderful car owners who allowed me to come out and document and photograph their cars. To Curt Collins, manager at Chevrolet Performance, COPO, and Performance Parts Licensing, and Mike Lawrence, plant manager at the COPO Build Center, who graciously granted access to their wonderful and high-tech facility, giving me a behind-the-scenes tour and full download of the COPO-transformation process. Thanks also to John Tinberg and Marlin Spotts Jr.

I wanted this project to be authoritative and historically accurate but still interesting to read and fun to look at. As such, I scoured the country for unique and creative locations for vehicle photoshoots. Special thanks in particular go to the Valiant Air Command Warbird Museum in Titusville, Florida, for allowing exclusive access to some of its incredible collection and a big thank you to its wonderful staff for helping with the setups.

Paul Johnson kept me on track every step of the way and a big thanks goes to him and his team for seeing my vision and helping carry it out. Other thanks go to Eddie and Donna Martin, for being so accommodating; Mark and Chris Riggsby, for taking my efforts to new heights and landing a cool photoshoot with Mark's Nova; and to Fred Eggers, for the keen editing eye. Thank you to Christo Datini, lead archivist at the GM Heritage Center, for sharing insider corporate documents and historical image access. Thanks to Diego Rosenberg and Rocky Rotella, who were both an open book about the writing process, lending valuable insight and help from their own experience.

And finally, it's not lost on me that I've been blessed with talents and abilities that could only have come from God, and I'm so grateful to Him for allowing me to pursue and enjoy my passion for automobiles.

INTRODUCTION

A loophole. A backdoor. A grey area. In a word: *COPO*. I am specifically referring to the COPO muscle cars of the 1960s and early 1970s that, officially, never should have been. These cars were built as a workaround to skirt strict corporate mandates banning their very existence. Grisly racing tragedies and negative press from too-fast highway incidents gave strong indications that building COPOs, or similar vehicles, would be tough, if not impossible. Chevrolet controlled the new-car marketplace and pushing race cars was a dangerous game. If Chevrolet continued to grow, the government was threatening to intervene.

But thanks to a culture where competition was king, street image mattered, and going fast moved inventory, COPO cars were quietly slipped out of factories and let loose on strips and streets. Despite being ground-pounding race cars through and through, they were amazingly available for sale at local dealerships, parked next to pickups and compacts. It was all a wild ruse, but it worked. Dreamed up and driven by a collaboration of diehard leadfoots and passionate office insiders, these legendary race-ready automobiles still stir hearts and souls today. You've certainly heard of the models Camaro, Chevelle, and Nova; when these street icons were given some COPO muscle magic, they became nothing short of motoring legends.

COPO: What Was It?

COPO is an acronym that stands for Central Office Production Order. It was Chevrolet's process of handling special, out-of-the-ordinary circumstances for new vehicle orders. A 1968 internal Chevrolet Introductory Sheet initiating the engineering center staff to COPO defined it as: A Central Office Production Order is the medium employed in the issuance of a specification for a given type of equipment being furnished on special order to a customer whose specifications requirements differ from those normally furnished for basic production, or a combination of basic production together with equipment furnished as a regular production option.

According to the GM Heritage Center's lead archivist, Christo Datini, COPO was established in the years following World War II. It was essentially a ticket submitted for a special request that was directed to GM's Central Office in Detroit. The primary use was for fleet vehicle sales, such as taxi companies, telephone companies, police departments, trucking firms, municipalities, and the like. Vehicles used in these applications could be specced with such components as heavy-duty suspensions or stain-proof interiors to make them better suited for the extended use and abuse they were sure to encounter in their daily travels.

RPO Versus COPO

During the 1960s, Chevy employed a regular production option (RPO) structure to its new car ordering system. In this structure, a base vehicle would be offered and then any available option that could be made for it was called an RPO. These would have been researched, designed, engineered, and marketed by General Motors for optimal market penetration.

Individual RPO options were designated by a letter and number combination. This combination appeared on a vehicle's window sticker, reminding the customer how much each cost. It was also found on the vehicle's build sheet, or what General Motors called the Broadcast Sheet. This sheet of paper was essentially a master list that stayed with the vehicle as it moved down the assembly line. Factory workers glanced at it to see what parts to install. For example, a customer told the sales associate what they wanted on a brand-new car and the order would go in. If you ordered a 1969 Camaro and wanted power windows (RPO A31), front accent striping (RPO DX1), and a heavy-duty radiator (RPO V01), it would go on the Broadcast Sheet. Several weeks later, the special ordered vehicle would be delivered.

COPO: How It Worked

The COPO process was different. It worked by allowing deviations to the configuration and combination of the available options on one condition. When a special request came through, the first internal action General Motors took was to have it evaluated to determine if the base vehicle needed a design change or additional parts in order to make it work. From there, the Special Equipment Design Group at the Engineering Center in Warren, Michigan, came up with an estimate for any tooling, fabricated assemblies, or additional research and development (R&D).

Next, the COPO Specification's Group tallied up the costs, weighed the benefits, and compiled a list of all the parts that needed to be sourced. Then, the COPO Specification's Group accumulated a master material sheet called an Engineering Parts List. On it would be all the part numbers, or RPOs, that needed to be removed from the base vehicle and the new ones that were going on. If a request was green-lit, a design work order was initiated and given a several digit COPO number that had the part or groupings of parts that were going on the vehicle. The Project Engineering and the Special Vehicle Group each signed off and the order went through.

The needed expenditures were spread out internally and absorbed across the budget. Records detailing COPO orders are very rare, but some examples have surfaced. One instance was a Forest Preserve Municipality special order for a batch of 1957 Chevy sedan deliveries. The vehicles were made with the rear hatch from a sedan delivery installed on a wagon with windows. When the vehicles were delivered, there wasn't any extra badging to identify the COPO process, and that term was buried in the paperwork. The vehicles were still covered under a factory warranty and could be serviced at any Chevrolet service department.

This process had never been done before, so few dealerships connected the dots to figure out that the COPO process could be used to build high-performance machines. Dealerships that may have seen the possibility passed because of the lengthy turnaround time and hassle involved. Another factor was that many performance-oriented dealerships had the resources to do their own modifications.

Hot-Rodding and Racing Get a Bad Rap

From an automotive standpoint, the years leading up to the muscle era of COPO (1965–1972) were volatile. Fast cars were an extremely popular but polarizing subject with an abundance of mixed feelings. These feelings were quickly becoming mostly negative because of over-the-top hot-headed drivers. Hot rodders had developed an image of being hooligans and hoodlums. Street racing was common and the participants were rowdy, out of control, and itching to go, often with disastrous effects. In 1955, one out of every four traffic deaths in the United States was caused by young speeders, despite only representing 15 percent of all registered drivers.

Some enthusiasts tried to change that negative image. One wrote in a 1959 suburban *Chicago Daily Herald* editorial piece that the hot rod industry contributes "valuable technical information" to the automotive industry. "A real hot rod is a car that is lending itself to experimental development for the betterment of safety, operation, and performance, not merely a stripped down or highly decorated car." It didn't help that all through the 1940s, 1950s, and 1960s, racing deaths, injuries, and crashes were common. Safety protocols were crude and elementary, and mishaps, mostly fatal, were frequent.

The most horrific accident took place at the 24 Hours of Le Mans when a speeding Mercedes catapulted at 150 mph into the air, flipping down a tightly packed row of spectators. In a matter of seconds, scores of bystanders were killed and many more were injured. More carnage occurred in nearby Italy at the treacherous endurance race Mille Miglia (1,000 Mile). Back in the States, NASCAR wasn't without its share of incidents. From 1952 to 1967, 14 drivers were killed on NASCAR tracks.

Fallout: AMA Ban

In the wake of all this turmoil, automakers made a major announcement in 1957 that separated themselves from the chaos. At the June Automobile Manufacturers Association (AMA) annual meeting in Detroit, the group drafted an unofficial agreement to back out of organized auto racing and motorsports of any kind. They also agreed to de-emphasize speed in advertising campaigns.

The AMA was a trade group with members being top brass from all the major automakers. Present for the decision were the chairmen and presidents of Ford, Chrysler, General Motors, Studebaker, and American Motors Corporation. Most of the car companies had been backing race teams for years, although it was usually referred to as experimental groups.

Citing the 1955 Le Mans disaster and other incidents, the AMA withdrew its sanction from every type of auto racing. The board announced that it "unanimously recommends to the member companies engaged in the manufacture and sale of passenger cars and stations wagons that they not participate or engage in any public contest, competitive event, or test of passenger cars involving or suggesting racing or speed, including acceleration tests, or encourage or assist employees, dealers or other, or furnish financial, engineering, manufacturing, advertising, or public relations assistance."

Another act the AMA banned was supplying pace cars or any official cars in connection with "any such contest, or test, directly or indirectly." All of this was a recommendation from all the member companies and few believed it would be enforced. There was strong motivation for the car companies to get their act together, as rumors persisted of racing being banned outright. One long-time foe of the sport was Senator Richard Neuburger of Oregon, who, in 1955 and again in 1959, tried to get Congress to ban all automobile racing in the United States.

1957 Black Widow

Chevrolet wanted to toe the line, but it also wanted to keep its cars selling. To ensure its models stayed out front in racing, General Motors sneakily created the Southern Engineering and Development Corporations Operation (SEDCO) in 1957. SEDCO was merely a shadow company with minimal ties to Detroit, partly for brand image and partly for liability. Chevrolet hired a former Hudson race engineer by the name of Vince Piggins and sent him to Atlanta. Piggins helmed SEDCO, which was run as a subsidiary of Nalley Chevrolet, a large dealership in the area. Bare-bones 6-cylinder passenger cars were delivered to Nalley in the fall of 1956.

Veteran racer Rex White was at Nalley as part of the crew picking up the cars. At the time, White was driving for Chevrolet and worked at SEDCO. "They [the cars] were business coupes—a cheap car sold as company cars," said White. "The whole deal was all about getting them to go fast." He and other colleagues caravanned the black-and-white painted cars to East Point, Georgia, where SEDCO was headquartered. "We rented a basement from a local body shop and set up shop there. There, we stripped them down and made them into race cars." While White was a professional wheelman, he was also skilled with his hands. He focused on chassis work, installing roll bars, shock mounts, and sway bars in the cars. The team worked all winter installing factory parts that were all available from General Motors.

A guide was created detailing the changes that had been made to the cars so anyone could head to his or her local Chevrolet parts counter and build one themselves. The guide was then mailed to more than 411 Chevrolet dealers. The *Black Widow* debuted in February 1957 at NASCAR's Daytona Beach and Road Course, where it performed extremely well, taking home the Manufacturers' Trophy. Chevrolet wasted no time spreading the news, taking out full-page ads proclaiming, "Chevy is America's 'hot' car—officially!" next to a picture of a 1957 with a checkered flag waving in the foreground.

After the AMA ban was signed, General Motors ordered SEDCO to be shut down. White remembers going into work one June day to find a lock and chain around the doors. He was informed that he had been fired. It wasn't all bitter; wishing the racers success, the cars (along with a tow vehicle) were given to the drivers. "It's just a shame that Chevy wasn't able to go the full year with it," recalls White. "We would have won the championship. It would have been one hell of season."

1960s: Easing Back In

As hard as the automakers tried to pretend to follow the mandates set forth in the AMA ban, no one was fooled. Most people knew the automakers continued their support of racing and speed in advertising. A congressional investigation kicked off again in the spring of 1962, spearheaded by Representative Oren Harris from Arkansas. He was quoted as saying that the House subcommittee on health and safety would "look into the matter as soon as possible" and asked the auto executives to furnish his committee with copies of all recent advertisements that stressed horsepower and speed. Tight-lipped representatives for the auto firms would not comment except to say, "We are conforming with the request and getting together examples of our advertising." Over-the-line ads included such pieces as a Chevrolet ad stating the 409 hp of a new big V-8 and a Dodge ad proclaiming the "Dart 440 handles like a perfectly set-up race car." Fears again lingered that Congress would step in and federally limit racing and the horsepower.

Horsepower War

This anxiety lingered as all the automakers entered a new contest to create the largest engine size and highest horsepower figure. With each passing year and the success of racing, the brands kept inching closer and closer to all-out speed. Each brand was clamoring to claim the crown of the largest cubic inch displacement, boasting the most horsepower. They kept reaching but wouldn't toot their own horn.

In 1959, Ford quietly debuted an engine capable of 360 hp, the highest to that point. A *Kansas City Star* report stated that "there was a time when introduction of such an engine would have been accompanied by blares from the publicity trumpets" but all that fanfare was quieted because

of the AMA ban. Pontiac, Plymouth, Ford, and Chevrolet all offered a 400-plus-hp engine and one overzealous engineer, seeing no end in sight, predicted 700-hp supercharged passenger car engines before too long.

Ford Caves In

Finally, Ford had enough. In the summer of 1962, Henry Ford II (also the president of the AMA) announced the brand was back into auto racing, this time officially. Ford cited the reason was that the resolution had been broken so often that, "It has come to have neither purpose nor effect. Accordingly, we are withdrawing from it." Chrysler followed, stating that with Ford's withdrawal, it "considers the resolution inoperative." General Motors made it clear that the brand "continues to endorse the soundness of the principle stated in the AMA resolution."

Some were still nervous about such brash actions. Roy Abernethy, president of American Motors, spoke to the Detroit Adcraft Club in January 1963. He stated "that those firms which had returned to auto racing and are touting speed in their ads despite congressional pressure are flirting with the likelihood of a stiff government crackdown."

GM's Unwavering Stance

Perhaps the greatest illumination on GM's position going into the 1960s comes from a news conference held on February 18, 1963. Chairman Frederic G. Donner and company president John F. Gordon fielded a battery of questions from a dogged group of media and journalists. One reporter asked, "In Washington, it is generally an accepted fact that the government is unhappy with the big share of the market that General Motors accounts for today in the United States, and yet General Motors's share apparently is getting bigger all the time. What effect does this knowledge of the government's being unhappy have on your operation?" Donner responded by questioning if the government being unhappy was fact, but he also confirmed that for 1962 General Motors accounted for 51.9 percent of the total passenger car market.

Another reporter asked about the policy that General Motors instituted in 1957, if it was still in effect, and if there had been any violations of it. Gordon answered that yes, there had been violations, but that there "have been violations of policy by everybody in the business." He stated the policy was still in effect, internally and in the AMA too.

This renewed commitment and anti-racing position was one General Motors was going to maintain for the next couple of years. Even though its competitors were dropping the flag and returning to racing, General Motors was adamantly going to stay out of it, at least officially. That stance changed once a few key individuals at the dealership level saw an opportunity to use protocols already in place to build performance-oriented cars that could skillfully slip between the cracks.

CHAPTER 1

YENKO CORVAIR STINGER

A Rear-Engined Compact Becomes a Road Race Weapon

Chevrolet Corvair Stinger

Total Production: 126
Dana Production: 3
Total Left: 70 (estimated)

While Chevrolet was proceeding gingerly around the racing scene, many outsiders were happily campaigning their products all-out at tracks around the country. One of those passionate enthusiasts was Don Yenko. Don's parents, Frank and Martha, owned Yenko Chevrolet, a bustling dealership nestled in sleepy Canonsburg, Pennsylvania, about 20 miles southwest of Pittsburgh. Don graduated from Penn State with a degree in Business Administration and served in the US Air Force before jumping into the family business. In 1957, he started racing Corvettes, quite successfully. By 1961, Don had "attacked and conquered just about every race course in the Eastern United States."

Clever Don Yenko took Chevrolet's Corvair and crafted it into an all-American racer; one that could properly mix it up on the track with the best of them. Ed Cunneen owns this striking trio (YS-119, YS-001, and YS-107).

Don made a name for himself by racing and modifying Corvettes, and he used that high-octane experience to launch his Stinger effort. Here, two Stingers undergo track testing. Note the dealership's field support truck, advertising "Specialized Corvette Service" on the rear fender. (Photo Courtesy the Barr Collection)

Don had his fill of staring down the rear bumpers of Mustangs he was trailing on the track. He was determined to make the Corvair into a winning machine and turn the tables on the naysayers, who doubted its performance proficiencies.

Because of this, his reputation, as well as the dealership's, grew. Don even helped form the Corvette Club of Western Pennsylvania, which was the largest of its kind in the country and still together today. That involvement paid big dividends when the vice president of Gulf Oil (headquartered in nearby Pittsburgh), Grady Davis, joined the club. In 1961, Davis agreed to sponsor two Corvettes in the 12-hour Grand Prix road race held in Sebring, Florida. Not only did he order the vehicles from Yenko Chevrolet, he hired Don to drive one of the cars. In 1962 and 1963, Don was ranked as the national Class B Production champion of the Sports Car Club of America (SCCA) and even headed to Puerto Rico to compete in the Grand Prix there.

Yenko's Corvette Center

While he enjoyed the intense wheel-to-wheel competition, Don was about sales. He leveraged the trackside publicity and credibility to push the store. As early as 1960, he ran ads offering "Corvette Competition" tuning and repair, stating the crew at Yenko Chevrolet were fuel injection and carburetion specialists. He lumped these efforts into what he called the Yenko Corvette Service Center and began offering competition preparation for Corvettes. Don offered upgrades for owners wishing to compete in the SCCA races as well as other performance items for "...the ultimate in Corvette competition preparation."

The dealership's performance group rebuilt engines, polished cylinder heads, and installed heavy-duty front and rear springs and heavy-duty electric fuel pumps. Some parts were designed by the team and designated as such: there was as a YENKO roll bar, a YENKO Plexiglass windscreen, and a YENKO heavy-duty bumper tow bar. An estimate from 1962 for the full tuning works rang up at nearly $6,200 for a complete overhaul. To put it into perspective, a 1962 Corvette's base price was around $4,200. Don focused on branding too and offered "Corvette by Yenko" license plate frames to show off their handiwork. Rumor has it this move wasn't well-received by Chevrolet. Protective of its model names, the carmaker asked him to stop using the frames.

Shelby Strikes: Mustang GT350

Yenko's world (and the rest of the racing community) was shaken up in 1963 after seeing what Texas-tuner Carroll Shelby had cooked up and rolled out. Shelby unleashed his Ford V-8-powered, British-bodied AC Cobra onto the A and B Production road racing classes. The track weapon proved potent, placing first in A in 1963 and 1964 and earning Shelby quite the reputation.

By now, Ford was full-steam ahead with its racing program, continuing to roll out its Total Performance campaign. There were high hopes that the recently released Mustang would prance with the best on the country's top tracks. Ford was shocked when the SCCA turned it down for classification. Because of its back seat, the Mustang was ruled a sedan and not suitable for competition. Ford contracted Shelby's team to get the vehicle race-ready. Besides the back seat deal, there was another SCCA regulation for the production classes: 100 examples had to be produced to prove the vehicle was indeed production and not a small batch of one-offs. To manufacturers, the production class was key. Winning was winning, but winning with a vehicle that inspired spectators to buy street versions right off the showroom floor. Now *that* was truly winning.

In late 1964, Ford shipped the vehicles (sans back seat) to Shelby's headquarters near the Los Angeles airport. He and his team worked their magic and had enough prepped for the SCCA to give them a green light and allow them to compete in the 1965 race season. The combination proved a winning formula. The Shelby GT350 R-Model nabbed the SCCA B/Production title away from Corvette. The year-end SCCA American Road Race of Champions (AARC) for A and B production categories looked like a Shelby parade as the Cobras and Shelby GT350 Mustangs galloped away with the first five finishes overall and the laurels for both A and B Production.

Shelby's Bumper: Seeing the Need

Having gone toe-to-toe with Shelby's speed steeds (and lost), Don's wheels were spinning. He was tired losing, despite his Corvette having

Chevrolet had made some styling and suspension tweaks to the Corvair to help it stand up to some negative press. Seeing a unique window of opportunity, Don felt confident it would be the right platform to build on.

received a full overhaul in 1963. In his mind, the 1957 Corvette was the ultimate. He was growing more and more frustrated as the model's curb weight kept climbing. In 1964, he voiced his frustration about the 1963 design. In June 1966, Don wrote a piece in *Sports Car* magazine, saying "After repeatedly looking at the rear bumper of Mark Donohue's [Shelby] Mustang, [he] decided the only way [he] could stay loyal to Chevrolet (they put food on my table) was to build my own car." Looking across Chevy's lineup, he settled on the Corvair, the brand's compact offering. A 1966 *Motor Trend* article quoted Don as saying he had grown to deplore "The trend of Detroit manufacturers to concentrate their design exercise on front-engine, nose-heavy, large-bore vehicles, the result of which is a fast-accelerating but poor handling machine."

Don had his work cut out for him. According to *Car and Driver*, while the Corvair had been rallied successfully and the engine was reliable in drag racing, in road racing it tended to overheat. That was to be expected because the engine was mounted in the rear of the vehicle and air-cooled. The publication observed that it would be a stretch for the Stinger to compete successfully in Class D and would have been better suited for slower classes. To be fair, the article's author remembers seeing Don race a few years earlier and remembers his "fierce determination to win against overwhelming odds."

Working in Don's favor, besides his tenacity, was that the Corvair had just undergone a redesign and updating for the 1965 model year. Part of that was a suspension upgrade, thanks to Ralph Nader's poignant *Unsafe at Any Speed*. In his book, Nader criticized the Corvair for being prone to suspension related accidents. To alleviate the quickly mounting bad press, Chevrolet swapped out the rear swing axle suspension for a fully independent suspension. Like Ford and its Mustang, in 1964 (and again in 1965) Chevy submitted the two-door Corvair to the SCCA to get it classed in for competition in the Sports Car production class. Like Ford, Chevy was turned down on the grounds that because it had four seats it, too, was a sedan-based car. Despite having two doors and looking sporty, it still had two rows of seating.

Clever Don was fed up and frustrated with his losing streak. He saw an opening window of opportunity. It would take a ton of work, but he was willing to make the effort.

Choosing the Corvair

For 1966, Corvair was being offered as a base 500, a mid-range Monza, and a top-of-the line Corsa (which had just debuted in 1965). One of the biggest changes in this second-generation economy car, besides its continental styling, was its nimble, fully independent rear suspension, which was derived from the Corvette Sting Ray. Since 1960, the car's rear suspension had been using a swing axle design, enhanced in 1964 with a cam-ber compensating transverse leaf spring, mounted horizontally between the wheels.

Overall, the 1964 vehicle didn't get high praise. *Car and Driver* remarked the Corvair was "one of the nastiest-handling cars ever built," saying the tail would give "little warning that it was about to let go, and when it did, it let go with a vengeance few drivers could cope with. The rear wheels would lose traction, tuck under, and with the tail end jacked up in the air, the car would swing around like a three-pound hammer on a thirty-foot string."

For the 1965 model year, Chevy set out to rectify the negative press. The swing axles that only pivoted in the middle at the differential case were exchanged for a four-link suspension. Universal joins were mounted at each end of the axle halfshaft, allowing for greater flexibility.

Lower links were added, too, so when the car went over bumps, the wheels wouldn't camber (or lean) out as before. As part of the overhaul, the front suspension got a new sway bar.

Don stated that the Corsa was "engineered so soundly that it can be made completely race worthy without major rebuilding. The usual route of providing a 'stiff as a board' suspension, as is done on the Mustang and pre-1963 Corvettes, isn't necessary in this case. The fully independent suspension system of the Corvair makes this compromise with handling unnecessary."

Don also saw a need for something like it in the SCCA. "We felt that there is a need for American representation in the lower speed-potential car classes of the SCCA racing. Our sampling of public opinion substantiated this opinion. And the idea of being able to race an American car for a reasonable initial investment, and then be able to procure parts locally, is intriguing even to the most avid foreign car buff." Power for the Corsa came from a reworked 161-ci air-cooled boxer 6-cylinder that was mounted in the rear of the car. It was fitted with four single-barrel Rochester carburetors and with redesigned heads, bigger valves, and improved porting that was good for a stout 140 hp.

Think Pink: Donna Mae Mimms

Don wasn't alone in this quest to bring the Stinger to reality. He was joined by Donna Mae Mimms of Bethel Park, Pennsylvania, who was his self-employed public relations manager. She was a racer through and through, having mixed it up on the track with him in the early 1960s. In 1963, as a 20-year-old, she was crowned the American Road Race of Champions winner in H/Production class, making her the only female race driver to ever win a national road racing championship up to that point.

Her association with the Yenko team began when she stopped by the dealership to get her personal car serviced. Don found her bold personality, charm, and wit key assets, to say nothing of her driving skills, and he added her to his team. Donning her pink helmet and jumpsuit, the Pink Lady

Donna Mae Mimms was a vivacious, creative marketer with a passion for racing and the color pink. She and Don made a great team, working to get the Yenko Super Cars known and distributed. Her affinity for pink was legendary; she always wore pink, drove pink cars, and even used pink stationery. Here she is talking up the Stingers at an unknown exhibit. (Photo Courtesy the Barr Collection)

The Yenko STINGER

This booklet was part of the promotional campaign to get the word out about the brand-new Stinger, touting all its performance capabilities. Don not only had the know-how to build something fast but also the marketing savvy to raise awareness of it. (Photo Courtesy Brian Henderson)

would go on to be a top driver for Don's team. She stayed with Don all through the glory years of COPO performance vehicles and played a key role in crafting the Yenko mystique and brand image.

Pizza Box Prototype

To build the Bonanza, Yenko and his team took a Corsa from the dealership lot and made some tweaks, including adjusting the bodywork to appear more coupe-like. As Don tells it, his friend John Salathe, an industrial designer, came to his shop to help the group modify the exterior. They drew lines all over the car and ordered pizza for lunch. In a fit of inspiration, they used the leftover boxes to fashion the rear window panels and decklid spoiler. They liked what they saw and decided to go with it.

The general plan for the vehicle was to boost horsepower, beef up the suspension, tighten the steering, add some fiberglass rear panels to alter the body line, and remove the rear seat and place the spare wheel into that location for better weight distribution. Yenko wanted the vehicle to be built as a multi-purpose car for racing, rallying, or touring. He also set out to offer it with three various stages of tune. He stated, "I think there's a real need for a comfortable, high-performance, low-priced grand touring production car with true dual-purpose capabilities. And, like all modern race cars, it's rear engined—the logical [layout] for the Stinger."

Stirling Support

A friend of famed race car driver Stirling Moss suggested to Don that they invite Mr. Moss himself to come drive it. Don was apprehensive about

If your idea of a gutsy Grand Touring sports car can be met by a nose-heavy, large bore bomb that has been beefed up to imitate sports car performance, then the Yenko Stinger is not for you.

Here is America's only air-cooled rear engine sports car with independent four-wheel suspension. Inspired by the inherently excellent design of the Corvair Corsa, the Stinger was created to handle in true GT tradition. It transforms sophisticated chassis engineering into a competition-bred road machine that will make **you** want to do the chauffeuring.

Inside there are two honest bucket seats (three-passenger removable rear seat included); a four-speed, full-synchro, closer-ratio gearbox; responsive, feather-light, quick steering (3.0 turns lock to lock). And that's just the beginning.

It corners like it "invented rails." Race-spawned dual master cylinders command the heavy duty brakes. A few racing modifications make the Stinger a winner in Class D Production of the Sports Car Club of America or Class H Stock (NASCAR) at the drags.

Even the basic Stinger (Stage I), a fine five-passenger family car, offers you an eager 160 horsepower in a race-suspended chassis. A dual-purpose Stinger for the serious rallyist and the occasional race driver boasts a Stage II tune that unleashes a husky 190 horses. Stage III is all spirit with 220 horses for the street — the "detuned" race car. Stage IV is something else — with ALL the racing goodies at 240 horsepower. For this one you'll need a competition license, a race course, and lots of trophy space. And, if it's brute horsepower you're after, try Stage V — up to 250 horsepower. Stinger anyone?

DON YENKO

On the inside cover of the booklet, Don personally wrote a letter explaining what made his little car unique, fast, and desirable. It was also meant to be practical; as evidenced in the lead photo showing five adults packed inside the car. (Photo Courtesy Brian Henderson)

The changes Don requested through the COPO system were to help the Corvair stay competitive. Don added to those improvements, such as inserting decklid cooling doors, which only made his stinger more potent while buzzing around a track.

what Moss would say to the press, but to his surprise, Moss came away impressed. Moss was in the country to attend the US Grand Prix, so on September 24 Don flew him to a race course in Marlboro, Maryland, to drive the prototype of what would become the Yenko Stinger. During a practice session at the final SCCA National championship races, Moss wrung the machine out on the course in front of an estimated 10,000 spectators. His tests on the 1.8-mile, 10-turn course included severe braking, fast cornering, and standing acceleration starts.

After returning home, Moss penned a letter on October 6, 1965, to Don with his impressions. He began by thanking Don for the opportunity, then he proceeded to say the vehicle used in the trials was one of the best handling production sports cars he had ever driven. He added that the Stinger "handles as well as any production sports car and better than most. There as virtually no indication of understeer or brake fade. It is a car that can undoubtedly be driven not only in the race, but also to and from the race."

Yenko's Fleet Account

To prepare for the ramping up and preparation of 100 vehicles, Don laid some groundwork. On October 9, 1965, he sent a letter to the Chevrolet Motor Division requesting that Yenko Chevrolet be recognized as a Chevrolet national fleet account. That would expedite the process of ordering a COPO.

On October 11, Don sent Jim Kaiser all of the necessary forms to have

the Yenko Stinger categorized. That same day, he also sent a letter to six top SCCA members to lobby for the classification of the YENKO Stinger. He began by stating "it has been the trend of Detroit manufacturers to concentrate their design exercises on front-engine, nose-heavy, large-bore vehicles, the result of which is a fast accelerating but poor handling machine." He went on to say that the Corvair is engineered so soundly that it can be made completely race worthy without a major rebuilding problem. Don praised its "already fine, fully independent suspension system" and stated that he didn't want to offer another high-powered monster but felt the need "for American car representation in the lower speed potential classes of the Sports Car Club of America racing." Don closed his argument by saying that "the idea of being able to race an American car for a reasonable initial price and then be able to procure parts replacement on a local basis is intriguing to the most avid foreign car buffs."

On October 28, an antsy Don sent a letter to Joe Pike, Chevrolet's National Sales Manager. Don wanted to tip him off about the fleet order that was going to be placed soon and see if it could be expedited. He also reviewed what he was looking for: 100 Corsa Coupes in color code CC (Ermine White, 3900CC) with blue interiors and the regular production options for special steering (3N44AA), special purpose front and rear suspension, and 4-speed transmission (3M20BB) with half of the order getting a Positraction rear axle. In addition, Don wanted them equipped with a brand-new component: a dual master cylinder. Yenko requested it as a fail-safe during racing, as it separated the pressure going to the front brake lines from the pressure going to the rear brake lines. During the heat of a race if a line blew out, due to the dual reservoirs, racers would still have the ability to slow and hopefully stop using the pressure from whichever set of brakes was still operable. With the Corvairs' stock single master cylinder, if you lose a line, you lose all brakes.

SCCA Endorsement & D Class

Don's next move was to talk to Don Sesslar, chair of the Car Classification Committee for the SCCA. Don asked him if it would help classify his car if he wined, dined, and sent him lavish gifts. Sesslar's reply was, "Certainly not; but you go ahead and try."

Even before getting the car approved, Don was working to get even more performance out of his Stinger. By November, he was armed with a list of (performance) options that would have made the Shelby Mustangs look like Shetland ponies. Word leaked that the Stinger would be raced in D Production, and, according to Don, he was advised by everyone to forget the idea. Don knew the car was lacking power and figured it would be placed in G or possibly F Production classes. It didn't help that the SCCA turned down most of his options to make it go faster. He almost decided to quit.

Don underestimated how many people had gotten wind of and were interested in the project. Jerry Thompson, from Detroit, called and gave Don a speed demonstration of his non-COPO Corvair at Nelson Ledges Road Racing Course in Warren, Ohio. Thompson had been competing in the SCCA's sedan class. Don was impressed and encouraged to move forward.

Don went back to the SCCA and agreed to conform to their regulations. On November 7, Don drove the first competition-prepared prototype Stinger at Nelson Ledges. His goal was to get it placed in the SCCA's race classes. The SCCA grouped production cars into classes according to their potential lap times. *Car and Driver* said, "The Corvair, even souped up, couldn't have much of a chance in class D against cars like the race-prepared Triumph TR-4A, which had won class D the last four years in a row." To everyone's surprise, the Stinger (driven by Don) buzzed around the 1.1-mile course and turned in a best lap time of 56.9 seconds, the best Class D Production time ever recorded in the three-year history of the Ledges. That was good enough for the SCCA, which officially placed it into the D Production class.

Don sent out a press release on November 12, 1965, stating that "Lap times compared favorably with other class competition cars." Immediately following the test, Don had one of the onlookers line up a 396-ci V-8–equipped Chevelle to see how the Stinger would compare in heads-up acceleration from a standing start. With the cars set up dragstrip style, the Stinger buzzed away from the Chevelle and had more than a two-car-length lead at the end of the straight.

While emotions were high, Don and his team were about to come up against another obstacle. As Don puts it, "It was at this point that [he] dis-covered that his naiveté had no bounds. It was then that he learned the 'good news' that, like Shelby, he too had to build 100 cars to be ready for inspection the start of the race season." In Don's case, that was before January 1, 1966. It was too late to turn back now, and Don went $500,000 in debt (or roughly $2.7 million today) to cover the cost of the cars. He spent four days discussing, deliberating, and cajoling to finally secure the financing from GM's financing division, GMAC. Don joked later in 1966 that they "still don't know what Stinger is."

Dealer Network

While Don was rushing to get the cars created, he was also rushing to get dealer partners set up to sell the cars. Within days of the Nelson Ledges test, Donna Mae sent out a press release announcing the coast to coast network of 12 dealers (including Yenko Chevrolet) that would be selling the Stinger. They had all regions of the United States covered. Don made inroads to Canada, too, with a dealer in Hamilton, Ontario, ready to sell and service the Stinger.

SPAN Inc. based in the Marina Towers in downtown Chicago, Illinois, was the exclusive US distributor for the cars. Jim Spencer lived in the towers and worked out of his home. He was an amateur racer who competed in his own Stinger. He connected with Don to be a salesperson, selling the Stinger to dealerships and getting a commission on each unit moved. In 1967, he also became the distributor for then-new Camaro, but the business relationship fizzled out not long later after the dealer-distributor network became robust. Initially, Don required new distributors to stock six autos of various stages, but he handled each case individually.

100 COPO Corvairs

While Don's dealership crew certainly had the means to build and prep race cars (they had been doing it for years), getting 100 cars race ready, and in less than month, would be near impossible. To help speed up the process, Don put in a COPO to have the vehicles built with a couple performance-oriented tweaks done right at the factory. His initiative would mark the first time the traditionally banal and utilitarian Central Office Production Order process would be used to build a vehicle with a focus on enhanced performance.

In early November, Don ordered 100 Corsa two-door sport coupes, all painted in Ermine White. Formula 1 racing utilized a standard set of country colors to identify their team's nationalities. There was British Racing Green for Great Britain, blue for France,

This Yenko Stinger was delivered to the dealership on December 8, 1965, and built into a Stinger on December 12. It was the first to be created, being assigned the YS-001 stock number. For some reason, it sat on the lot before being sold on July 8, 1967. It's rumored it was used as a display car or perhaps as a track tester.

By removing the front chrome bar between the headlights, Don gave his Stingers a sleeker look up front. It also drew more attention to the addition of the special hornet sticker, painted headlight buckets, and lower valance.

red for Italy's prancing horses, and white with blue stripes for the United States. While strict adherence to the code wasn't required in the SCCA, many racers followed suit and emulated it. The Corsa's blue interior color was swapped to black (3758DA) before production started for the Stingers.

The cars were built at Chevy's Willow Run factory near Ypsilanti, Michigan. They were equipped with a stock Corvair air-cooled, rear-mounted, horizontally opposed 140-hp 6-cylinder engine. A heavy-duty suspension (different spring stiffness and shocks, under RPO F41) was installed along with a special "feather-light" quick steering gear box ratio (RPO N44) that allowed drivers to go lock to lock in 2.8 turns. Under COPO 9861E, the brake cylinder was swapped out for the one from Cadillac, sporting dual master reservoirs. This marked the first time a dual master brake cylinder was used in a Chevrolet model. Fifty of the cars came with a Positraction axle with 3.55 gearing while the other 50 came with specially made 3.89 gears (under COPO 9513A).

Don wasn't certain where his Stingers would end up. For racers on small tracks with fast curves, the 3.89 would be ideal, while those on much longer, higher speed tracks, the 3.55 would be most useful. The 3.89:1 ring and pinion wasn't available as an RPO for other Corvairs in 1966, but because the parts were initiated by Yenko and the COPO, it became available as an over-the-counter part. In the Chevrolet parts catalog, the line item even stated it was a Yenko part.

In the May 1966 edition of *Sports Car Graphic*, the magazine reported that when they talked to Don about his undertaking, he didn't hesitate to tell that General Motors was not supporting the project. The article also said that they got the idea that "he had to do some pretty fast talking to interest the people who call the shots in selling that first batch of 100 white Corsas."

Setting the Stage

Even with the help of the COPO process, there was still a lot of work to be done. On average, Yenko Chevrolet sold an average around 190 cars per year at that time. This massive influx of inventory was quite an undertaking. To prepare for the arrival of 100 Corsas, the field behind the dealership was graded and turned into a makeshift parking lot. The first batch of 27 cars arrived on December 8, and they continued to pour in through December 18.

A new building was constructed on-site, where two shifts of employees working 16-hour days assembled cars around the clock, ensuring the vehicles would be done by the end of December. Only Christmas Day was taken off. It was hectic, but they got it done with no time to spare.

Because of that frenetic work pace, the quality of the final cars varied. Owners today will tell you the only thing consistent with their Stingers is that they're inconsistent. The varying results could be attributed to the compressed schedule but also because Yenko contracted several area body shops to help with final assembly. Undoubtedly because of the rush, communications must have been fuzzy in the breakneck speed to get the vehicles done.

Exterior

Some of the changes made during that December included exterior modifications. Up front, the chrome lock bar located between the headlights was removed. Fiberglass sail panels were installed over the rear of the side quarter windows to widen the rear pillar. These panels were painted

The biggest alteration to the profile of the COPO Corvairs was this special sail panel, installed at the rear of the window. It gave the cars a more coupe-like design, helping to sell the illusion to the racing sanctioning bodies that this was indeed a legit and distinct automobile. This one is a 1967, hence its blue paint color.

in the body color, giving the Stinger a more coupe-like profile. At the rear, the steel decklid engine cover was replaced with a lighter fiberglass piece. It featured two built-in air vents that were held in place with a small, narrow strip of metal and cabinet magnetic catches. The vents could be opened to direct cool air into the engine compartment. It was crude and simple but effective. To add downforce, the decklid had a small spoiler on the rear edge that supposedly was reminiscent of the one on the Ferrari GTO.

Most Corsa and Chevrolet emblems were removed, such as the C (for Corsa) found on the lower rear quarter panels and the Corsa script on the front fenders. The holes left behind from their mounting pins were filled in with lead and plastic filler and then painted white. Naturally, the "140 hp" emblem

The stripe setup consisted of a wide center flanked by two thin stripes. The blue hue was not consistent across the full fleet of Stingers, more than likely because of the rush to complete them and some were done by local body shops.

Don was hoping this was the view most of the competition would see once his Stingers were let loose on tracks. The blue stripes running down the middle of the car tied in nicely with the painted rear panel.

The hardware Don used for his vent doors on the custom-created fiberglass decklid were just that, hardware. They were simple magnetic catches you'd find on household cabinet doors. A thin bar of metal held the door in place.

The clever little hornet insignia was a nice touch and helped to shape the brand for the Stinger. Because this car did not have the sail panels installed, the stickers were relocated to forward of the rear wheels.

and Corsa script on the decklid were removed when the decklid was exchanged for the custom fiberglass one.

The headlight buckets, rear taillight panel, lower door sills, and front panel under the bumper were all painted blue. From there, a trio of blue stripes were painted on: a fat, wide stripe ran down the middle of the car and was flanked by thinner stripes. There wasn't a standard hue, and Stinger owners have compared numerous original paint cars to confirm that no blue was the same shade. Others have found that even the stripes varied in their appearance. Some gradually draw closer together toward the front of the car while others remain evenly spaced all the way down.

New Stinger badging came in the form of an embossed aluminum circle sticker, complete with a little angry black hornet with an oversized stinger. Don originally wanted a zinc die-cast emblem, and in early November 1965 reached out to several companies (L. F. Grammess & Sons Inc. in Allentown, Pennsylvania, and LaFrance Precision Casting Company in Philadelphia, Pennsylvania) for quotes. Don received samples, but due to hectic production schedule, he changed plans and went with what he called an etched type of trademark medallion.

The stickers were stuck on the new sail panel as well as the front panel on the driver's side. Later reproductions often incorrectly replicate the sticker with a silver hornet. This was the result of original stickers' black coloring wearing off, revealing silver underneath. Above the Stinger logo on the front and on the rear spoiler (also on the driver's side) script detailing what stage (one through four) the car had received was applied.

Handling was a high priority for Don, who knew firsthand the value that added while blasting around a track. Additional suspension modifications were offered to customers who wanted to further enhance their car's capabilities. The sail panels on this Stinger were removed by an early owner.

Suspension

The updated suspension in the stock Corsa performed quite well on the track, but it was even better with the heavy-duty rear suspension (3F41AA). If a customer requested it, Don would add Monroe or Koni shocks. No sway bars or other "bolt-on gadgets" (as one ad hyped) were added. Don was quite proud of the car's road-hugging abilities, touting that it "corners like it invented rails." Don added heavy-duty brake shoes for better stopping. The result was nearly neutral handling.

Interior

Inside the cabin, the back seat was removed and replaced by a plywood board covered with a mat, essentially making for a carpeted luggage shelf. The goal wasn't cargo space but to make the car lightweight. However, many cars had their back seats left in place, more than likely due to the frenetic schedule of completing the cars. It's also plausible that some own-

With the rear seat removed, there was quite a lot of room in the Stingers' cabins. Space wasn't the goal, and neither was lightness; the car had to be presented as a coupe to clear the SCCA class restrictions. This car is equipped with the optional Yenko roll bar.

ers weren't as track-focused as others and wanted the ability to carry passengers. Sometimes the heater was removed for weight savings, but, again, some were left in. The Corvair emblem on the glove box was removed and a Stinger embossed decal that matched the exterior stickers covered the holes.

Performance

Don made sure to offer the Stinger with a varying degree of performance, Stages 1 through 5, based on buyers' wants and needs. As he explained in a brochure: Even the basic Stinger (Stage I), a fine passenger family car, offers you an eager 160 horsepower in a race-suspended chassis. A dual-purpose Stinger for the serious rallyist and the occasional race driver boasts a Stage II tune that unleashes a husky 190 horses. Stage III is all sprint with 220 horses for the street—the "detuned" race car. Stage IV is something else—with ALL the racing goodies at 240 horsepower. For this one you'll need a competition license, a race course, and lots of trophy space. And if it's brute horsepower you're after, try Stage V—up to 250 horsepower."

All engines had the factory air cleaner replaced with four individual chrome air cleaners on top of the four carbs to increase airflow. This modification alone increased horsepower by 15 hp at the rear wheels. In addition, the carb jets were increased to 0.006 inch to compensate for the increased air intake. The flat, stamped steel oil pan was swapped out for a bigger, finned aluminum unit. This increased oil capacity by an additional 2 quarts, bringing the total to 7 quarts. The engines came equipped with a Tufftrided crankshaft, standard in the turbocharged 180-hp engine, as well as M-400 Moranie connecting rods and special main bearings. Other enhancements included high-velocity exhaust headers, steel pack exhaust mufflers, and chromed dual tailpipes.

A belt-idler spring tensioner was added to maintain a constant tension of about 10 pounds on the fan belt. Corvairs had a nasty habit of throwing the belt in high RPM situations, such as when drivers came in hot into a track's corner, braked hard, and quickly downshifted, letting the clutch speed the motor up to up around 5,500 rpm. Don's team substituted

Buyers could dial up their Stinger's performance by opting for higher stages of tuning and modifications. A Stage II (shown here) featured a high-performance camshaft, a modified fan, 10:1 compression heads, a lightened flywheel, and modified carburetors.

Four chrome air cleaners were part of the Stinger package and dressed up the engine compartment while also serving to get more air into the carburetors.

Don knew the first step in getting the Corvair to move was to ditch the restrictive factory air cleaner. This 1967 example is a Stage I and was recommended for street use or for the customer who wanted to do his or her own performance enhancements.

A 7-quart finned aluminum oil pan came standard with all stages of performance and helped keep the engine cool.

A simple spring (like these found on a screen door or on a child's hobby horse) kept pressure on the fan belt, which was necessary when racing the Corvair. In marketing, Don called it a "Daytona-type constant tension belt retainer."

the 3/8-inch nut on the back off the stock tensioner pulley for a bushing, allowing the pulley to float back and forth and compensate for lapses in load. This spring (which looks like ones used on period hobby horses and trampolines) was installed at the rear of the engine to a core support and to the top of the tensioner pulley bracket.

A customer ordering Stage I received all of the previously listed engine modifications plus their choice of other options that were available for additional cost. They could select items such as competition seat belts ($35.00), special metallic brakes ($79.45), power brakes ($73.80), heavy-duty valve

guides ($102.00), a Yenko-designed roll bar ($150.00), and an AM/FM radio ($133.80). A base Stage I vehicle rang up at $3,520.

Stage II built on the Stage I, receiving all those modifications plus a high-performance camshaft with heavy-duty valve springs and retainers. It also received a lightweight 9-pound flywheel, a modified engine cooling fan with about 1 inch cut off its diameter, and reworked cylinder heads for high compression (10:1). A baffle was installed in the oil pan to keep oil from lifting into the cylinders during hard cornering. Final touches were high-capacity ignition secondary wiring; oil pressure, ammeter, and

A Yenko Chevrolet employee makes an adjustment on the dealership's engine dyno, coaxing more power from a Corvair's engine. (Photo Courtesy the Barr Collection)

The Stingers ended up being capable little cars with the improvements reflecting Don's knowledge of garnering success on the track.

temperature gauges; a polished crankshaft; select fit main bearings; and a deep sump oil pan pickup. Total weight savings was about 250 pounds. Yenko claimed the Stage II engine was tested at 190 hp and would "easily out-accelerate all of the street variety V-8s and most of the so-called high performance cars."

Move up to Stage III and the engine was completely dissembled. High-compression cylinder heads (10.5:1) that had been polished, ported, relieved, and shaved were installed. The engine's cylinder walls were honed to race clearances and high-compression forged pistons were installed. The piston deck height was adjusted and a high-performance distributor installed. The flywheel was lightened to 8 pounds and balanced, and a high-tension clutch pressure plate was installed. The vibration damper was engraved with degree markings. Larger carb jets and heavy-duty fuel lines were installed along with special fittings. A heavy-duty oil cooler was installed and the Stage I headers were reversed for an even more direct flow of exhaust gases. Output was rated at 220 hp. During Moss's test, he drove a Stage III and reported 0–60 in 6.8 seconds and the standing-quarter in 13.6 seconds at 97 mph. Yenko rated top speed at 127 mph at 6,200 rpm with a 3.55 axle. The Stage III was the Stinger designed for the SCCA Class D Production.

Stage IV cars had displacement increased from 164 to 176 ci and was rated between 185 and 230 reliable horsepower, depending on what other racing options the customer selected. It was for the "customer who wants all-out performance in Class D Production Competition." Stage IV was intended primarily for modified competition, both in road racing and at the drag strip. It received all of the Stage III parts, was bored to 176 ci, and featured fuel injection with individual ram tubes.

It all worked very well. A *Car and Driver* track test from June 1966 commented that the first thing the driver noticed was how quickly it responded to even the smallest steering input; it tracked "instantly and exactly where its aimed." The report also stated that to get the maximum out of the car, it had to be tossed into each corner with as much bravery and gusto as the driver can muster and that it felt more like a designed racing car than a production car prepared for racing.

Top dog was supposed to be a Stage V, which was never fully rolled out. The engine was going to boast individual ram tube fuel injection and upgraded pistons and be rated at 250 hp. A Stinger equipped with a proto-type engine tested in one race in Canada. No sanctioning body would allow the fuel-injection motor, so development was soon dropped. Don tested it himself at a special press preview held in Daytona, Florida, and posted impressive times. The standing-quarter mile came in at 12.8 seconds at 108 mph, 0–60 mph came in 6.1 seconds, and top speed was 135 mph.

Pricing

As *Car and Driver* put it, "the most astounding feature of the competition Stinger is its price." It went on to say that "there are few classes in racing today where you can buy a top-notch competitive car off the shelf for $4,781.07, ready to go. And how many manufacturers will race prepare the car for their customers and then show up at the races with spares and technical assistance?"

The base price for a 1966 Stinger in Stage I trim was $3,278. Stage II cost $3,692.33, Stage III cost $4,099.33, and Stage IV cost $4,154.33. In 1999, Donna Mae Mimms stated that Don sold the cars for slightly over his cost so people could afford to buy them and enjoy them. In one instance, Don even offered financial assistance for cross-country traveling expenses for Stinger owners who qualified for the SCCA American Road Race of Champions runoffs held in Riverside, California. That wasn't all; he also agreed to send a Stinger Nest, which was a "well-equipped van loaded with parts and spares, and staffed with a team of top-notch factory mechanics." These mechanics helped with any entrants' mechanical difficulties free of charge. In 1967, the cars sold for $3,450 plus destination.

Warranty

Yenko offered the standard 24-month or 24,000-mile Chevrolet warranty on Stage I vehicles. The Stage II and higher vehicles were given a 90-day or 4,000-mile parts warranty on the drivetrain. The standard Chevrolet warranty applied to the rest of the car. Don also made sure to emphasize that parts and service were "readily available at your local dealership at low cost."

In his Yenko Stinger booklet, Don wrote: "The Corvair itself has been labeled as a 'fun car,' a 'sport car,' a 'car for the wife,' and of course, 'unsafe at any speed,' but seldom has the marque been identified with high performance." Don changed that perspective by getting these cars out on the track.

Opening the driver's door on a Stinger would reveal this tag, located on the front of the doorjamb. YS stood for Yenko Stinger, while the digits were the vehicle's stock number. These tags were necessary for competition.

YS Tags

When a vehicle was completed, it received a special Yenko Stinger serial number plate. These were attached on the driver-side front doorjamb and followed the format of YS-001 through YS-100 (YS standing for Yenko Stinger). On November 30, 1965, Don placed a $41.38 order for the stamped aluminum plates with a company in Pittsburgh. Don was optimistic about how many he would sell, and he had the company produce 1 through 200. The SCCA required any competing Corvair in D Stock Production classes to have one of his tags, and it kept that rule in place through 1986.

Ever the salesperson, Yenko offered the Stinger components in a special Stinger Stuff catalog. Owners could take their stock Corvair and "Stingerize" it. On occasion, Don would issue YS tags when buyers bought a kit and include a letter of certification. This group of vehicles has become colloquially known as tagged cars.

Ready to Race

Even before the SCCA came to inspect the Stingers, Don was already showing them off. He debuted his prototype Stinger in downtown Pittsburgh on December 8 in the lobby of the ALCOA Building. Don even showed up to discuss the new car and his new role as an automobile manufacturer.

The SCCA's Greenlight

While moves like that were good for PR, the real test was on December 28, 1965. Claude C. Cardwell, a member of the SCCA National Competition Board, arrived in Canonsburg. He had three main jobs given to him by James E. Kaiser, competition director. Cardwell was to inspect the amount of floor space being utilized under construction or expected to be added during 1966. He was also to tally up the number of employees and anticipated hires. Finally, he was to review the present rate of production and the projected production for 1966 of the Yenko Stinger.

Don recalls his crew looked like a bunch of zombies but they had got the cars all done. While the race was on to complete the vehicles, Don went through another hectic endeavor; getting them back. Eager to move the inventory, he had already sold some off (perhaps not fully expecting the SCCA to actually send someone out to physically count the final products). A few urgent phone calls went out to customers, asking them to bring their vehicles back to the dealership to be tallied.

Cardwell walked out to the frozen, snowy field behind the dealership and counted 96 cars (4 had already been sold and shipped). He informed Don that his recommendation to the Competition Board meeting would be that the Stinger qualifies.

Don wasted no time in sharing the good news. Just a day later on December 29, 1965, he sent a letter to Ted Lobinger and the Automobile Competition Committee for the United States. Don informed Lobinger that Yenko Sportscars Inc. was a "wholly owned subsidiary of Yenko Chevrolet and is presently engaged in the manufacture of a grand touring coupe designated the YENKO STINGER." He also mentioned Cardwell's approval for the SCCA. Don wanted to be recognized as a bona fide manufacturer of automobiles, allowing him to compete in events.

Stinger Gets a D

On January 6, 1966, Don received a letter from James Patterson, assistant competition director. In it, he informed Don the Yenko Stinger was recognized by the SCCA in the Production Category, class D, for the 1966 competition season. A second letter was also enclosed "in the event . . . there was trouble convincing potential customers."

This is a sight Don liked: his Stingers out ahead of the competition. Here, a Stinger blasts around a track with other racers nipping close behind. Many Stingers had their hoods painted solid to help cut down on glare and reflection. (Photo Courtesy the Barr Collection)

A Bona Fide Automaker

More good news came on January 17, 1966, in a letter from G. William Fleming, executive director for the Automobile Competition Committee for the United States, Federation Internationale de l'Automobile (FIA). Fleming informed Don that with the SCCA's inspection his organization was pleased to certify that Yenko was a "bona fide constructor of production vehicles" and granted him international homologation.

The Yenko Stinger was considered a Prototype Sports Car in Group 6, Category B of the 1966 FIA Appendix J. This would allow Yenko Sportscars's products to be entered in international competition. In short, Don and his Stinger were off to the races.

Marketing the Stinger

"If your idea of a gutsy Grand Touring Sports car can be met by a nose-heavy, large bore bomb that has been up to imitate sports car performance, then the Yenko Stinger is not for you," said Don about his newest creation. Lots of different slogans and phrases were used to push the Stinger. From calling it a "Corsa with hormones" to "Meet the Boss—the Stinger." Other eye-catching ads boldly asked, "A Stinger for $15,000?" which quickly pointed out "That's what you'd pay if a great handler of a car like the YENKO STINGER was produced in Germany." The ad went on to say viewers could "Buy a $15,000 YENKO STINGER for only $3,450." During races, such as the 1966 12 Hours of Sebring, Yenko handed out pins that said, "Be a Swinger in a Stinger," saying they were worn by Stinger disciples.

Don also had designated areas, called Stinger Nests, were owners could gather. In preparation for the big Riverside race, Yenko set out to psych out the competition for the Riverside revolution by selling T-shirts and buttons that said such things as The Stinger is Coming, Help Stamp Out Tea-Are-Fours, and, of course, the main catchphrase, Be a Swinger in a Stinger.

Don was eager to help out those who were using his cars, and, even though funds were tight, he vowed to lend any assistance. "We're not big enough to subsidize racing on a grand scale," said Yenko. "But we're planning to be liberal with help to Stinger drivers. First, we'll keep everybody informed of the latest tuning developments. In other words, we won't keep any secrets for our factory cars. Second, we're making the Stage III engines available at cost, and parts for it will be sold at cost too."

Press Reaction

Australian auto publication *Sports Car World* got its hands on a Stinger for a full Stage I test for its January 1967 review. The magazine editor led off with a poke back at Mr. Ralph Nader stating: "I have seldom felt so compactly safe in a production car—it corned flat with mild and predictable

final oversteer, stopped clean, and had the torque to get out of trouble." He also found that "as a road car, the nicest thing about a Stage I Yenko is its tractability when puttering about town. With the back seat replaced you can even carry four somewhat cramped."

One negative was the reduced rear-quarter vision, as the Yenko-installed piece blocked visibility. They found that their Stage I test car would do 35 mph in first gear, 45 in second, 68 in third, and 100 in top. It returned better than 24 mph driven "good and hard," and they found 0–60 potential with two passengers of 12 seconds "in normal street rubber and observing the red line scrupulously." The brakes proved up to hard open road driving, but the author didn't have the car long enough to descend an alp. The piece closes with "Fie on you, Nader. At the expense of a very little more bouncy ride Yenko has proven that the Corvair is anything but inherently instable. In fact, it has all the potential of a first-rate travel companion for reasonable money."

Car, a British magazine, got its hands on a Stage I and wrote up a full review for its March 1967 edition. The car was borrowed from an American owner who had imported it to Germany to tow a Stingray 427, and the vehicle still had its trailer hitch in place. Their impressions were generally positive but did state that with the brakes being stock they had doubts about storming any European Alps. They loved the stripes, saying it was the nicest thing about the Stage I besides its tractability round town. They found the floor "gear change" has a taut gate and quick action but the four gears were spaced wrong for competition. Even though theirs was geared to be a tow car and for US speed limits, they reported they got 35 mph in first gear, 45 in second, 68 in third, and then 100 in a hardworking top gear.

Despite the odd spacing, *Car*'s driver returned 24 mpg with the 2.7L engine. For day-to-day use, they wanted Yenko's optional brake-limiting valve to prevent rear wheel lockup. They also wanted bucket seats. All told, their time in the Stinger revealed to them that "Yanks aren't quite so bad at building civilized, interest performance machines . . . without resorting to extravagant quantities of cubic inches at that."

Stingers in Action

Yenko wasted no time getting his Stinger out and competing. Its first time out was on a chilly January 9, 1966, for the inaugural road racing event of the year: the Refrigerator Bowl. Traditionally, the Washington, DC, Region of the SCCA sanctioned the first US sports car race of the year on the demanding, twisty, 1.7-mile circuit. It was the same course Moss had blasted around just a mere 90 days before. It was also the first outing for newly classified production sports cars.

The event was held in 20 degree weather near Upper Malbro, Maryland. During practice, Don and driver Jerry Thompson, the project engineer, turned lap times within a half second of the best posted in its class. Don recalls surprising everyone, including themselves.

Don pokes his head in the engine compartment of a Stinger at an unknown track. Donna Mae is behind the wheel. The Stinger was a real workhorse, hauling around the track and hauling in the pits. Check out that trailer connected to it, no doubt pulling a load of additional tires and parts. (Photo Courtesy the Barr Collection)

Reigning D Production champ Bob Tullius even commented skeptically that there must have been a monorail from Detroit to Canonsburg, implying that Don and his crew were getting direct support from General Motors. Don replied that "Certain Chevrolet people were asked what they thought of the project. Their reply was 'We sold you (Don) 100 Corsas; that's good business for us. What you do with them is your business.'"

When the green flag dropped for real, the Stinger finished third behind the 1965 champion Mark Donohue and his Shelby GT350 and DP runner-up Bob Tullius in his Triumph. Throttle linkage troubles caused the Stinger to retire from the Northeast Division opener.

Major Victories

The Stinger crew continued to charge ahead, and a few weeks later won first overall and first in class in the D-E Production race at the Vineland National Races in New Jersey. The Yenko team was especially excited, as the Triumph entries were "the best cars that Triumph could offer in Eastern competition." Apparently, the "Stinger overwhelmingly outdragged the pack from the start line and it appeared that there would be no competition."

The next major victory was at the Danville National Sports Car Race in Danville, Virginia. Driver Dr. Dick Thompson won the Class D Production

Stingers did well when put out in competition, and many are preserved in track-ready condition. This Stage III Stinger (YS-086) was sold new at Yenko Chevrolet to Jim Spencer of SPAN Inc. and was a dedicated race car.

race on the 3.2-mile road course. His final time was 36 seconds ahead of second place finisher Buzz Marcus, driving a Triumph TR-4, and only 10 seconds behind the Class C Production Porsche Carrera. Thompson led the race from the drop of the green flag, and the victory surprised even Don, who said the Stinger's strong points were handling and braking. "No one believed it would ever take the Triumphs down the long 1-mile straight, let alone run away from them." The Yenko press release went on to say the "Danville win undeniably (made) the Stinger the boss of class DP."

Creating Buzz

Don, Dick Thompson, and the rest of the Stinger drivers caused quite a stir wherever they went. On May 13–15, an estimated 50,000 spectators watched the Cumberland Championship Sports Car races, held at a municipal airport in Cumberland, Maryland. While Don opted to pilot his Sting Ray Corvette, much buzz was around Thompson. He was the man to beat in D Production with his much-talked about Yenko Stinger. A Stinger was also the official pace car and the Stingers Nest area was set up.

Don also entered the Stinger in endurance contests such as the Daytona Continental Test held February 5–6, 1966, at the Daytona International Speedway. Here more than 40 sports, sports prototype, and GT cars representing the fastest makes in Europe and the United States competed. The Stinger averaged more than 80 mph with no mechanical difficulties and placed 23rd overall out of 60 entries. According to a Yenko press release, the car was "ridiculously outclassed in the sports prototype category, being forced to run with Ford GTs, the Chaparral, and Ferrari prototypes." Don stated it was entered as a test of durability "where, as a matter of fact, it outlasted or finished better than a goodly number of the world's fastest cars including all the Cobras, a variety of Ferraris, Ford GTs, and Porsche prototypes." The Stinger made two unscheduled pit stops (one because a crew member had forgotten to tighten the lug nuts and another to repair a throttle rod which was broken while running over a stray pylon). Don reported that after the race the car was in unbelievably excellent condition with both drivers reporting that "the engine was, if anything, stronger than at the beginning of the 24-hour grind."

Later that month, a Dallas Chevrolet dealer and Yenko distributor drove a showroom stock variety Stinger 25 miles in traffic to Green Valley Raceway to compete. With Jerry Thompson behind the wheel and with no practice session, the car moved from 30th to 4th in the class in the preliminary race. It then went from 7th overall to a class 3rd in the main event.

On February 27, a Long Island, New York, Chevrolet dealer drove a Yenko Stinger in the SCCA National Races held at the Palm Beach International Raceway. In the 30-lap competition, he placed 2nd overall and 2nd in Class D Production. The driver lapped the entire field of 13 entries.

On March 26, Donna Mae joined one of two teams competing Stingers in the 12-hour Grand Prix of Endurance at Sebring. On February 12, 1966,

Don wrote a letter to the executive director of the Corvair Club of America informing him that "the Stinger project has gotten off to a real good start." Don went on to say their only problem with the Stinger seemed to be a limited promotional budget.

On June 7, 1966, at the Mansfield National Races in Mansfield, Ohio, another Stinger racer won not only the Class D Production but also "thundered flawlessly up through the ranks of the Class C Production cars." Track officials said his time of 1:56.6 demolished the existing track record (a 1:58.8 set by a Triumph TR-4) and for the first time in the track's history, every lap of the 30-minute race was completed under the old lap record. The other DP competitors were more than 35 seconds behind. According to the *Mansfield News-Journal* the "car just goes. It is perhaps one of the few race-ready cars in the world which you can buy off the shelf and take to the track ready to win your class, come Triumph-or-high-water."

In August, a Chicago Stinger owner drove to Pewaukee, Wisconsin, to compete in the Lynndale Farms SCCA National Road Race. He started in the 29th position (the last in the combined C-D Production grid) to a 3rd overall and 3rd in the Class DP.

Autocross and Other Events

Road courses weren't the only places Stingers were showing well. They were also netting victories in autocross. Around Pittsburgh, a Stage II Stinger finished first in SCCA Class D Production in three consecutive autocrosses. The driver excitedly called the Yenko factory and went on about the win for 30 minutes, saying, "I never received such an ovation for winning a race let alone coming in third. And I'm still running the street carbs! No one believes that I drove the car up here. It's a fantastic way to go racing."

Stingers could also be found competing in gymkhana, which are single car runs over a tight, serpentine course. One family from Indiana competed and was interviewed about the experience. Its Stinger ran the course, but it also doubled as the family car, with the owner's wife saying it was "just the thing for a trip to the supermarket."

Even when the weather turned cold, Stingers could still be found competing. One owner competed in a Rochester, New York, hill climb, equipping his Stinger with spiked snow-tread tires. The Stinger roared into first place, beating a TR-4, which came in third on the 1-mile climb on snow-packed country roads.

On September 19, 1966, another racer took first place in Class D Production and third overall in the SCCA race at the Bridgehampton race circuit, breaking the current TR-4 holder's time. Prior to the race, the driver had decorated the Stinger with signs reading "Unsafe at Any Speed," which all blew off. When asked if he had any problems with the Stinger, he thought hard and mused, "Yes. It was going sideways down that hill."

The Dream Fulfilled

The crowning achievement for Don and his Stinger program occurred on Sunday, November 27, 1967, at the fourth annual American Road Race of Champions (AARC), the world's largest race meeting, held at the Daytona International Speedway in Florida. Jerry Thompson, in his YS-005, captured the SCCA's D Production championship. He was the only Stinger and started 3rd in the field of 18 racers, including Triumph, Jaguar, and Healey. This was a remarkable achievement, considering his Stinger (and any others competing around the country) had no factory backing.

NHRA Racing

On March 8, 1966, Don Yenko went after getting his Stinger classified in stock production in National Hot Rod Association (NHRA) competition. In a letter to the NHRA, he referenced both the SCCA and the FIA's certification. He heard back on May 24. The national tech director stated the modifications made would not permit classification in the Stock Sports classes but possibly C or D Modified Sports classes.

A frustrated Don sent another letter on September 6, asking if they had reviewed the "official documents which prove beyond a shadow of a doubt" that his team was in fact "manufacturing the automobile known as the Yenko Stinger." Another irate letter was sent out on December 2, 1966, after more months of no reply. Finally, on December 19, 1966, Don received a response. The NHRA informed him that, according to their Basic Ground Rules for 1967, any manufacturer of less than 500 units would automatically exclude entry from the Stock class competition. They went on to say that the Stinger couldn't compete because of the advertised power-to-weight factors being in excess of 9.49 pounds per advertised horsepower. Despite Don pointing out several times the approval from the SCCA and the FIA, the NHRA wasn't going to budge, saying their allowances are far in excess of those set by the Competition Committee of the NHRA.

1967 Yenko Stingers

By summer of 1966, Don was ready to look ahead to the 1967 model year. In a letter to Ed Cole on July 2, he gleefully stated that "by this time, we feel we have really hammered D Production to a pulp and are ready to take on the C Production boys if we're reclassified next year." Don went on to say that he had received word that the Stinger was classified in the NASCAR Drag Division in the H Stock category, making their Stage III "an almost automatic winner."

All his excitement at what was ahead was soon dampened by a major setback. Chevrolet had found the high-end Corsa wasn't selling well (totaling around 10,000 and making up about one-tenth of total Corvair sales) and dropped it in the new 1967 model year, leaving just the lower-tiered 500

and Monza series. That wasn't the worst of it; they also trimmed the 140-hp engine option. That was a major blow to Don, as he needed it for his Stingers to remain competitive on the track. Not to mention all of the time and resources he had spent developing additional parts for it.

"All in all, prospects look good for the '67 Stingers," Don wrote to Cole, "With the exception of the fact that I understand that the 140 engine is to be deleted from the 1967 line. If so, this will present a big problem for me. As you know, the 140 engine is our standard Stage I engine and also the engine which we modify for the Stages II and III. The 110-hp engine has a single port head which is useless for our purposes; the cost of replacing the cylinder head on each of these engines would be prohibitive." Don then proposed if he could purchase Corvairs with the 140-hp engine as a COPO in quantities of 25, scaling up if necessary to meet demand.

While the new year ahead looked uncertain for the Stinger, Don wasn't out of the woods yet with his first batch. In his letter to Cole, he said, "If

The 1967 Stingers are easily recognized by their red or blue paint colors. This Marina Blue Stinger was built on March 20, 1967, and sold new through Anderson Foreign Motors, in Swampscott, Massachusetts. Customers were charged $45 for the competition tri-stripes.

The sail panels and fiberglass decklid would still be installed on the 1967 Stingers, but the stage designation was moved from the driver-side corner of the spoiler to the center. This car's owner, Ed, and his son, Ted, have raced this Stinger at vintage track events.

Tech Insight: 1967 YS Door Tags

The first 1967 Yenko Stinger received the YS-107 door tag. The reasoning for the jump in sequence (as opposed to picking up with 101) was to fill some holes and to cover a few special circumstances.

Tag 101 went to the 100th 1966 car, which was bumped up because the prototype car was built from a stock, non-COPO Corvair and was slid into the Stinger sequence.

Tags 102 through 104 were reserved for 1966 Corvair requests put in by City Chevrolet of Canada. The dealership wanted Stingers but had to order them in Canada to avoid heavy tariff charges and thus, they weren't ordered as COPOs but rather stock Corsas. Cars 102 and 103 were converted at City Chevrolet to Stingers and got the appropriate YS door tags. Car (and tag 104) was used by Maurice Carter, owner of City Chevrolet, for his Stage IV Stinger race car, which was converted in Canonsburg at Yenko Chevrolet.

Tag 105 went to one of the original 100 COPO Corvairs of 1966, though the sequencing is unclear. Similarly, tag 106 went to YS-065 but was never used. The doubling-up of tags could most likely be attributed to Don trying to update and revamp the lingering 1966 Stingers on his lot, reselling them as 1967 Stingers.

On November 30, 1967, Ed Cole praised Don again. A Stinger won the National road racing championship at Daytona, and Cole said Don was to be congratulated and he had "done a terrific job with Corvair." By this time, word had seeped out about how the Stinger came to be. A *Cincinnati Enquirer* piece in July 1967 said, "Just about everybody connected with auto racing is in agreement that General Motors is coming back into racing. . . . I know for a fact that Yenko has the full blessing of Chevrolet on his sports car projects which help to solidify the idea that GM will soon be racing."

The sequencing of the tags put on Stingers after the initial 100 can get a little hairy and hard to follow, due to a couple peculiar circumstances. The tags were still installed in the driver-side door-jamb, just like on the 1966 cars.

This 1967 Stinger YS-119 was sold new at Jay Kline Chevrolet in Minneapolis, Minnesota, on July 27, 1967.

you can think of any way to help me dispose of 50 Corsa coupes, I'd be indebted to you." It took Don most of 1966 to sell the initial batch of Stingers.

That summer, Cole agreed to let the 140-hp engine be installed under COPO 9551B. Don felt 1967 would "be an even better year" (which it was, thanks to Jerry Thompson winning the D Production championship). He told Cole that he already had a firm commitment for 20 units from his Midwestern distributor with his Canadian distributor, City Chevrolet, projecting wanting 100 cars.

In December 1966, Don placed a COPO order for 25 Corvairs. Even though approval came in the summer, the cars weren't built until the fourth week of February 1967. Typical vehicle production called for the engines to be built sometime soon after the body so the cars aren't sitting, but these 1967 Corvairs had some sort of delay. Their engines (bearing code T0306RM) were all built on March 6, meaning the Corvair bodies sat for nearly a week before final assembly. The cause of the delay is unknown.

The 140-hp engines weren't exactly the same from the year prior and did need some modifications, mostly related to new carburetors that were installed. The 1967 batch also received a heavy-duty suspension (3F41AA), a 4-speed transmission (3M20BC), special steering (3N44AA), black interior trim (3758AA), the 3.89 Positraction differential (9513A), and a wheel cover delete (9551B). Interestingly, all 1967 Corvairs (COPOs and not), got the dual-master brake cylinder that had been installed under the special COPO for 1966 Stingers.

The redesigned gauge cluster caused a hiccup for Don and his team when creating a new batch of Stingers for 1967. Their solution was to add a tach in the center of the pod and offer customers additional gauging down low on the dashboard.

Adding an optional set of Stewart Warner gauging (for $50) helped drivers stay informed of their engine vitals. Don was doing the same thing on the 1967 Camaros he and his team were converting to 427 power.

The dropping of the Corsa line caused another hiccup for Don. The 1966 Corsa offered a multi-gauge pod, with a cluster of two large gauges flanking four smaller ones. In total, drivers could monitor six vehicle vitals: speedometer, clock, fuel, oil pressure, oil temperature, and tachometer. All that data was helpful for drivers who wanted to mix it up on the track. However, the Monza, being a lower trim, had a simplified cluster of three large gauges: speedometer, an optional clock, and fuel. Don had asked that summer for the Corsa dash to be installed under a COPO but never heard back. He ordered Stewart Warner 970 tachometers and had his technicians install them in the center pod (where the optional clock was located). For $79, Stinger buyers could also select an optional gauge cluster from Yenko, giving them a trio of gauges for oil temperature, ammeter, and oil pressure. The cluster was mounted down low at the bottom of the dash, just ahead of the gear selector.

One of the Stinger's shortcomings was with the transmission. Racers complained about a large gap between second and third gears. Don recruited help from R.S.T. Engineering, which was a group of GM engineers that had set up a side business in Utica, Michigan, tuning Corvairs. R.S.T. developed a close ratio transmission, building several units for $350 each. Don would also use R.S.T. Engineering for additional projects, such as his Z28 Camaro (non-COPO).

One exterior change made on the 1967 Stingers was the Stage script was moved from the driver's side of the decklid to the center of the decklid, within the center stripe.

Of the 25 Corvairs Don ordered, 11 were painted Marina Blue (3900FF) and 14 were painted Bolero Red (3900 RR, a new Corvair paint color for 1967). Many thought 11 red cars were sold to the Canadian mar-

ket because Canada's racing colors were red and white. But these sales have never been confirmed and none have been located. The remaining 3 red cars were sold in the United States.

Non-Stinger COPO Corvairs

Don was aiming to expand his sales network when he connected with Dana Chevrolet in South Gate, California, with plans of having them become a West Coast distributor. One hindrance was transportation costs. Each vehicle in a load of six cost $250 to be transported cross-country. The solution was shipping the COPO Corvairs from the Willow Run facility directly to California.

At the end of January 1967, Donna Mae advised and facilitated the Dana staff with their order in requesting the proper COPOs. The dealership ordered three COPO Corvairs, but the partnership dissolved before the cars were converted to Stingers.

Yenko Camaro Stormer and Yenko Chevy II

Less than a year after the start of his Stingers program, Don was already hitting up General Motors to support additional road-racing programs. Don saw potential in the Camaro Z28 and began developing a program he called the Z28 Camaro Stormer. He aimed to get it competing in the SCCA's A Sedan class. In September, he asked Chevrolet for help fabricating special wheels, exhaust systems, and oil coolers.

Don also pitched and idea to do the same thing to the Chevy II, "in addition or perhaps in place of the Camaro," which he declared would be

Don's creative wheels were always turning, and he already had ideas to improve the Stinger. This sketch, drawn by Don, shows what he had in mind for the Mark II version of the Stinger, one he was going to call the Yenko Scorpion. (Photo Courtesy the Barr Collection)

Don wanted to ditch the Stinger's decklid doors in favor of twin snorkel scoops that would direct fresh, cold air to the engine. He was really going to play with airflow, planning on installing additional scoops ahead of the rear wheels, air extractors in the hood, and spoilers on the front fenders. (Photo Courtesy the Barr Collection)

a "sure winner." Always thinking big, Don wanted to roll out the kits and merchandise the unit as a package that was ready to race similar to the manner in which Carroll Shelby offered the fully prepared Mustang for sedan racing. He stated the organization handling the project would be called Yenko Sportscars, with no connection to Yenko Chevrolet. His grand ideas were ignored, but he didn't give up.

Super Stinger

As 1967 and 1968 rolled around, it became obvious that the market wasn't into the Corvair anymore. Sales dwindled and interest faded, but if there was one person who eagerly saw a massive resurgence, it was Don. Not that he had time on his hands to fantasize; he was busy making his 427-equipped Camaros, but it was clear his heart wasn't in it. The drag racing scene made him money but his passion was road racing, and he wanted to get back into it.

On May 31, 1968, Don wrote Ed Cole, lamenting the lack of interest in the Corvair, which he deemed "one of the finest production machines ever built" and asked how Yenko Sportscars could help boost the Corvair image. "We promote the Corvair as a great-handling, trophy-winning, performance-packaged Tiger—all of which are certainly seldom associated with the Corvair description," wrote Don. "Frankly, it is a losing battle. Stinger sales have dropped to a standstill because we don't have the ability to carry on a full-blown promotional job."

Don knew his team could coax a lot more horsepower out of the Stinger. He said this would generate interest by beating the factory-backed Triumph, Datsun, and Lotus team. Don wanted to combine forces to create an undercover factory team. His goal was to have Chevrolet build a special Corvair with striped tires, vinyl top options, special trim, a fiberglass hood, disc brakes, and the reinstatement of the Corsa instrument panel. He wanted help from General Motors to create a prototype, the Super Stinger, that he was hoping to compete in the six-hour FIA race, held July 13–15 at Watkins Glen to attract attention and promotion. Don figured if it went well General Motors could justify doing a whole remodeling program where to upgrade the Corvair image. Don even offered to purchase 500 of them to get them reclassified as Mark II Stingers.

Don closed his letter to Cole by saying that his ideas had "worked for Shelby, Kas Kastner [driving for Triumph], Colin Chapman [the founder and manager of Lotus], and even American Motors. I think we can easily steal their stuff. And nobody will know we're even doing it." Don's enthusiasm couldn't overcome outside forces. Even though automotive experts refuted Ralph Nader's concerns, GM's legal department grew disenchanted with the car, as did dealers, who, worried about lawsuits, stopped stocking them. With buyers flocking to the Chevy II, the Corvair was offered as a special-order item. Finally, in 1969, production stopped as did Don's dreams of a Super Stinger race car.

This 1969 Goodyear Corvair is truly a one-off and unique twist to the Stinger story. While it lacks any of the visuals that made the Stingers stand out, it was still a COPO, having been ordered with specific performance goals in mind through the Central Office. Bob Dunahugh is the car's proud owner.

Swan Song: 1969 Stinger

In a moment of poetic irony, Don would get his chance to build an over-the-top, all-out, COPO-built Corvair race car in 1969. This final swan song was for the most unlikely of customers: Ford. The Blue Oval boys were developing a high-speed car for their Australian division and the plan was to equip it with Goodyear tires. The only problem was Ford didn't make a model that ran 13-inch tires and could hit targeted speeds of up to 140 mph.

In the fall of 1968, Goodyear started talking with Don and Donna Mae about what exactly the Stingers could do, seeing it as a great high-speed testing platform. In a series of letters that were exchanged in November, they discussed details for Goodyear to buy a Stinger outright to own, have it converted into a full-fledged race car, and use it at their private facility. On November 18, Donna wrote S. H. Clark of the Tire Testing Division that they could build a Stage IV for around $5,000. It would be equipped with good carburetors, the Stinger cam (although they had a "wild one" they were going to try which "may be better"), oil pressure and temperature gauges, and 7-inch rims all around (bigger than the 5.5 standard wheels).

Goodyear needed a vehicle that could attain triple digit speeds in order to test a new 13-inch tire that was going to be installed on a Ford vehicle that was to be sold in Australia.

Donna Mae and Don suggested the car be equipped with a Stage IV engine with additional add-ons, including high-flow racing carbure-tors ($300), heavy-duty valve guides ($102), and, at one point, long exhausts. Donna Mae felt confident it would attain nearly 145 mph after hearing local Stage II owners report they could hit 120 mph on the turnpikes.

Unsure of their exact plans for the vehicle, she cautioned that "noise alone would prevent this car from being licensable for street use." She estimated that on a long enough straight (like the oval at Daytona), the car "will attain almost 145 miles per hour," but to do that, the car would need a few extra days and a couple hundred extra dollars to lighten it up.

Clark wrote back on November 25 saying his team wanted a detailed quote for a Stage IV but with additional modifications. They requested a roll bar, oil cooler, long exhaust outlets, 14-gallon auxiliary fuel tank, a tachometer, and a tall 3.27:1 axle ratio. The gear ratio was different from the other COPO Stingers, which under COPO 9513A all had 3.89:1 gears. When it came to tires, the car was to be fitted with Goodyear 6.50/11-13-inch Sports Car Special tires in the rear and Goodyear 5.6/10-13-inch Sports Car Special front tires. While the car could have been lightened, they opted to forego any kind of weight reduction. They wanted the tires to have a load on them for proper testing.

Donna Mae worked up the quote for this special vehicle, which was to be built on a Corvair 500 coupe. Building on the base price for the Stage IV Stinger, which rang up at $4,420 and included a COPO 3.27:1 rear end, a quick steering gear box ratio, special heavy-duty suspension, long exhausts, and full competition engine. The car also got head restraints ($15.80, and now government mandated), the SCCA–approved Yenko roll bar ($134), metallic sintered brakes ($79.45), four high-flow racing carburetors ($79.45), special heavy-duty valve guides ($102), extra heavy-duty clutch disc ($52), and four 7-inch double reinforced steel racing wheels ($104). Instead of using their idea for a 14-gallon auxiliary fuel tank, Yenko recommended going with a 24-gallon Corvette tank ($80.00). When under full throttle, the powerplant sucked down fuel to the tune of 3 mpg.

The interior was left intact, as Goodyear did not want the car lightened. During testing, around 660 pounds were on each tire, which were usually run until they blew. A roll bar ($134) was installed for safety.

Modifications to the special test car included a "Big Red Light" that was mounted in the middle of the dashboard. It would come on if anything went wrong with the engine during testing.

Open the front hood and you'll find the remote oil cooler that Don's team installed. The option cost $250 and included heavy-duty armored oil lines that ran back to the engine compartment. Fresh air was funneled through a vent in the lower valance and routed up into the metal housing.

The special Corvair sits parked at the Goodyear testing facility. It was equipped with hood pins but, naturally, no fiberglass sail panels in the rear windows. That cosmetic touch was not needed for the serious testing this car underwent. (Photo Courtesy Bob Dunahugh)

Even though Don and his team were busily ramping up their Yenko Supercar network and efforts in 1969 crafting their Chevelles, Camaros, and Novas, they made time for this special project. It was the closest Don would come to building the all-out Stinger he had envisioned.

Don charged hard with his Stinger, moving from passionate racer to custom car creator. The success of the program only came about because of lots of exhausting work and just as much ingenuity and determination. Mark Pieloch owns this example.

Besides being thirsty, the hopped-up powerplant made some heat. To help it run better, Don's team installed a special remote engine oil cooler made by Harrison Aircraft. It was mounted in the car's trunk (at the front of the car, as the Corvair's engine is in the rear) and came complete with heavy-duty armored oil lines that ran the length of the car back to the engine compartment ($250). A special inlet in the center of the lower front valance routed fresh air to blow in a special duct, cooling the oil. An electric fuel pump was also mounted up front.

Goodyear got a Don Yenko discount of $650, but with taxes, the total came to $5,021.65. At the bottom of the paperwork, Don reminded them that "this car will not be licensable for street use, in our opinion." Goodyear selected the car to be painted white paired with a blue interior. The order was processed in the end of January, and the car was delivered in March. It went to Goodyear's proving grounds and 5-mile oval track in San Angelo, Texas, where it ran high-speed laps all spring and summer. It took some effort to get it dialed in. During testing in June, the engine blew and needed to be rebuilt with new pistons, rings, spark plugs, and other items. After some tweaking, the testing team was able to get the car up to very satisfying 125- and 130-mph speeds. The vehicle was also used to test a line of studded snow tires and received scatter shields in the fender wells, which would prevent them from being thrown through the bodywork in the event the studs came loose.

Engineers racked up just over 2,300 miles on the test-mule before selling in 1976 to Bob Dunahugh, a budding racer. He tore it down and performed a complete overhaul. In 2007, he took the car to Talladega, Alabama, for a day of all-out running. His average top speed was 142.2 mph, and all from a non-turbocharged, no nitrous 6-cylinder. "It's terrible on short tracks," said Bob. "It doesn't really get kicking till it's warmed up and over 6,000 rpm. But let it loose and it really moves."

Stinger Summary

Don Yenko accomplished quite a lot with his Corvair Stinger. To go from nothing but a vision to a full-fledged, certified, international race car in a matter of months was a truly monumental task. His love of racing (and winning) knew no bounds, driving him to overcome arduous hurdles. While he would have preferred to come out of the gate hard charging to victory in the 1966 season, surely he felt vindicated when that moment arrived soon after in 1967. While the Stinger program was driven by passion, dollars and market demand would drive Don's next venture.

CHAPTER 2

1967 CAMARO 427 CONVERSIONS

BUILDING THE PERFECT BIG-BLOCK BEAST

Just as his Stinger venture was getting underway, Don already was on to something new. If the Stinger was a passion project fueled by Don's love for road racing, his next undertaking was strictly a case of following the money and keeping up with the competition. Realizing its Corvair wouldn't be the machine to properly compete with Ford's Mustang, on September 29, 1966, Chevrolet debuted its entry into the quickly heating up pony-car segment, the iconic Camaro.

After a false start with Dana Chevrolet, Don revved up his operations and started cranking out his own 427-converted Camaros. Dick Harrell built this Royal Plum example (the only one known in that color) for Don Yenko. It was supposed to be delivered to Canonsburg. Instead, it was shipped to Harrell and then to Jay Kline Chevrolet, where it was sold new. David Boland currently owns it.

While the muscle car had been engineered to accept a rumbling big-block V-8, because of the brand's continued adherence to its self-imposed engine displacement restrictions, as well as the AMA ban, it wasn't about to put one in. In 1967, *Car Life* magazine declared for a while, it seemed like the Camaro was "to be a second-thought car," citing how for a time, Chevrolet "preferred to ignore Ford's highly successful Mustang, but then had second thoughts."

Then, once the Camaro was designed and built, the biggest, hottest engine option was to be a newly developed 350-ci V-8 (the L48 option). General Motors was still abiding by its unwritten policy limiting engine displacement to 10 hp per 100 pounds, so the Camaro would have no more than 295 hp. When Ford announced its 1967 Mustang could come equipped with a 390-ci engine, Chevrolet woke up and announced the 396-ci V-8 option. More shots were fired when Carroll Shelby broke the news that his new GT-500 package was powered by a 428-ci V-8 engine. Chevrolet later added a 375-hp L78 396-ci V-8 big-block engine option to the lineup in an attempt to compete but wouldn't go one step further.

That wouldn't stop others from seeing the potential for the space between those front fenders, just begging for bigger engines to be shoehorned in. *Car Craft* magazine, in its February 1967 edition, discussed how Ford and Chrysler were putting high horsepower engines into their small cars and the growing concern that Chevrolet fans would be left "out to lunch with worthy" competitors.

Any fears for the Bowtie faithful were put to rest as soon as Camaros began showing up at dealerships, where, in no time, engine transplants began taking place. In the revved up era of the 1960s, engine conversions were common across the nation, and Camaros everywhere were getting the 427 treatment. With the popularity of the sporty model and the boom in demand for performance upgrades, dealerships were doubling down on their tuning and enhancing efforts and it was paying handsomely. That caught no one off guard. *Motor Trend* reviewed one such 427-Camaro transplant, saying "What everyone knew all along would happen has." *Car Craft* called that kind of move inevitable. Just because Chevrolet wasn't going to move forward with making the Camaro an all-out performer didn't mean others wouldn't. While the 1967 cars weren't ordered through the Central Office, they certainly deserve an honorable mention for paving the way for the muscle-oriented COPOs that would soon follow.

Speed and Supercar magazine discussed the growing trend of 427-swapped Camaros in its August 1967 edition, saying in general, no matter who builds it, the "427 Camaro is the quickest and fastest supercar on the market . . . and it's more streetable and easier to live with than some of the lesser powerful, production-line models coming out of Motor City." The Camaro needed help. Even in the hottest factory shape with 396 ci and 325 hp, the Camaro is no match for the Shelby GT Mustangs or the special 440 Barracuda, which is on the plans board as of this writing. The

actual conversion from 327-, 350-, or 396-cube shape to SS-427 condition is a simple one with the end product looking as stock as any line Camaro. The actual changes are minor as compared to the average small-to-large-cube engine conversion. Besides, the price is right!

1967 Conversions: "A friendly musclemobile unbeatable on the street!"

Gearheads within Chevrolet dealerships around the country were racing to not only assemble these special and desirable vehicles but also to get them marketed and distributed. They all had the same conclusion of where to start: the SS350 Camaro. That foundation offered a heavy-duty suspension and radiator, metallic brakes, a 4-speed Muncie transmission, Positraction, and red stripe tires. From there, they all knew where they wanted to end up: have the car equipped with the Corvette's 427-ci V-8. That was a winning combination and one buyers had to have. No matter where enthusiasts were located, 427 Camaros could be had all across the nation. *Speed and Supercar* attributed this small group of dealers scattered across the nation as salvaging Chevrolet's rapidly sinking performance image.

West Coast: Dana's 427 Camaro

Out on the West Coast, there was Dana Chevrolet, located south of Los Angeles in South Gate, California. Its Hi-Performance center was stocked

The dealership's main showroom was located a little under a mile away from a separate Hi-Performance Center. It was advertised as featuring "race-bred service mechanics," new and used "hi-performance street, strip, and track cars," and a complete line of Chevrolet high-performance parts and accessories. (Photo Courtesy the Barr Collection)

The 427-converted Camaro wasn't the only hopped-up Camaro Dana's performance center created. They also built Z28 Camaros for rallying and auto-crossing, offering additional speed parts for it, such as fuel cells, roll bars, and mag wheels. (Photo Courtesy the Barr Collection)

full of hot cars and its ace technicians could readily be found performing engine swaps on Camaros. One of the dealership's owners, Peyton Cramer, was a former Shelby American employee who had played a key role in starting the GT350 Mustang project.

Cramer sought out another Shelby alum, Don McCain, a drag racing specialist who had helmed both Cobras and GT350s in competitive drag racing. Together they set their sights on dethroning the Ford tuner's steeds and

put together their Dana 427 Camaro. They partnered with Yenko Sports-cars to build the Dana Camaro under license and get it distributed on the East Coast. "My experience with Shelby has shown me many of the pitfalls of this business, and I'm sure that there's a steady market for this type of high-performance machine," said Peyton. The relationship between Dana and Yenko was reciprocal; the West Coast dealer built and distributed the Stinger.

The hopped-up Camaro, which was designed by Don Yenko and the Dana guys, even had the same base price as that of the GT350. Dana advertised Its hot sportster as "Looks like a Camaro . . . drives like a Ferrari!" Starting with a Camaro SS, they swapped out the factory 350-ci V-8 for that 427-ci V-8. The 427 engines arrived without carb, clutch disc, and bellhousing. Starters and alternators were sourced from 350-ci engines and the original 350 was removed and the 427 bolted in with "plenty of room . . . for ease in maintenance and servicing."

Other components (some part of the SS package) included 6-inch-wide wheels, special springs and shocks, badging, a 4-speed transmission, a heavy-duty radiator, and redline tires. Extra Stage packages (similar to the Yenko Stinger) could be tacked on, boosting capability, with top dog being a Stage III intended for racing. Knowing the stock gauging needed improvement, for $79 buyers could have a Sun Tach installed on the steering column and a pod above the console with Stewart Warner oil pressure and water temp gauges. The biggest cosmetic change was an optional custom-made twin-inlet, fiberglass hood, which buyers could have for $125.

Motor Trend got its hands on one for a road test for its July 1967 magazine and came away impressed at the performance. "No matter how many 'hot' cars you've driven, the first time you really uncork a Dana Camaro you're

Converted Dana Camaros had fenders full of badging, with the dealership lettering at the top. Nickey Chevrolet did the same thing. Next, wedged between the factory Camaro script and the crossed flags, would be Corvette hood numerals, showing 427 and ultimately what was under the hood. (Photo Courtesy the Barr Collection)

Car Life's Dana Road Test

Car Life thoroughly tested a heavily optioned Dana 427 Camaro retailing at $5,500. According to the magazine, "swapping engines is a snap" as the Camaro engine compartment was "obviously designed to accept the 396 and external dimensions of the 396 and 427 are exactly alike." During Car Life's test of Dana's creation, it found it was not the best for "round-town junketing" with the lack of power steering making the Camaro very difficult to park. They approached the throttle with caution and, as to be more than expected, found that wheelspin happened in any gear when full throttle was applied. The test crew pulled some runs at Carlsbad Raceway and found it difficult to get the Camaro off the line with "any semblance of order" and wheelspin was happening all through third gear. They thought with better traction (via chassis mediation and suitable tires), a full 2 seconds could be knocked off the 14.2 second elapsed time in the quarter mile.

Dick Harrell

Dick Harrell was a name that surfaced several times throughout the heyday of the muscle-oriented COPO vehicles. He was attached to several of the iconic vehicles and worked with other key COPO-related figures.

Harrell grew up in Carlsbad, New Mexico, and got into cars, racing, and going fast while stationed at the Fort Sill, Oklahoma, army base. "I bought a new 1956 Chevy," said Harrell. "They had a strip in Oklahoma, and I started running on weekends just for the fun of it." After winning a couple trophies, he was hooked, moving to a new 1961 Chevy and competing at drag strips in Texas and back home in New Mexico. Until 1961, he was racing for fun, making just enough to cover expenses while also bringing in cash from a second job as a machinist.

Later that year, Harrell struck out with his sights set on making a name for himself on a national level, managing to acquire backing from Chevrolet. The obscure youngster headed to the AHRA Winter Nationals and let his driving do the talking as his lightning quick reflexes propelled him into the winner's circle. Ready to move on and keep the momentum going, at the end of the 1963 season, he made the decision to truly go professional. He embarked on a touring circuit, competing at nearly every major strip in the country, smoking many of the big-name racers off the line. The likeable country boy quickly gained a following, taking time in the pits to put down his tools and answer questions from his growing fan base, his genuine passion for his occupation evident.

The crowds and spectators also loved him because Harrell was the king of wheel standing, and, despite the fact that his runs were usually made with the front wheels high in the air, he rarely lost. "The front end comes off the ground every time I start," said Dick. "Of course, now I'm used to it, but I still don't take it for granted. You can never lose respect for the car. Oh, I've kept the front wheels off for an entire eighth of a mile and the left front tire is generally off the ground for an entire race."

Naturally, things got tough in 1965 when General Motors officially dropped out of racing, pulling all financial and speed parts support from its racers. Soon Harrell was the only major driver left competing in a Chevrolet. "We scrounged around with what we had," Harrell explained. "But it made it pretty hard not being able to get any parts." Instead of jumping to Ford or Chrysler, the diehard Chevrolet fan stayed with the brand, earn-

Dick Harrell (left) was a passionate and serious competitor and drag racer who loved speed. He was the driving force behind some of the vehicles crafted through Chevrolet's Central office. Here he is with Don Yenko. (Photo Courtesy the Barr Collection)

ing the nickname Mr. Chevrolet.

In the fall of 1966, Nickey Chevrolet in Chicago, Illinois, was looking to expand into drag racing and hired Dick as a professional driver and performance adviser. A "fantabulous salary" lured him to the Windy City, where he set up a thriving performance car program for the dealership. In 1966, he jumped back in to become a driver and the performance advisor for Nickey Chevrolet in Chicago, Illinois, soon moving to the Windy City because they offered him a "fantabulous salary" to set up Its performance car program. Besides campaigning a highly successful Chevy II drag car and Camaro, one of his projects was pioneering the 427-ci V-8 Camaro transplant. Nickey fully leveraged Dick's credibility with potential buyers, running ads like one in the *Chicago Tribune* touting that "'Dickie' Harrell would be at the store year-round to help you select the correct (speed) equipment."

bound to be awe-stricken if not outright panicked at the sheer magnitude of the forces unleashed," wrote John Ethridge. "At about T plus 1/2-second you begin to wonder if maybe you hadn't ought to have done it, a feeling which persists until you either chicken out and get off it or shift into third gear."

Ethridge found a restrained throttle foot was the order of the day, both on the strip and street. First gear was useless for acceleration runs as it would spin the stock tires. The *Motor Trend* crew bolted on a set of Goodyear slicks, uncorked the headers, and posted 12.75 seconds in the quarter mile at 110

Like a lot of the other 427-converted Camaros, there weren't major identifying marks on the front of a Dana Camaro indicating what was rambling behind the grille. (Photo Courtesy the Barr Collection)

cars, fielding Corvette teams for years and stocking its 20,000–square foot parts area (the largest in the country) with high-performance drag racing merchandise.

Nickey's strategy was tried and true: get the word out that the place to go fast is back at Nickey and sell all those eager fans performance upgrades and parts. In turn, that income was reinvested right back into racing, and so the cycle went. Inventory was flying off the shelves and the store was constantly making improvements to its parts area, which had the world's largest inventory of Chevrolets parts. In 1967, it had 27 employees working the parts counter, managing more than 200,000 parts. It used ads with such phrasing as "From accel to zoom," "from mild to wild," and "if it's for speed, we sell it."

The dealership hired Dick Harrell to be its performance advisor in 1966. As the story goes, before the first Camaro had slipped off the transport at the dealership, he and the parts manager were out measuring the engine compartment. Like everyone else, they knew the stock 350 ci wasn't going to cut it. Dick removed the hood, battery, radiator, and 350 and found the 427 slipped right in, perfectly matching the engine mounts with no cutting, bending, or welding required. "I thought the 427 would adapt well so I tried it," explained Dick. "It just fell in."

The 427's extra weight dropped the front of the vehicle 1 inch, so Harrell installed heavy-duty spacers to fix this. Wanting customers to be able to race in stock racing classes, Nickey and Harrell got the car classified for competition in the American Hot Rod Association (AHRA) for use in their

mph. They were confident more performance could be extracted. While at the track, numerous bystanders called out to know if the car was driven to the strip and the answer was yes and "without the slightest difficulty."

Ethridge wrote: "The 427 always came to life on the first or second turn on chilly mornings. And although the engine is hooked on super-premium gas, highway mileage of around 12–14 mph qualifies it as a social drinker. To be perfectly frank, the Dana Camaro is not everyone's motor car and it was never intended to be. But to the enthusiast who can afford it, it offers a combination of the highest order of performance and utility value that is hard to match." Production numbers on how many conversions Dana performed remains a mystery, although Peyton claimed 60 dealers were handling the Dana Camaro. Records of total vehicles converted were not saved and best guesses today indicate less than 100 vehicles were made. At some point, Yenko and Dana fell out of sorts and the relationship was cut off.

Midwest: Nickey Chevrolet's 427 Camaro

In the Midwest, Nickey Chevrolet, located in Chicago, Illinois, also wanted in on the action. It teamed up with several key individuals to launch its own super car. Nickey was no stranger to fast

A young man from Morton Grove, Illinois, bought this 1967 Emerald Turquoise SS Camaro new from Humphrey Chevrolet in nearby Evanston, Illinois. Wanting to go even faster, in 1968 he went to Nickey, plunking down top dollar to have an L88 427 installed. Slicks were installed too. The unrestored car has never left the Chicagoland area, and today it's owned by Jim Pearse.

The original owner and his brother-in-law, Pete, took the Camaro drag racing, posting times in the 11.50- to 11.60-second range. At some point, an aftermarket Sun Tach was installed but later removed. The car has a factory tach in the right gauge pod and factory gauging ahead of the shifter.

On the way home after Nickey's engine upgrade, the owner eagerly launched hard from a stop sign, wanting to see what his ride could do. Not only did the tires break free, all that newfound power broke the rear axle's center section, twisting it loose on the tube sections. The dealership's tow truck retrieved the vehicle and a new rear end was installed.

The car's block was built in the end of August and is identified as an L88 by the IT at the end of the stamping. It wasn't standard protocol for Nickey to paint engine blocks yellow, but the owner wanted it done after seeing a magazine article showing Bill Thomas standing next to one.

new Super Stock class. The NHRA wouldn't allow anything built outside the factory to compete. The goal was to have it run in the NHRA's Super Stock class and, since the work was done before the customer picked the vehicle up, Nickey offered it with a warranty. The dealer also offered a kit for individuals to do the modification at home, but the NHRA would place those home-built cars in Modified Production, Gas, or Factory Experimental classes.

Nickey wanted to go big with the venture and looped in Bill Thomas. Thomas, a racer and car-tuner, was located in southern California and had been preparing road racing Corvettes since the late 1950s. He opened a shop, Bill Thomas Race Cars in Anaheim, California, and was approached several times by General Motors to help develop performance options for the Corvair and Chevy II. In 1963, he even built what Chevy was hoping to be a dead-on Shelby Cobra-killer: the ultra-fast Cheetah. Nickey set up his shop as its West Coast associate and stocked him with the complete Nickey high-performance parts line as well has had him build 427 Camaros. The Camaros carried the Nickey nameplate and were classified as stock by the AHRA.

East Coast: Baldwin/Motion Performance 427 Camaro

Out on the East Coast, racing enthusiast Joel Rosen, owner of Motion Performance, convinced the management at Baldwin Chevrolet, in

Car Craft's Nickey Road Test

The crew at *Car Craft* could hardly wait to try out Nickey's 427 Camaro for its February 1967 edition. The crew came to Chicago and found that on cold mornings, it started right up, and after a short warm-up (outside temps neared 30 degrees) they blasted down the street. They found "almost no foot pressure was necessary to paste you to the back of the seat, and the engine worked smooth and effortlessly in moving the Camaro through the gears." The manual steering seemed completely unaffected by the added 90 pounds of the 427, and it had the quick response of a race car. It cornered like you had that "glued-in feeling," with the Camaro going into corners flat and stable with no sway. They found that the 427 Camaro "as a gymkhana machine should be pretty wild."

The crew headed to Great Lakes Dragway at Union Grove, Wisconsin, to run the car down the track. As it turns out, it was "everything you could ask for," posting 11.4 seconds at 126 mph in the quarter mile. In September 1967, *Car and Driver* got around to testing a Nickey 427, saying "no doubt about it, (it's) an attention-getter" and it "looks exactly what it is—a Camaro with Mr. America musculature." The potential of this combination seemed ". . . almost unlimited, leaving a lot of room for experimentation. In street trim the Camaro is a wild, going concern, and on the strip it will keep you right in the thick of the competition."

Unlike COPO-created cars that had to hide their identities and capabilities, Motion machines proudly proclaim their high-performance lineage. The speed shop went to flamboyant measures to make sure its cars stood out. Anything that called out the 427, L88, or its SS-roots was welcomed. Mark Hassett owns this Lemans Blue 1968 example and that's his son, Mark Jr., behind the wheel, lighting up the rear end.

This Phase III's L88 V-8 is equipped with aluminum cylinder heads and an aluminum high-rise intake manifold topped with a dyno-jetted 950-cfm Holley 3-barrel carburetor. Customers who wanted this kind of performance had to pony up close to $5,000 for a Phase III Camaro.

The dealership grew to embrace the partnership with Motion, eventually calling themselves the East Coast Headquarters for the Chevrolet Racing Division. All the attention the hot cars received was good for business and helped drive traffic back into the showroom.

This car was given a full suite of Stewart Warner gauging, including a 160-mph speedometer and tach in the factory cluster and, down below, additional instrumentation. Another unique add-on is the toggle switch below the ignition. The original owner, from Texas, bought the car to dominate his street racing scene. Flipping it killed the taillights, allowing the car to disappear during those late-night, highway pursuits.

The Motion Supercar Club quickly became the "in" place for serious performance enthusiasts. Benefits of paying your annual $5 dues included getting a cool status sticker (such as this one here) and other perks, such as a membership card, jacket patch, and discounts on speed parts.

Joel Rosen and the Motion crew employed all the tips and tricks of the trade, including bolting in traction weights in the trunk, adding much needed grip during hard launches.

Baldwin, Long Island (located some 30 miles east of New York City) to team up. Initially, the young man's plan was to get Baldwin Chevrolet to sponsor a new 1967 Camaro for use in Modified Production race classes, which was difficult as the store had no background in speed or racing. A tentative deal was struck and the small dealership provided a gold Camaro to the shop for modification. Rosen and his team quickly swapped in an L88 427-ci V-8 and put it to use competing on tracks.

With that as a foundation, a larger roadmap was developed to scale the program. Starting with a second Camaro and then several more, the relationship grew as the dealership saw the potential in foot traffic of showcasing high-output machines in the showroom. Camaros and soon other Chevrolet vehicles were sold at Baldwin (with financing available from GMAC), and then they would get the engine swap with Rosen and his team, located less than a mile down the road. It wasn't just powertrain changes, Motion also crafted custom bodywork and exterior design touches into their creations.

The SS427 Camaros they built could be had in either SS trim (good for 425 hp) or, starting in 1968, Phase III (putting out more than 500 hp)

When it came to branding its Camaros, Motion repurposed the white and red badging found on 1968 Impala SS427s, mounting one on the deck-lid and one on the hood. Traction bars were a must-have accessory on a big-power car like this.

configuration. The Phase III featured a Muncie 4-speed transmission, any ratio Posi-rear, heavy-duty suspension and radiator, redline wide oval tires, chrome valve covers, striping, bucket seats, and special emblems. It also got Super-Bite suspension kits, designed and engineered by Motion. Shocks, front coil spring risers, and traction bars were also installed. They were track tested and guaranteed to stop axle and spring windup and wheel hop regardless of tires and the engine output. The Phase III cost around $5,000 and, thanks to a whole host of additional speed parts, was guaranteed to run 120 mph in 11.50 seconds or better. Rosen and his marketer, Marty Schorr, claimed it could "out-handle any domestic production car (including the Corvette)" and it could hold four, had a trunk, and was tractable enough for daily transportation. If the car didn't live up to its expectations, the customer could get their money back, but Rosen states that never happened.

The Camaro was just one 427-creation the New York duo churned out. Their "Fantastic Five" lineup grew to include not only Chevrolet's pony car, but also the Chevy II, Chevy Biscayne two-door sedan, Corvette, and Chevelle. Each car was custom-built to owner's specifications, was warrantied, could be financed through GMAC, and had the L72 427-ci V-8 as standard power. The L88 aluminum head 427-ci V-8 was available too.

Yenko's 427 Conversion

In Pennsylvania, Don Yenko was destined to lead the Camaro big-block conversion movement. After he and Dana Chevrolet went their separate ways, he connected with Dick Harrell. Harrell had become a free agent, leaving Nickey Chevrolet in the summer of 1967 and moving from Chicago to St. Louis, Missouri. There, he set up his own performance shop in a vacant service station, calling it the Harrell Speed Center. Seeing a great opportunity, Don approached Harrell about selling his modified Camaros through the Yenko-dealership network, established from the Stinger project.

While Don advertised buyers could opt for "special aluminum or mag wheels," this example wears factory mag-style covers (RPO N96) over its steel wheels, wrapped in redline tires. (Photo Courtesy the Barr Collection)

A deal was struck, and sometime later, production commenced. Stock SS396 Camaros would be sent by rail to St. Louis, along with additional branded parts, and Harrell and his crew would perform the transformation for cars for the Midwest and Southwest markets. Don's crew in Canonsburg also completed builds, and in advertisements, Don publicized the cars came from "two strategically located assembly plants for lower freight costs." He went on to say the vehicle featured "Dick Harrell engineering and preparation" and that the vehicles

Buyers had the choice of two horsepower levels for 427-equipped Yenko Camaros: the 450 and the 410, both based on horsepower output. Note the connection to Dick Harrell under the lead image. SPAN Inc. was a marketing firm in Chicago, owned by Jim Spencer, who was a racing buddy of Don's. For a while, he helped distribute the cars and get dealers connected to the network. (Photo Courtesy the Barr Collection)

Personal Perspective: Warren Dernoshek, Yenko Technician

Warren Dernoshek grew up down the road from Yenko Chevrolet and was hired on through his childhood friend, George Furda. Furda was Bill Hartley's assistant. Hartley ran the race shop for Yenko, preparing his race cars and serving as chief mechanic. Dernoshek and Furda grew up together, both loving cars. In November 1965, Furda mentioned to Dernoshek that he and some of the Yenko race team were going out to Riverside Raceway on a loaded-up transport truck bearing three Corvettes and a couple of Corvair Stingers. "He asked if I wanted to take a ride out to California," said Warren. "That sounded like fun, so of course I said yes. We ended up getting back a month later, making for a very interesting experience."

After that first encounter with the Yenko organization, Hartley hired Dernoshek to work in the race shop. "I had to first prove myself," said Dernoshek. "He set me out on some used cars, mainly Corvettes, bringing them back to life. After a few successful efforts, Bill accepted me, and from then on I was part of the team." Dernoshek's employment started right in the thick of the Stinger kickoff, but he recalls there not being much to do. "The cosmetic work was too much for the Yenko dealership to handle and was farmed out to body shops all over the place," recalls Warren. "I would go around the lot with an awl to punch and rivet the tags in place." The gearhead did do some of the Stage modifications but found a whole

lot more work to do in 1967. "When those Camaros came in for engine swaps, we threw everything we had at them. Everyone got the works. They're an absolute treasure and, in my mind, the premiere Yenko collector car. It was a total engine transplant, including bellhousing, scatter shield, an L88 clutch. We had to do everything to them. The first few were small-block cars, so we changed the coil springs too."

All the work was done in the race shop, which was located toward the back of the dealership. "People think it was a big-time operation with assembly lines but not so. We had a bay and a half and could get four cars in the space. We didn't have a rack or lift. Everything was done on the floor. What used to be a paint booth was converted to our dyno area. There was [sic] few air tools, if you wanted them, you had to buy them. Hanging from a roof truss was a single chain block that we used to pull engines and put them back in. It was a real workhorse."

Given the conditions, Dernoshek recalls a constant turnover of employees. "The place was like a revolving door with people coming and going, sometimes working for just days at a time after experiencing what it was like. People think I had quite the deal, being there full-time, working on and traveling with the race cars, but it was tough. As a 20-year-old, it was just a job but even then, I could feel it was important and there was extreme significance. That was my reward."

Any kind of license plate or frame aside, it would be difficult to spot a 1967 Yenko Camaro from the front. With the factory SS badging left on, most would assume it was still a factory setup. Hood pins were a part of the Yenko package.

Nothing on the back screams modified, save for the distinct rumble of a 427 engine. If you missed that, be sure big smoky burnouts would give it away. This car has special homemade Yenko/Harrell traction bars. Super Car Workshop restored this Royal Plum example.

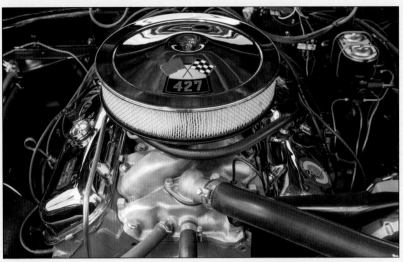

This Camaro had its stock crossed flags and 396 fender badges swapped out for ones from the 427-equipped Impalas. This was one of the few times that Don repurposed stock Chevrolet badges; in later years he had custom pieces created.

The 427 powerplant looked right at home under the hood of the Camaro. An install like this seriously woke up Chevy's pony car performance game. An early owner applied the period-correct Stinger sticker on the driver-side valve cover.

Don and an unnamed associate read up on a new Z28 Camaro. While his 427-conversions were designed to dominate drag strips, Don wanted to try his hand at getting Camaros into road racing too. The package was called the Stormer, featuring a special track-designed suspension and Corvette disc and drum brakes. Under the hood would be the stock 302 but tuned to pump out 400-plus hp. It's unclear how many were ever made. (Photo Courtesy the Barr Collection)

featured technical know-how from a functioning research and development program, coming from the combined knowledge of Corvette road racing champion Don Yenko and drag racing champion Dick Harrell. The deal was Don would supply the cars and parts and Harrell would lend his expertise and credibility in assembling them. Don called it the Super Camaro and the modified vehicle could be had in either 450 or 410 trim, based on the horsepower output.

Both utilized the 427-ci V-8 and cost around $4,200. Don and Harrell also offered additional options, such as a scatter shield ($54), Traction Masters traction bars ($46), tuned exhaust, an L88 engine option, side exhaust ($250), a Yenko 2 4-barrel high rise intake, a lightweight fiberglass hood featuring a 1967 Corvette inspired scoop, performance-tuned intake and exhaust headers ($175), heat-resistant spark plug wires ($25), and a fiberglass rear deck with spoiler. Special 4:10, 4:56, or 4:88 rear ends and aluminum or mag wheels could be installed. The cars came with a 5-year/50,000-mile factory warranty and were capable of 7 second 1/8-mile times at 109 mph and 11 seconds at 128 mph in the quarter mile. The vehicle received official AHRA Super Stock classification and was highly competitive on the drag strip.

Don also had a custom fiberglass hood with a 1967 Corvette scoop made, which buyers could purchase. Harrell was planning on building about 92 Super Camaros for Don and, after moving to a permanent location, had plans to ramp up to 300 cars by the end of 1968, a lofty goal given the months remaining in the year. However, only 23 builds were completed

Parked inside the tight Yenko Chevrolet showroom in front of the parts counter is one of the converted 1967 Camaros. A fiberglass hood styled to look like the Corvette's was available, but this one here has kept its stock SS hood. Just like the car used in the brochure, it's been equipped with side exhaust. (Photo Courtesy the Barr Collection)

Mounted on the front fenders were the same individual numerals used on the hoods of 427-equipped Corvettes. Don took lots of inspiration from the 'Vette, including the Camaro's available fiberglass hood, which even advertised it had a 1967 Corvette scoop. (Photo Courtesy the Barr Collection)

before the relationship between the two businessmen fell apart. Don's crew back in Canonsburg completed the rest of the run, which as another 30 or so cars.

The cars didn't follow an exact protocol for final assembly. Some wore 427 badging (individual black numerals) on the front fenders, sourced from the Corvette, while others wore the crossed flag and "427 Turbo-Jet" badging from the 1967 Impala SS. Some received repurposed Yenko Stinger circle stickers, which were stuck on valve covers. While Don had the artwork for the red, white, and blue Yenko shield (designed by Donna Mae) painted on the door of Dick Harrell's sponsored red Camaro funny car, the shields weren't used as badges on the fenders of the 427 Camaros until the spring of 1968.

Dealer Network

To get the cars into the hands of buyers, Don worked his Yenko Sportscar dealer connections and set up a network. "We feel that we're the only ones who have even tried this," said Harrell in a 1967 interview. "And we've found the Chevy dealers are accepting this program even better than expected. We've signed up 34 dealers in the East and Midwest, and we expect to have 75 to 100 by the time the new cars come out." The dealer network included dealerships in Illinois, Indiana, Kentucky, Massachusetts, Michigan, Minnesota, Ohio, Oklahoma, Pennsylvania, Texas, Utah, and one in Ontario, Canada.

The marketing campaign included calling the vehicles "the Boss of the Road" and holding some personal appearances by Dick and Don together. One such occasion was in August 1967 when they both went to Jay Kline Chevrolet and met with enthusiasts. The ad touting the occasion said come

see Mr. Chevrolet of Drag Racing, Dick, as well as Don, Mr. Chevrolet of Sportscars. The partnership between Dick and Don lasted until at least November, at which point the two parted ways.

One of the standout exterior add-ons to this Camaro was its side exhaust, resembling the Corvette. This option wouldn't be offered on the Yenko cars that would be created in the years to come. (Photo Courtesy the Barr Collection)

Chevrolet didn't offer a great solution for monitoring engine vitals in the Camaro, leading car builders, including Don, to add in their own gauging. Throughout his years of crafting cars, he primarily stuck with Stewart Warner products.

Typically, the Camaros converted at Yenko Chevrolet would have the aftermarket tach installed on the steering column, while Harrell's team screwed them into the metal dash, next to the gauge cluster. Starting in 1968, Don would follow suit and do that too.

The Yenko Chevrolet dealership wasn't the largest, and space was at a premium. Don knew he could move a good amount of inventory from his modest showroom but dreamed bigger, developing his dealer network to get his cars distributed. (Photo Courtesy the Barr Collection)

This high vantage point across the street from Yenko Chevrolet shows the entire work space Don had at the time. An unknown employee added the black pen emphasis. For sure, this tiny thoroughfare was filled with the rumblings of Chevy power. (Photo Courtesy the Barr Collection)

which by 1968 included Courtesy Chevrolet's California stores in Los Angeles, San Diego, San Jose, and Thousand Oaks, as well as their Phoenix, Arizona, location. Other participating dealerships included Fred Gibb Chevrolet in La Harpe, Illinois; Bill Allen Chevrolet in Kansas City, Missouri; Ed Black Chevrolet in Albuquerque, New Mexico; Crawford Chevrolet in Ventura, California; and Burt Chevrolet in Englewood, California.

Interested buyers could also pick up the phone and call Dick to make special arrangements for delivery. The cars carried a 90-day/4,000-mile warranty on the powertrain and the rest of the car carried the standard Chevrolet warranty. They also were accepted AHRA classes; the Camaro was placed into A/Stock, and the Chevelle was put into D/Stock.

By 1970, the operation had grown to include 12 full-time employees supporting 5 Chevrolet race cars competing in AHRA meets across the country. On Saturday, January 31, 1970, Dick held the grand opening for an outlet center called the Dick Harrell & Associates Hi-Performance Parts in Las Cruces, New Mexico, across the state line from El

New Digs: The Dick Harrell Performance Center

Dick relocated again to Kansas City, and on January 1, 1968, he opened the doors to the Dick Harrell Performance Center, located at 11114 Hickman Mills Drive, adjacent to a small shopping center. The location was chosen because of its centralized location. Business was good and after just one year, the facility doubled in size and added many more machinery items.

It was a one-stop shop for going fast. The parts counter carried all kinds of top speed parts: there was a custom machine shop on-site as well as a chassis dyno, and vehicles could be readily serviced and tuned up. Everyone from novices to professional competitors could have vehicles built from the "tires up." At one time, custom "soul paint" was available by John "Oop" Fensom, who did everything from mild to wild, using pearls, candies, lace panels, metal flake, glass flake, and multicolor spectaculars. Oop also did bodywork, including fiberglass, and painted Dick's race cars, as did the other painters who came after him. Dick developed his own dealer network,

Paso, Texas. It was to be the first in a series of high-performance shops, featuring all the "latest California speed and hi-performance parts" while also giving out professional tech information to help buyers select the right parts the first time and at the right price. Dick also set out to sign up more Chevrolet dealers to sell his finished cars.

Dick's colorful racing and professional automotive career ended suddenly when a racing accident took his life on September 12, 1971.

Conversion Conclusion

All of these efforts, dealerships, performance shops, and key figures helped shape what came next. While the conversion car business was good and demand was high, the process was labor intensive and difficult to scale. Numerous parts were often leftover and hard to repurpose or resell. Conversions would continue to happen through the end of the decade and into the 1970s, but the real game changer came about when the idea was formed to have more of these performance parts bolted on before the cars left the factory assembly floor. That idea came from the mind of Don Yenko.

Don assigned his 1967 Camaros stock numbers, similar to the Corvair Stingers, using a YS and number format. The Camaros started with 7, for the 1967 model year, and then the next two digits would indicate the car number. This one was the sixth Camaro built. The Camaros would not get a door tag.

CHAPTER 3

1968 YENKO SUPER CAMARO

SUPER CAR PRODUCTION GEARS UP AND EVOLVES

While Don would have happily spent his days crafting road-racing rockets, the buzz and excitement surrounding the brand-new Camaro was too loud to ignore. So was the possibility for profits to be made off of Chevy's pony car entrant. Yenko Chevrolet built the right foundation in 1967 with its Camaro 427-conversions, but in 1968, it would take a huge step forward in streamlining costs and scaling its potential for inventory. If there was anything that Don loved more than mixing it up on a packed track, it was making money.

By skillfully using the COPO system, Don was able to get Chevrolet's partnership in facilitating Camaros that could not only hang with the 427-Corvette crowd, like the Rally Red 1967 'Vette, but more than likely beat them. The Miller family has owned and operated this Dog 'n Suds drive-in, located in Ingleside, Illinois, since it opened in 1967.

The 1968 Yenko Camaros started to develop a consistent look and feel as Don worked to expand his sYc brand. Branine Chevrolet, located in Mulvane, Kansas, sold this YS-8023 when new, and now Kevin Suydam owns it.

Yenko Chevrolet sold this Camaro to Ranide Berton of Bridgeville, Pennsylvania, who traded in a 1967 Chevelle on the $5,445.20 deal. The 1951 Chevy 3100 pickup is neither Yenko nor COPO. Darrell Meister Jr. owns it while his dad owns the Camaro.

Based on his experience with the Stingers, Don saw a golden opportunity that no one else did. He grasped the potential for these Camaros to have some of the necessary components bolted on right at the factory through a little backdoor process he had learned back in 1965 called a COPO order. In doing so, he managed to inch Chevrolet closer to a line it swore it would never cross and get the carmaker to build something it swore it never would. That magical moment wouldn't come until 1969, but only because of the groundwork laid in 1968.

Chevrolet was standing by its policy of limiting cubic inch displacement to 400 in its intermediate line of cars. It wasn't quite ready to bolt in anything bigger than a 396-ci V-8 into its Camaros. After a few talks with Don and hearing his cajoling, Chevrolet decided it was willing to test the waters. The ice had already been broken and was melting fast with the success of the 50 Novas that Fred Gibb had ordered for his dealership and, no doubt, that helped get the brand excited about Don's ideas. What resulted was the Yenko Sports Car Conversion Package, filed under COPO 9737. This gave a batch of Camaros a collection of performance-oriented accessories to put on while the car was built. They'd all support the L72, 427-ci V-8 that Don's techs were going to be installing once the cars got to his dealership.

sYc Is Refined

Just as Chevrolet was trying new things for the first time, allowing its Camaro to be modified through a COPO, Don, too, was trying new things, venturing further out of his element. He was a deeply creative guy who had turned the Corvair into something to call his own, crafting vivid, colorful imagery, branding, and wording to set the Stinger apart. That vibrant imagination was seemingly restrained in the development of the 1967 Camaros. The cars were effective yet simple and understated, lacking the pizzazz and sparkle that Don could deliver.

After a year in this new tire-smoking scene, he had gotten his footing, adapting quickly and learning lessons from the field of fierce competitors. The first was harnessing the power of visual branding. Everyone knew Nickey Chevrolet because of its logo with the backward and red-lettered K. Dana Chevrolet stood out with its medieval font, and the Motion Performance brand had no shortage of identifiable marks. Not only did the speed shop have a funky look and feel for its lettering, it developed a sense of exclusivity through its Motion Supercar Club. A tire and checkered flag logo was created and placed on its doors as well as on stickers for members to adhere to their rides. It was seen as a badge of honor and leadfoot drivers wanted in.

Once Don grasped that simple YENKO text wouldn't be enough to stir emotions, the same mind that originated a heated hornet saw the need for an easily identifiable and iconic trademark for his customers to rally behind. It was decided the Camaros would be marked in several specific locations with the Yenko crest medallion that had previously only graced his sponsored race cars. That would set them apart and help him build the brand.

Another move Don took was going beyond the one-off mentality that prevailed in so many other shops and dealerships (including his). With his 1968 Camaro, he sought to move away from the image of the full-service shop telling incoming customers, "We'll build you whatever you want" to a much more proficient "Here's our highly developed line of performance offerings." There was a budding sense of standardization as Don revamped and rebooted his efforts. While saving costs and maximizing profits was always at the forefront, Don also began sly ways to have his cars stand out with unique parts and offerings sourced from unlikely means and measures. Building straight-line performers wasn't his favorite thing to do, but Don figured out how to get behind it and excited about it.

Motoring Milestones

The cars that resulted from his efforts were truly significant but not purely in what they were but also what they represented. They weren't just converted 427 Camaros but rather a bridge to something bigger and better and something no one at the time thought possible. Through Don's prompting, these 1968 COPOs opened the door for the Chevrolet brand to take the first step in going all the way in building the Camaro that the masses were demanding but staunch corporate edicts prevented. Don and his team managed to prove value in the venture, and in time, their efforts were rewarded.

Ordering the COPOs

Just like he and his 427-swapping competition had been doing, Don knew he wanted to work with SS Camaros, which aided the soon-to-happen conversion process. He placed an order for 70 coupes, equipping them with the Super Sport package. The SS equipped them with multi-leaf rear springs; a special hood with simulated chrome; stacked, boxy air intakes; and an SS grille emblem and SS badging on the front fenders and fuel filler cap. It also included a front striping band graphic, which came in either white (for darker colored cars) or black (for lighter colored cars). The styling element wrapped the front edge of the car and curved sharply to run a spear down either side of the vehicle, ending just before the rear edge of the doors.

Around back, the SS package included a blacked-out tail panel surrounding the taillights. Don didn't request any special wheel, at least not from the factory, and as such, they came equipped with the base hubcap and steel wheels. They were painted body color and covered with a "dog dish" hubcap with a Chevy bowtie logo in the center. Don equipped some of the cars with black vinyl tops and the later cars got RPO D80, giving them a front lower and rear decklid spoiler.

RS Package

Roughly a dozen of the cars had the RS package added on as well, giving them additional dress-up items. Up front, they had hideaway headlights hidden behind a full-width blacked out grille. The front parking and direction signal lights were moved down from inside the grille to underneath it, mounted below the front bumper. There was molding on the roof drip rails, wheel openings, lower body side, along the belt line, and at the top of the doors. At the rear, the backup lights were relocated from the inboard taillights to down under the bumper. Rally Sport script would have been installed on the front fenders but superseded by the SS package, giving them "Camaro" script above SS badging. Likewise, the RS emblem in the grille was replaced by an SS emblem, and the RS emblem in the gas filler cap would be swapped to one showing an SS.

RS-equipped Camaros came with the easily identifiable, full-width grille, and hidden headlights. The marker lights were moved from inside the grille to down below the bumper.

The RS package relocated the reverse lights from the inboard taillights to the lower valance, underneath the bumper. This particular car was once equipped with an unusual not dealer-installed accessory: a trailer hitch. Its current owner, Bill Emmerich, bought the Camaro in 1979 and, after daily driving it for a year in Florida, relocated to Illinois.

The origins of the custom speedometer that the COPO included are not clear. Obviously, his car was going to run faster than the stock Camaro top speed, and Don wanted to make sure he didn't undersell the car's performance. (Photo Courtesy the Barr Collection)

COPO 9737

Where Don was able to deviate from any other dealer placing an order for Camaros was the ability to tack on COPO 9737, called the Sports Car Conversion Package. This allowed him to make significant changes from the typical RPO structure, and in some cases, get Chevrolet to engineer one-off parts.

140-mph Speedo

Knowing his future buyers would be keeping the hammer down for out-all blasts, Don had the stock 120-mph speedometer swapped out for a unique 140-mph speedometer not offered in anything else in the Chevrolet lineup. The Chevelles' speedometers also topped out at 120 mph, while the Corvettes' jumped to 160 mph (as did Pontiac's Firebird, which also came with a 160-mph speedometer). While seemingly insignificant, an exchange like this would involve some serious legwork for the final end product. Not only did a designer have to sit down and come up with completely new faceplate artwork for the gauge, but calibration would also have to be factored in for just a few dozen cars.

Drivetrain Upgrades

The COPO also upgraded the suspension, added front disc brakes, and included a larger 1 1/16-inch sway bar, M21 close ratio 4-speed transmission, QD 4.10 posi rear differential, and a higher CFM carb. Underhood, the cars came with a MV-coded L78 396-ci 375-hp big-block. While the engine would have been fitted with the L78's standard 780-cfm carb (4053 PN 3923289DZ), that component was deducted from the engineering parts list and in its place went a 1968 L88-sourced carburetor (PN 3935519).

Magic Mirror Trim Tag

Another item unique to the batch of COPO'd Camaros was the trim tag, mounted (like other Camaros) on the driver's side of the firewall. Underneath the standard "Chevrolet, General Motors Corp., Detroit, Michigan" text and then the body number, paint code, build date, body style, there was a unique line. The bottom of the tag, above Body by Fisher, read "This car finished with Magic Mirror Acrylic Lacquer." General Motors used the Magic Mirror phrase to advertise its paint finishes as far back as the early 1950s, even using it to describe the 1953 Corvette's finish. It wasn't anything special in and of itself. In 1968, the phrase only showed up on Camaros that were exported in certain markets overseas. Camaros sold in the United States had text showing that "General Motors Corporation certifies to that dealer that this vehicle conforms to all federal motor vehicle safety standards applicable at time of manufacture." It's thought that since these COPOs skirted the rules, the Magic Mirror tag was used as an additional method of internal tracking for Chevrolet to see how well Don's program did and if it was worth scaling up.

Tech Insight: MV Engine Code

The MV-coded engines that were shipped in the cars to Yenko were unique. Usually, Camaros equipped with the L78, cast-iron heads had an MQ stamping, while the L78 aluminum heads had a QT suffix. For years the MV suffix baffled enthusiasts before it became common knowledge about the engine swaps taking place at the dealership. For a long while, it was assumed the code stood for a factory-installed 427-ci V-8, as MV shows up on all the factory paperwork, including the Protectoplate. It turned out to be a 396 replaced by a CE-stamped 427. That didn't stop many from grinding down their 427's engine code and incorrectly stamping it with MV, thinking they had returned their car's factory-correct accuracy.

The "Rosetta stone" confirming 1968 was a conversion year for 427 Camaros was found to be a 396 stamped with MV that was directly traced to Yenko's records. The car was YS-8006 and its VIN was linked

This 396-ci engine block was discovered at a Pittsburg-area swap meet in the early 1990s. Upon closer inspection, it was revealed it contained a secret, unlocking a vital part of the Yenko story. This special engine belongs to Brian Henderson.

This engine block's stamping of 2520 matches up to Yenko's internal paperwork, showing that it once belonged to the 396 Camaro that became YS-8006, before a 427 short-block was swapped in. The completed car would go on to be sold through Roy Stauffer Chevrolet in nearby Scranton, Pennsylvania.

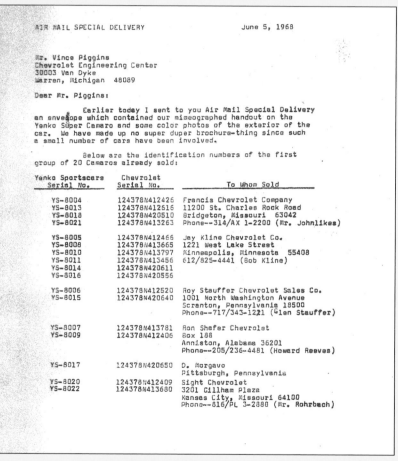

Donna Mae wrote this letter to Vince Piggins, informing him of how the first batch of COPO Camaros had sold. Halfway down the page is the line about YS-8006, confirming its MV-stamped 396 block. The color photos she references and included with her letter would have been from the photoshoot of the green Camaro, included elsewhere in this chapter.

to a letter Don sent on June 5, 1968, to Vince Piggins (of SEDCO fame), identifying the dealerships of the first 20 cars that had been sold. The 11th car was 8006, showing the VIN and that it had been sold at Roy Stauffer Chevrolet in Scranton, Pennsylvania. That VIN matched the found 396-ci V-8 block and solved the puzzle, confirming there was not, nor ever should be, a numbers-matching MV-code 1968 427 Yenko Camaro. (Note: Several of the SS COPO Camaros were ordered but never converted with 427 engines. They would still have the MV-396/375 engine underhood.)

As for the rationale of having a dedicated code, it's thought it was an internal tracking program to follow the success of this pilot program. GM insiders knew Don's intentions of swapping out the 396s for bigger engines, and perhaps it was a way to judge interest from consumers by monitoring final sales. As for the leftover blocks, Don would sell them to trucking firms, racers, and the like.

Canonsburg Changes

Once the cars arrived at Yenko Chevrolet sometime during the late spring of 1968, Don would further modify them both mechanically and cosmetically.

Under the Hood

The biggest change was underhood, where his techs removed the MV-coded L78s and would replace the short-block assembly (block, pistons, crankshaft, and rod assemblies) with one from an L72 427-ci V-8. The L78's cylinder heads and aluminum intake manifold were retained and installed back on the converted motor.

Warren Dernoshek was working back in the race shop and performed a lot of the motor work. "Compared to 1967 when the whole small-block was exchanged for a 427 big-block, it was a big relief. We didn't have as much to do to them, which made it a piece of cake." Customers were charged $100 to have the 427 engine installed and then another $24 to have the hood mounted and the car cleaned.

As it had in 1967, the 427 and Camaro combo still proved wildly successful and made the coupe a true drag strip performer.

These COPOs had the unique line on their trim tags about Magic Mirror acrylic lacquer. The 04B designates this car (YS-8023) was built in the second week of April; the 12437 indicates it was a Sport Coupe; NOR means it was built at the Norwood, Ohio, plant; and the CC paint code states that it received Ermine White paint. The TR 724 is for the interior trim; in this case, red with standard buckets. The green inspection stamp was stock Camaro.

Don advertised his 1968 427 Camaros as being capable of 450 hp, a big jump in power from the stock 396's 375 hp. Underneath the air cleaner is the same Holley carburetor that was installed on the L88 427-ci–equipped Corvette.

It sure seems like it would have been fun to be wrenching in the back of Yenko Chevrolet, swapping high-performance motors all day long. Former employee Warren Dernoshek attests it really wasn't. That area of the dealership had no lift and only a single chain hoist to remove engines. Any glamour wore off fast; Dernoshek recalls some new employees sticking it out for only a few weeks before moving on.

Exterior

Don wanted these cars to turn heads as well as have a somewhat uniform look. Exterior changes included swapping out the fancy SS hood for a special fiberglass hood that Don had custom made. Stylistically, it was very similar to one offered by Dana Chevrolet on its 427-converted Camaros (which they sold for $125 and may have even been designed by Don while he and Dana were in cahoots), featuring twin functional air inlets. Before it was installed, it was painted the body color to match the rest of the car.

No doubt knowing how hard it was to drive muscle cars in wintry weather, Don included a block-off plate that would close the scoop vents, allowing the engine to heat up faster for cold-weather driving. The plate slid over a permanently affixed center stud and was held in place with a wing nut. Hood pins were installed too. The custom-designed hoods didn't accommodate the stock hood latch, and some original owners were simply given a flat piece of wood (similar to a yardstick) to hold their hoods open. Technicians also swapped out the factory hood springs for lighter gauge springs or eliminated them altogether. The stock springs' tension would have been too much and, if left on, would bow the custom hood. Initially, the first dozen or so were made at a shop in Atlanta, a connection made through fellow racer, Fred Eggers. Don then switched to a local Canonsburg manufacturer for the rest.

Another issue with the hood was with radio interference. Some frustrated owners took it upon themselves to relocate the antenna to the rear fender. Also, around back, Don experimented with two different looks for the gas cap located in the center of the rear tail panel. For a promotional photoshoot, the tester had just the center painted in flat black covering the "SS" badge but retaining a silver outer circle. Most likely due to time savings, the rest of the cars' entire caps were painted flat black.

Decklid and Rear Spoiler Options

Another exterior change was with the rear decklid on the Super Camaros. Through a variety of circumstances, three different treatments were applied to the rear decklid to achieve one final visual look.

First, Don created and had made a custom rear fiberglass decklid, just as he had with his Corvair Stinger. It was a one-piece design, integrating the decklid and spoiler together. Only a handful were actually made and installed

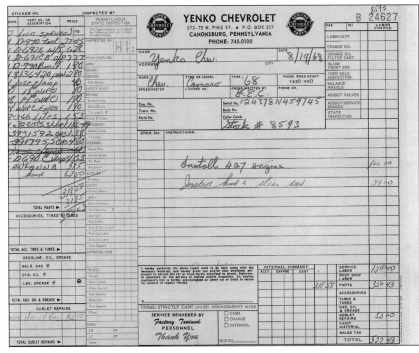

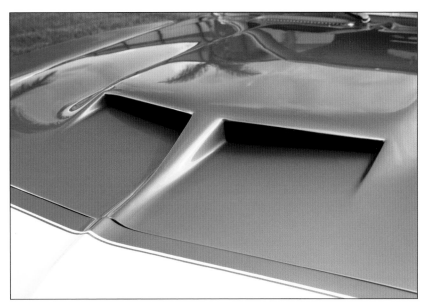

Here are seldom-seen billing records showing how much the services performed at the dealership cost customers. This particular Camaro received the work late in the year, being done on August 19, 1968. Note the list of other assorted parts like wire ends and clamps in the upper left corner. *(Photo Courtesy of the Meister Collection)*

The hood design was similar to the one found on 1967 Dana Camaros, which makes sense because Don partnered with Dana for a while that year. He could have very well designed it himself. For his 1968 Camaro, Don made the custom hood sleeker and better integrated. Those big scoops could be closed with a cold weather block-off plate.

The green car featured in this promotional photoshoot had a blacked-out center portion of the gas cap surrounded by a silver ring. While it looks cool, going with this look did require an extra step for Don's technicians. *(Photo Courtesy the Barr Collection)*

Here's an outtake from the photoshoot for the brochure on page 63, showing a Camaro with an entirely blacked-out gas cap. It was much simpler for techs to twist off the cap, spray it black, and then reinstall it. This angle also shows the custom decklid, evidenced by the high-pointed spoiler. *(Photo Courtesy the Barr Collection)*

on a few of the early cars that hadn't been equipped with RPO D80 spoilers. Don's decklid showed up on a brochure advertising the 1968 Camaro, but it is readily apparent that it doesn't fit well. At some point, Don stopped using them. While it's unlikely that when he ordered the cars, he didn't know about RPO D80. Perhaps he figured, just as he had with the Stinger, he'd create a superior, lightweight, custom-crafted unit to upsell to customers. It wouldn't have taken long to see that getting them made, fitted properly, painted, and then installed back on the vehicles wasn't efficient or cost-effective.

Second, Don scaled back, choosing to craft a custom lip spoiler that would fit to the factory steel decklid. It mounted flush, peaked slightly higher in the center, and the rear edge extended to and covered the rear edge of the factory decklid. The unit was held on with five wood screws. Cars equipped with spoiler had the "Camaro by Chevrolet" badge removed. Only a handful of vehicles received it.

The third option was retaining the factory D80 rear spoiler. Cars that came equipped with it would still retain the "Camaro" badge, but at the factory it got moved up the decklid, ahead of the spoiler.

Rally II Wheels

Those stamped, base wheels that were on the cars when they arrived from Chevrolet weren't going to cut it for Don. He devised a clever solution to swap them out to give his cars a unique look. The hip trend was

When paired with the SS Camaro's F70-14 redline tires, the wheels and red center cap showed well. Don used a simple and straightforward sans serif font for the letter Y.

Don pulled a fast one, connecting with his bud down at the local Pontiac dealership to score a bunch of the Firebird's Rally II wheels. After slapping his Y center cap on it and getting them shipped off, no doubt more than a few prospective buyers came to Chevy dealerships to kick the tires and found the wheels oh-so familiar but unable to place them. (Photo Courtesy of Barr Collection)

for muscle machines to have true mag wheels, but Chevrolet didn't offer anything that came close. They did have a simulated mag-style wheel cover, but Don knew that wouldn't get any street cred. Any less than the real thing wasn't boss. There was a rally wheel, which was the only optional wheel on the SS Camaro, but Don didn't want that either.

What he had in mind was to connect with a friend who worked at Arnold Pontiac in nearby Houston, Pennsylvania. The dealership was less than a mile from his and, allegedly, the two often swapped parts and extended deals to each other. Pontiac had its steel mag-type Rally II wheel, which could be had on the Firebird. Don purchased enough sets from Arnold to bolt on all his incoming COPO'd Camaros. The SS Camaro's F-70-14 redline tires were installed around them.

Knowing his audience, Don advertised the Rally II's as "mag-style wheels" and, to make them distinct, he covered Pontiac's black plastic disc center cap, showing PMD (for Pontiac Motor Division). He overlaid it with a special emblem showing a red letter Y (in a sans-serif font and standing for Yenko) on a black background.

Atlas Wheels

For owners who wanted to swap out the Rally II's, Don offered an option he called the Yenko Atlas, available in both 14x6 and 15x6 sizes, and cast in aluminum. Just as the Rally IIs, the Atlas wheels also have a unique origin. The wheel was a direct knockoff of the popular American Racing Torque Thrust D five-spoke wheel with peaked, sharp edged spokes. As legend has it, Don was good friends with a Corvette-loving regional rep

Mag wheels were all the rage in the 1960s, and Don wanted the look but without the price. Here he proudly stands next to one of his Camaros wearing a set of his Atlas-created knockoffs. Surrounding him are Atlas employees, including Dominic Esposot, the owner of Atlas (standing). The photo was taken on July 8, 1968, on Route 19 outside of Canonsburg. (Photo Courtesy Mark Kickel)

for the Atlas Foundry in nearby Atlasburg, Pennsylvania, about 15 miles northwest of Canonsburg. Atlas was an industrial aluminum manufacturer and wasn't in the business of making automotive parts, but, because of the rep's love of cars, he convinced them to give it a shot.

One of Don's employees showed up at the dealership one day in his personal ride, equipped with the American Racing wheels. Don took a liking to them and took the set to his contact at Atlas for them to cast his own version, sans the American Racing text cast on the backside inside lip. The finished products were dropped off to Yenko Chevrolet with no fanfare or special packaging, all in the name of saving a buck.

Atlas took it upon themselves to go all out, even creating a custom logo for the center cap of the wheels. The design they came up with was a red center foil circle, showing "A×a" font (for Atlas alloy) above crossed checkered racing flags. Its attempt at branding was cut short by Don, who, upon receiving the wheels, covered the center with a white sticker showing a Yenko crest. The creation of the wheels at the foundry likely happened in late spring/early summer, as by July 8, 1968, Don had a finished set installed on a 1968 Camaro. The final products were poorly cast, porous, and leaked air. Few sets were sold, making them a rare option on the 1968 Camaros.

Because of their nondescript nature, the wheels are prone to forgeries, with instances occurring of American Racing wheels having their rear side logo ground off and then attempted to be passed off as authentic Atlas wheels.

Badging

Special cast 427 badging would be installed on the front fenders ahead

If Don wanted 427 badging, he could have gone to his parts department. Picking up what 427-equipped Corvettes received: individual numerals filled in with black. While the font is similar, out of necessity, he went a different route, getting them custom made.

By connecting the custom-made 427 digits, installation on the front fenders was a whole lot easier. They used the same holes the stock 396 badging, which, after the swap, was no longer accurate.

of the wheels in place of the stock 396 badging. It would also be installed on the rear panel. Don had the badges custom made; the 427 digits are solid chrome and are connected underneath by a straight bar. One unique aspect of the finished vehicles was that nearly everything Don used to make his Yenko Supercars came from within 50 miles or less of Canonsburg. He was all about using local suppliers, probably because of the cost savings than of his sense of hometown pride.

Red, White, and Blue Crest

Behind the front wheels, Yenko crests were installed right above the Camaro script and SS factory badges. This was the first time the red, white,

The Yenko Camaros of 1968 marked the debut of the red, white, and blue crest as a badge, and the first time it was mounted anywhere on Don's cars. For this batch of vehicles, he was okay with showing their Super Sport roots, leaving the SS badging on.

The blacked-out gas cap blended in better with the blacked-out tail panel on the Camaros, helping the Yenko crest and custom 427 badging stand out. Don and Donna Mae advertised this rear angle as the "last look of Super Camaro" most folks would get. Chances are, when drivers mashed the throttle, it was.

and blue crest, which had been designed by Donna Mae, was turned into badge form and installed on a Yenko Supercar. The iconic logo showed up a year earlier, painted on the door of the Yenko-sponsored Camaro race car driven by Dick Harrell. To mount them, two holes were drilled into the fender and the badge's twin studs slid in, held in place by tubular clips. On the Camaro's rear panel, the same Yenko crest would be mounted to the left of the center fuel cap, while the new 427 badge would go to the right, both flanking the center gas cap. After seeing the new look, a few previous owners wanted to dress up their Yenko rides. At least one Stinger owner installed a colored crest on his vehicle, and surely it happened with others, including 1967 Camaros.

Interior

Inside the cabin, black textured trim was the standard finish. A Stewart

This promotional photo, likely snapped by Don or Donna Mae, shows just where the techs installed the crest on the front fenders. Now, when drivers were cruising around in their hopped-up rides, people would know exactly where they came from. (Photo Courtesy the Barr Collection)

Looking ahead, drivers were greeted by the big tach in the right of their vision and the 140-mph speedometer in their left. The cute little SS emblem was retained on the steering wheel. (Photo Courtesy the Barr Collection)

The lower cluster of gauges blended in nicely when surrounded by woodgrain trim, matching the rest of the dash. Also visible from this angle is how the aftermarket Stewart Warner tach was screwed up and into the dash. (Photo Courtesy the Barr Collection)

The exact origin of this Camaro (YS-8023) remains murky, but the thought that it was used for internal emissions testing is given credence because of its standard steering wheel, blocked-off center stack, and lack of a radio or climate controls (besides the Special Drag Car tag). Chevrolet wasn't about to install those creature comforts in what they deemed a test mule.

Unless RPO U17 was ordered, relocating the fuel gauge to the center console and installing a tach in its place, the only way to monitor the engine's RPM was to install an aftermarket part like this Stewart Warner tach, which all 1968 Camaros received.

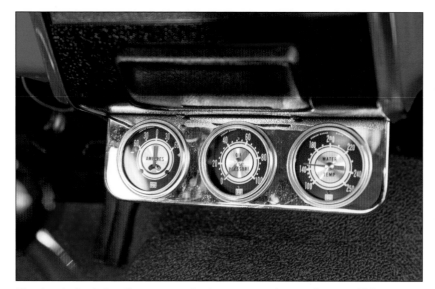

The basic look for the gauge cluster surround was chrome. This extra set was a helpful addition because none of the COPO Camaros ordered had the center console and RPO U17 instrumentation, adding four extra gauges down below.

These are the standard gauge faces while the ones in the left image are the custom faces.

Don continued his use of affixing tags to the driver's door-jambs. He changed up the numbering though, using four digits after the YS, reflecting his desire to scale his output or, at the very least, to give the illusion of massive amounts of inventory sold. The numbering series started with 8 because of the 1968 model year.

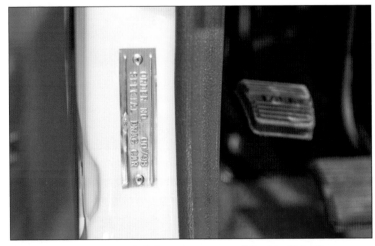

Not one but two special door tags were fitted to this Camaro. Besides getting the YS-8023 tag, it was the only car to receive this unique door plaque installed at the Chevrolet factory. It's generally thought that this vehicle was the first COPO 1968 Camaro built and, as such, was used for R&D and additional testing. To skirt the brand's internal edicts, it was given this Special Drag Car tag as a workaround in case anyone asked questions. Note the tiny bowtie under the text.

Fred Eggers did outside sales for Yenko and assembled this brochure. The featured car is his Corvette Bronze demo (seen elsewhere in this chapter) that he drove all throughout the Southeast region. Fred took these photos in Orlando in front of one of the many inland lakes. (Photo Courtesy the Barr Collection)

George Edwards purchased his Camaro brand new in June 1968 from Roy Stauffer Chevrolet in Scranton, Pennsylvania. "I didn't know a Yenko from a lawnmower," laughed George. "All I knew was it had a big-block 427 and that's exactly what I wanted." Here, the classic is parked outside of Massey's, a charming ice cream stand in Carlisle, Pennsylvania, that opened in 1949 and served as a popular gathering spot for muscle machines in the 1960s.

Warner tach would be screwed into the dash above and to the right side of the gauge cluster. A tri-gauge package containing Stewart Warner gauges for amperage, oil pressure, and coolant temperature was installed down low, under the dashboard, ahead of the gear selector. The gauge faces came in either standard or custom faces and the surrounds were mostly chrome, but some had woodgrain surrounds to match the walnut woodgrain on the center console and ashtray door. On some cars, the glove box Camaro script in the bottom right corner of the door was swapped for a Yenko crest emblem.

Finally, like the Stingers, the Camaros received identification tags, located in the driver-side doorjamb. Don used the same format, starting with a YS (for Yenko Sportscars) and then a hyphen followed by numerals. His Stinger series had three numerals, reflecting his sales projection. The first two digits were 8 (signifying they were 1968 models) and 0, and then sequential numbers to indicate the 64 made. The whole concept was a carryover from the Stinger program, designed to comply with the SCCA requirement. It was dropped for 1969 Yenko vehicles.

Pricing and Distribution

It's important to note, that while Don was making strides and taking risks, all the changes made to the cars at the dealership were not standardized across the completed line. Original owners and dealership employees will attest that not all cars were created equal. The processes put in place for not only recording the cars but also what was to be done with them wasn't as refined or polished as today's record keeping, and slight irregularities do exist.

Approximately 64 Yenko Camaros were built in 1968 and sold through the Canonsburg dealership as well as to Don's dealer network. Building on the success of his Stinger program two years prior, he and Donna Mae (his trusted right-hand PR manager) worked hard to use existing dealers while also constantly adding new ones to the network. By June 5, 1968, he had sold 20 Camaros that were sent to dealerships around the country. The vehicles weren't cheap, with final examples ringing up such prices as $5,052 and even $5,445.20.

Super Camaro Conclusion

The 1968 Super Camaro marked a transition year of vehicles for Don and his team of 427-converting techs. It certainly was an evolution from their efforts in 1967 and, at the same time, a direct launching pad for what was to come in 1969. Don's determination from a few years back in developing the Corvair Stinger, and the subsequent knowledge of taking advantage of the COPO program, paid off.

While the rest of his dealer competition kept their noses to the grindstone, churning out conversions, Don struck four-wheeled gold by working with Chevrolet to take first steps in getting performance-oriented parts installed right at the factory. Once the connection was made, his mind soared with the possibilities. For 1969, Don would go even bigger, adding more cars to the list, more dealers to his network, and, most importantly, having Chevrolet add the 427 under the hood.

The 1968 Super Camaro wasn't some watered-down custom creation, but one built to both move and sell. This Grotto Blue example was shipped to Francis Chevrolet in Bridgeton, Missouri, which got at least four vehicles as part of its order. Mark Pieloch owns this one.

CHAPTER 4

THE GIBB CHEVY II NOVA SUPER SPORT

A MUSCLE CAR OF EPIC PROPORTIONS

On paper, Chevrolet was adhering to its promise of refraining from motorsports involvement. But behind closed doors and up and down the hallways of General Motors, talk was always present about how to stay not only in it but also on top. The adage "Win on Sunday, sell on Monday" was ringing true more than ever, and for those on the inside such as Vince Piggins, it was a forbidden fruit too irresistible to simply ignore, even while toeing the company line.

The 1968 COPO Nova wasn't some cobbled-together hack job. Chevrolet engineers put in the time to get the powertrain combo right, resulting in a tough-as-nails competitor. This car (number 28) spent time racing in the Colorado Springs, Colorado, area, at such tracks as the Denver International Raceway and Mile High Raceway Park.

An outside Corvette enthusiast wrote to Vince Piggins asking if Chevrolet would be hosting any performance clinics (like the competition had been doing) at his local dealership. Piggins wrote back in August 1968 stating, "My personal feelings are in agreement with you on the benefits of a high-performance clinic such as being conducted by Chrysler, Plymouth, and others. Under our present policy, it is impossible for any division of General Motors to directly or indirectly participate in racing or race-oriented activity. It thus would be out of the question for anyone in Chevrolet to underwrite an activity of this nature. We at Chevrolet Engineering are quite cognizant of our performance image and the necessity of ever improving our stock performance vehicles. I can assure you that we have no intention of letting you down in this area." He closed by letting the gearhead know that any clinic at their closest dealership would have to be an independent endeavor.

As product promotions manager, Piggins's main concern was keeping Chevrolet products in the limelight. Naturally, with his racing past, he determined that winning races was the best way to do that. But not wanting to infringe on the company's rules, he set his sights on improving Chevrolet's portfolio of stock performance vehicles. As 1968 dawned, he spied an untapped racing opportunity in which General Motors could do just that, muscling in and stealing the show. He set his sights on the upper classes of NHRA drag racing and made it his goal to not only compete but to dominate, and all in a stock vehicle.

Chevrolet advertised that the Super Sports package gave the Chevy II "sports car handling" while the available powertrains made for "custom made performance." In all, it made the perfect foundation for what Vince Piggins and Fred Gibb had cooked up.

A New Nova

Piggins's plan started with the fully redesigned Chevy II Nova that had just been released for the 1968 model year. Gone was the sharp, boxy, slab-sided style of years prior and in its place a flowing, modern look. The updated looks weren't the only thing new. The car could be had in a Super Sport package, which gave the compact a newfound sense of serious muscle. Buyers of SS Novas could select a 396-ci V-8 that came in two output ratings: 350 hp (L34) and a solid lifter 375 hp (L78). All told, in 1968, a total of 234 Novas were equipped with the L34, while 667 got the L78.

To be clear, the L78 wasn't anything new; Chevy had been making it available in full-size and intermediate cars for the past couple of years. What was new was that the Chevy II would mark the first time it was available in a compact car. It made for a hot setup; up until then the L78 was the highest horsepower engine available through Chevy's option ordering system as a regular production option (RPO). When it was paired with the smaller, lighter Chevy II, it made for a fast combination. Officially, horsepower was rated at 375, but realistically it cranked out more like 425.

Shifting Gears: A New Turbo-400

The limitation with the package was with transmissions. Buyers of L78 Novas had three transmission offerings and all were 4-speed manuals:

If Chevrolet was going to stand a chance against the race competition, it had to kick its automatic transmission R&D into high gear. Piggins came through in the clutch, spearheading the efforts to get it done, get it done right, and then get it out the door into the COPO Novas.

the wide ratio M20, the M21 close-ratio, or the heavier-duty M22 Rock Crusher. Widespread speculation and rumors circulated that Chevrolet would never put an automatic transmission behind a solid lifter engine. Solid lifter–equipped engines produced higher output than a common flat tappet production V-8. They featured such things as a high-lift camshaft allowing the valves to be open longer, rectangular port heads allowing more air in the combustion chambers, a high-rise intake, and a 780 carb. By contrast, lower output engines used hydraulic lifters, which ran smoother but didn't pack nearly the punch.

Whereas Chrysler, pairing its Hemi engines with TorqueFlites, and Ford, with its automatic-equipped 428 Cobra Jet, had experimented with putting automatics behind their higher performance engines, General Motors held back. As with any new technology, there was a learning curve to master and a juggling act to perform to make it all work. On the one hand, engineers needed to dial in stall speeds so that when drivers came to a stop, the transmission would reign in the rumbling muscle machine, preventing bucking and bouncing unmercifully.

On the flip side, they had to make sure at higher speeds the transmission gearing stayed tight and didn't slip when under heavier loads. For one reason or another, General Motors hadn't moved forward with getting it right. With this new car and its new performance-oriented engine option, Piggins set out to do what he could to help the process along. Besides bragging rights, winning the super stock automatic drag racing classes held an added benefit of increased foot traffic to dealerships. A winning, automatic transmission–equipped race car would open up the market of potential car shoppers. The notion that only manuals were for racing would be shattered, making the auto more relatable and more desirable. Piggins had a vision, but to bring it to fruition, but he'd need a partner, and one at the dealer level, to make these stock vehicles a reality.

Fred Gibb Chevrolet

Piggins turned to Fred Gibb. Fred owned Fred Gibb Chevrolet in the tiny little town of LaHarpe, Illinois, located near the Iowa and Missouri state lines. Fred had grown to be good friends with GM president Ed Cole, occasionally hunting with him and sharing holiday meals together. Fred's ties to the industry started in 1948, when he began selling Chevrolets. With business good, in the fall of 1963, he opened a brand-new building for his dealership.

LaHarpe was in rural Illinois, so the focus was on offering customers simple, reliable transportation. Up until then, Fred had little interest in competitive racing. His change of heart came once he saw the monetary gains that could be had from the sport. It started with one of his longtime salesmen, Herb Fox. Fox was a drag racing enthusiast and all-around performance car diehard. Beginning in 1963, and for the next couple of years,

he purchased a new Corvette to drive. When the Camaro debuted in 1967, instead of grabbing a demonstrator to use, he purchased one outright, selecting a Royal Plum Z28 model. The vehicle arrived on May 27, 1967, and soon thereafter he was racing it in D/Gas classes at Beardstown Dragstrip, in Beardstown, Illinois, as well as at the St. Louis International Raceway in East St. Louis, Illinois. He campaigned it under the name *Little Hoss* and did quite well.

Sometime around then, Bill Krable, who ran the parts department at Fred Gibb Chevrolet, starting stocking more and more of the available performance parts. The once-quiet parts department was soon buzzing with excitement as enthusiasts came in to scoop up carbs, camshafts, wheels, and more. Sales began to boom, enticing Fred to look more into racing partnerships. Simple lettering was applied to Herb's Camaro, advertising the dealership, which Fred would soon call the "Tri Sports Sports Center." Fred's competitive nature was stirred through the venture and for good reason; Fox's race team went on to post a 35-0 record in the 1967 racing season. Fred wound up buying the car back from Fox for the 1968 race season and had it painted red. With Herb still behind the wheel, the combo would go on to become the AHRA World Champion, running a quarter-mile time of 11.75 in the Top Stock Class.

During the 1967 race season, Herb connected with the friendly and very talented Dick Harrell, most likely at a track competition. Congenial Harrell invited Fox to check out his shop, which had started performing the

In the most unlikely of locations, the Fred Gibbs Sports Center sprang up in rural Illinois. Based in a tiny farming community known for trucks and basic transportation, Fred Gibb Chevrolet soon became a hub of activity, selling go-fast parts and accessories and, soon, some of the most desired and collectible Chevys of all time.

Appearing understated and docile, these COPO Novas were ready to be driven. Other than the lower Super Sport and fender 396 badging, the dog dish hubcaps and lack of other performance upgrades didn't give anything away at what these cars could do. Mark Riggsby owns this example.

427 conversions for the Yenko Camaro. Fox was so impressed he convinced Fred to return to see the racer's operations. While he grew to like the sport, Fred's ultimate goal was to sell cars, and with Harrell's renowned name, he saw potential in a relationship. Fred returned a few weeks later and bought two of the Yenko Super Camaros, bringing them back and selling them through his dealership.

COPO 9738

With input from Harrell, Piggins and Fred Gibb crafted a plan to help the Chevy IIs out. It involved equipping an L78 Nova with a fully redesigned and still experimental 3-speed Turbo-Hydramatic 400 automatic transmission built specifically for competition. Engineers at General Motors put in the R&D to get the heavy-duty unit just right, and their hard work paid off.

The final product was designated CY and was one tough transmission, which included a new, special six-lug higher stall speed converter to help get the L78's power to the ground. All told, the transmission was able to handle

more than 400 ft-lbs of torque, making it a great choice to back the punch from the 7,000-plus-rpm 396-ci engine. While Chevy was willing to do the legwork to make it work, Piggins needed buy-in from Fred both literally and figuratively. To be eligible to compete in the stock race classes, NHRA requirements dictated that 50 completed vehicles had to be built in order for the vehicle to be recognized as legal and available to the general public as a production vehicle.

Just as with the Stinger, it was the NHRA's way of ensuring the Stock race classes had some semblance of street-ready machines. Willing, committed, and eager to take the gamble, Fred placed an order for the necessary 50 COPO Novas, financing all of them through his GMAC account. His confidence was bolstered by his newfound partnership with Harrell, who he knew would be a valuable asset in getting the dozens of cars sold. The special paperwork for the automatic L78 combo was filed under the designation COPO 9738. Piggins approved the order, and the cars were built in the first two weeks of July at Chevy's Willow Run Plant in Ypsilanti, Michigan. The transmission received a special tag stamped CY while the engine was stamped with an engine code of E3.

All of the cars came with the base Super Sport package, offering dual exhaust and deluxe bucket seat interiors. Besides the transmission, Fred (likely with input from Harrell) requested additional race-specific components as part of the COPO, including a heavy-duty cross-flow radiator, a BV 4.10-geared Positraction rear end, and a center console with a floor-mounted shifter. Other options included 14x6 painted steel wheels, E-70x14 Firestone Wide Oval Redlines, and heavy-duty power drum brakes. Knowing tunes aren't important at the track, the radio was left out, streamlining the build process and saving weight. The cars came in four exterior paint colors: 10 Matador Red, 10 Tripoli Turquoise, 10 Grecian Green, and 20 Fathom Blue. Blue cars got a matching blue interior while the rest got black. "They were really cars," recalls Helen Gibb, Fred's wife. "Fred believed that race cars should be sleepers because he figured they would be used on the highway as well as the drag strip."

All 50 cars, including number 15 seen here, received the Super Sport package, which added dual exhaust and SS badging.

For the debut of the Super Sport option, this lower script on the bottom of the front fenders was affixed to the 1968 Nova SS. It was a one-year-only feature and removed for the 1969 model.

Simple and straightforward, all 50 COPO Novas were equipped with bucket seats and a center console, complete with floor-mounted shifter. Underneath that T-handle and transmission tunnel was where all the promising straight-line magic was.

For the 20 buyers who purchased Fathom Blue COPO Novas, interiors were color matched to the exterior and received blue cabins. The extra gauges were add-ons, mounted lower, and installed by the crew at Dick Harrell's speed shop.

To accelerate the process of getting the cars cleared for racing, in May GM wrote the NHRA stating that all 50 vehicles had been built. In reality, they wouldn't be assembled until the first two weeks of July. They then were shipped to Fred's dealership, making for a massive influx of inventory. To accommodate them all, Fred rented space from the other three dealerships in LaHarpe—the AMC, Chrysler, and Ford stores—where he temporally moved all of his used inventory. Novas were everywhere, and Fred stacked them on every square inch of available asphalt, all the way to the cornfield behind the dealership.

The cars didn't sit for long. They were stickered around $3,500 and moved fairly quickly into eager buyers' hands. While Chevrolet was going to build them, because of their extreme performance capabilities, they wouldn't receive the brand's normal 5-year/50,000-mile factory warranty. Instead, they were given a 90-day warranty. They were sold to customers around the area, as well as to buyers in California, Kentucky, Michigan, Kansas, and Michigan.

As to the Novas' performance, Fred said, " . . . they were really hot. And you could be sitting still, and just stand on it and the tranny would shift, shift, shift. You didn't have to let up like you do with most automatics. You just had so much pressure there, and extra springing behind everything, like your drive plates and so forth, that it was just bam, bam, bam, bam. It beats anything you've ever seen for an automatic transmission." A recent Gibb Nova was put on a dyno and put out 499 hp at the flywheel.

The combination worked so well that for the 1969 model year, Chevrolet offered the Turbo 400, now using the CX code as an RPO for L78 Novas, as well as other performance-oriented models. It made the announcement to its dealer networks on July 12, 1968, stating that they were rolling out the heavy-duty transmission on the 425-hp V-8 in Chevrolet models; the 375-hp V-8 for Chevelle, Chevy ll, and Camaro models; and the 430- and 435-hp Corvette. Up until then, only manual transmissions were available, but Chevrolet felt the Turbo 400 was sufficient because of its ability to handle greater engine torque, higher RPM, and "generally more rigorous operation anticipated with these high output engines."

The Super-Chevy II

A handful (the best estimates ring up at around a dozen) of these track-oriented Novas got further

This COPO Nova (number 44) went to Courtesy Chevrolet in Anaheim, California, and it was purchased new by Beverly Warren of Pasadena, California. During the 1980s, the second owner added fender flares and front disc brakes and swapped in a black interior. During its recent restoration, current owner Tommy Kusmiesz made changes (like the white hood accent) that he felt would be in the same spirit of how these cars were modified when new.

tuning at the hands of Dick Harrell. Fred and Harrell had cooked up a deal in which buyers who wanted it could have Harrell and his two technicians supertune the 396 by rejetting the Holley 3310 carburetor, putting a differ-

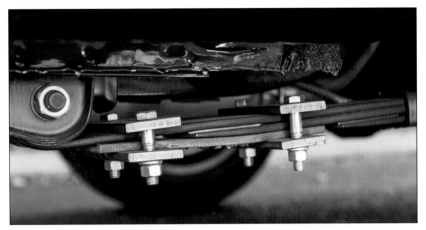

Dick Harrell and his techs (as well as many other enthusiasts) installed clamps on the Novas' rear leaf springs, attempting to keep the rear wheels planted and grabbing traction during hard launches.

Under the hood, the car was equipped with a 4-barrel carb, which Tommy swapped to tri-power. Throughout the restoration, he stayed in touch with Dave Libby, one of Dick Harrell's technicians, to ensure the alterations were period correct. "They would do anything a customer requested," said Tommy. "I wanted to do it right. All of my changes were things they did back then."

ent advance curve in the distributor, checking the rocker adjustment, and performing an overall check of the car. No doubt Fred strategically looped in the star racer, thinking the name recognition would help move the massive inventory of track-focused Novas.

In addition, go-fast goodies, including rear spring clamps and headers could be installed too. It wasn't over the top, but Harrell would add simple badging to his creations. On the outside, an etched plaque proclaiming, "Built by Dick Harrell," was riveted to the front edge of the hood on the driver's side. A similar plaque was riveted inside, ahead of the gear selector on the center console.

Each completed car would be road tested for overall performance, braking, shifting, and all-out acceleration. Once orders came in, Harrell made a couple of trips to Fred's dealership with an empty race-car hauler to load up a few cars and return them to his shop to perform any additional modifications.

Chevrolet's Hot 427

The 396 wasn't the hottest Nova to roll out of Harrell's shop. Just as he had with the Yenko Super Camaro, the seasoned tuner quickly assessed that the Nova could easily accept an engine larger than the L78. He turned to either the L72 or L88 427-ci V-8, converting a select few. The process involved replacing the 396's short-block with the 427 short-block but retaining the top end of the motor, including the intake, cylinder heads, and other components.

The engine was then super-tuned for drag racing performance, so the carburetor, distributor, and the shifting characteristics of the automatic transmission were all finely tuned for this application. A Sun tach was standard equipment and

The only exterior element advertising the Harrell treatment was this simple plaque riveted to the driver-side front edge of the hood. While similar to the one inside, this outside one is elongated slightly.

If a car passed through Harrell's shop, it would get one of these plaques riveted just ahead of the floor-mounted shifter. It was the only source of branding on the inside.

These stickers were often stuck to both valve covers of cars' engines that Dick and his crew had modified. Note the shield logo with three stars across the top and a solid bar through the middle. There's no denying the similarities between it and the design used by Fred Gibb and Don Yenko. Here, underneath it reads "Super Camaro Chevelle Dealers."

Harrell's team commonly installed these lower gauges, oftentimes made by Stewart Warner. Chevrolet did offer its own special instrumentation that gave a "flight deck look," adding four gauges ahead of the center console.

mounted on the steering column, along with a specially prepared rear suspension and a fiberglass Stinger–style (Corvette, not Corvair) hood. The hood was for weight savings as it featured a center vent that was blocked off and purely cosmetic. For buyers with deeper pockets who wanted more, Harrell offered additional optional performance parts including Jardine headers, custom mag wheels, gauges, and racing slicks. Steel clamps were added to the front of the rear leaf springs for extra strength.

Dick ran ads touting the Chevy IIs, proclaiming output ratings of "up to 500 horsepower." While Dick may have been the pioneer to figure out how to get the 427 installed, it wasn't his crew that performed the majority of the swaps.

Popular Hot Rodding Track Test

Popular Hot Rodding headed to Dick Harrell's shop as part of a feature on his Chevy II's for the publication's November 1968 edition. They took three different Chevy II models to the Kansas City International Raceway, home base for Harrell's test of the cars. In their shoot-out was a stock L78 396 with street tires ($3,590), a tuned L78 396 with slicks ($3,790) and the monster street/strip prepared L72 427 with slicks ($4,412). The best they could run with the stock version was 14.26 at 101.46 mph. The tuned 396 turned in times of 13.64 at 102.38, and the 427 came in at 12.05 at 115.78. Their conclusion was that the Chevy II "seems to be an ideal car for a quick street/strip machine."

Personal Perspective: Jim McPeake, Gibb Repair Technician, 1967–1974

Jim McPeake made many of the repairs to the various COPO cars. He watched all of the COPO Nova saga unfold firsthand. He grew up in nearby Blanksfield, Illinois, and was hired by Fred in 1967 as a scrawny 17-year-old gearhead. "My first day on the job was putting a 427 V-8 in a 1964 GTO," recalls McPeake. "The shop foreman pulled it out of the crate and said, 'Make it fit.'" From there, McPeake just tried to keep up with the busy repair garage. Working at Gibb's wasn't his only source of income. McPeake worked second shift at the Bauer Bearing factory in Macomb, Illinois. "I'd go to Fred's from 7:30 a.m. to 2 p.m., come home, change, and then go to the factory for a 4 p.m. to midnight shift. My weekends would be full of rebuilding additional customer's motors and cars. It didn't leave much time for playing," said McPeake, laughing, thinking back to his hectic schedule.

Things got even busier when 1968 rolled around. "The Novas were a fun deal," said Jim. "They were neat little cars with lots of power. But the whole dealership's persona changed once we got into racing. That became our focus. After the order went through, they just kept showing up, and we had them stacked up everywhere. But they moved pretty fast.

The COPO additions and Harrell touches were just the ticket to keep this batch of special Novas on track in recapturing first place finishes in drag races around the country.

The sweptback roofline resulted in massive C-pillars but still offered loads of headroom in both the front and rear seats. The integration of the aftermarket tach into the Nova's elongated, narrow dash wasn't as seamless as in the Camaro, which featured taller gauge pods. It would fit but blocked the speedometer.

them and, not used to being able to leave the throttle down, starved the front bearing of oil, blowing up the engine.

This was the same story with the service manager, Glenn Wright, along with countless customers who loved this newfound, hammer-down power. A quick, short-term solution was to dump in more oil, but Fred tasked his techs with coming up with a better solution. "The cars came from the factory with 5-quart oil pans," said Jim. "Customers would take their new cars out, nail the gas, and suck the pan dry, spinning the bearing. When they came back, we'd replace the bearings and swap out the factory 5-quart oil pan for a 2-inch deeper 8-quart oil pan and the longer L88 pickup tube. For the most part, that'd fix the problem. The Chevrolet-offered 90-day warranty wasn't much, but Fred was always good to take care of customers."

People were buying them regularly. There was a couple that stayed in LaHarpe that were bought for the street. They were reasonably priced cars that normal people could buy."

McPeake was also one of the technicians responsible for performing many of the 427 swaps, which happened right in LaHarpe. "We pulled a bunch off the showroom and yanked the 396 and dropped in the bigger motor, saving the 396," said Jim. "I could put in a new short-block and roll it out the door in seven hours. I hustled through them pretty good. Fred charged customers $75 for the swap. It wasn't uncommon that I would have several tore apart at the same time. Most of the 427 conversions were done at Gibb, but I do recall Dick walking out every once in a while, visiting with us in the shop and checking on the progress."

After the cars left in the care of new owners, McPeake remembers many coming back for a common problem: oil starvation. The L78 featured a hemorrhaging oiling system in place of a closed system with no efforts for restriction to keep oil in the bottom end of the motor. Because of this, when eager drivers got behind the wheel, stuck their foot in it and stayed on full throttle, the mechanically driven oil pump would continually pump oil to the top. It didn't take long for the number one main bearing at the front of the engine, the farthest away, to overheat and fail. Conditioned to 4-speed manuals, where protocol is putting it into gear, getting on the accelerator, backing off, shifting gears, and then getting back on it, many drivers didn't know how to handle the readily accessible power that the new auto afforded. Herb got behind the wheel of a couple of

For owners who really wanted to move, Harrell and his team swapped a 427's short-block into the COPO Nova. Even more power could be squeezed out through the addition of exhaust headers and super-tuning and calibrating the powerplant.

McPeake also went above and beyond to remedy another oiling issue. Even with the larger oil pan, the L78s still burned oil. With all of his weekend tinkering and knack for mechanics, McPeake diagnosed it as piston rings with too light of tension against the cylinder walls. He took it upon himself to bypass the parts counter and head down to Shannons, the

If somehow competitors missed such clues as racing slicks or the rumbling exhaust when pulling up to the start line, they'd get one last chance to see what they were about to tangle with before the light changed to green. If the numbers read this combo, they'd better hope, pray, and give their ride all its got. (Photo courtesy Brian Henderson)

While certainly looking tough, the fiberglass stinger-style hood wasn't functional and was added on purely for weight savings. There's no denying the design inspiration came from the 1967 Corvette equipped with the factory 427-ci V-8.

local auto supply store, to purchase aftermarket and higher quality Hastings piston rings. When Fred learned he had a bill at an outside vendor, he wasn't too thrilled. He stormed to the back of the dealership, asking McPeake, "Why are we buying rings when I have them on the shelves?" McPeake informed him the stock rings weren't working and he was curing the oil burning problem. Fred paused and then, realizing Jim was fixing a problem, allowed him to keep doing it.

Another conversation between Fred and McPeake happened one summer afternoon with an offhand comment that didn't go so well. A happy customer who had just completed the paperwork to purchase one of the L78 Novas was in the process of transferring his belongings from his trade-in vehicle to the new ride. McPeake, knowing full well all the work involved with keeping Novas on the road, walked by as he was loading up a portable toolbox in the new car. "I made a smart comment, yelling out, 'You're going to need that!' He heard me and ended up being madder than hell. He went back up front and tried to back out the deal. Fred calmed him down and he ended up buying the car, but Fred chewed me out pretty good. The biggest problem with the cars was the oil pan. I don't remember having a single transmission issue; it was bulletproof."

A tach became a crucial element in getting the COPO Novas down the track. A factory gauge was available as part of the RPO U17, but the option was pricey, and the gauge was small and hard to read. The better route was to install a large, aftermarket unit, like this one, on the column, front and center ahead of the driver. A Sun tach, such as this one, was standard equipment on Harrell-prepared 427-equipped Novas.

Personal Perspective: Dave Carpenter, Gibb Repair Technician, 1968–1972

Dave Carpenter, who came on board in October 1968, joined McPeake in the back repair bays. Carpenter had gone through an auto tech school while in the air force and was ready to put his skills to good use. "Many of the Novas had already been delivered," recalls Carpenter. "But there were still some on the lot. I remember seeing all the colors; some red, some blue, and some green." While Carpenter's training was for mechanics, Fred needed a body technician. He tasked Carpenter with running point for the collision and paint and body repair.

Being just one of a handful of repair techs, Carpenter still did a lot of his first passion: mechanics. At the time, the state of Illinois had a required test for trucks 1 ton and over, and Carpenter remembers getting a lot of them ready, given the farming community and heavy trucking environment Fred Gibb Chevrolet was in. Still, he also did a good amount of work to the COPO Novas. "Most of the customers I saw were buying them to drag race and coming back with the oil starvation problem on the bottom end," said Carpenter. "While I never drove one on a strip, I did do my fair share of test drives, and they did run pretty good," he added with a chuckle. Carpenter spent time up front too, befriending Herb Fox. Carpenter left Fred Gibb Chevrolet in 1972, but his path crossed with Fox again. In 1990, Carpenter got a job across town at LaHarpe Motor Sales (the local Ford dealer) and Fox was one of its salespeople. "We spent a lot of time talking about the old days," said Carpenter.

A couple of slick remedies quickly surfaced to help with the L78's oil issues. At the most basic level, the engine could be slightly overfilled with oil but a more long-term solution was for techs to add a deeper oil pan.

The 396-ci V-8 engine, while potent, packed a design flaw that left it starving for oil. When eager new buyers climbed behind the wheel of their new COPO Novas, their first move was to put it into gear, mash the gas, and hang on. All that did, besides afford a wild ride, was to overheat the engine bearings.

Personal Perspective: Nancy Gibb

"Dad used to go with our family doctor up to the Dakotas to go pheasant hunting. Every year they'd go out there and stay in a friend's hunting lodge. That's where he ran into Vince Piggins and Ed Cole and became good friends. After we started racing the Camaro, Mom kept track of all the points and clipped out all the articles in *Drag World*. She even drew the sketch for the Fred Gibb logo and wrote all the copy for our ads. She was very bright and creative. After getting into the competition, Dad liked the idea of finding one class to focus on and win. He also liked the idea of a 'sleeper type' car and the Nova was perfect. When they came in, they sold fast. After they were all gone, Dad kept saying, 'I'd knew they sell, I knew they'd sell.'

"There was a stretch just outside of town we called the Fountain Green blacktop. It was the best, newest road and always in good shape. Dad would take cars out there for test and tune. The cops were good about it and would sometimes even block it off. Dad always wanted to drive the car first; he had an ear for mechanical parts and was a good shifter. The whole town was great and behind us and what we were doing. There were always 'blackies,' the twin pairs of rubber marks, on the stretch. I'd go to school and kids in my class would come up and say, 'Your dad and Herb were out last night laying blackies!' after they saw or heard the loud cars."

Dick Harrell Dealer Network

After receiving the Harrell touch, the completed cars were then sold through a network of dealers, similar to Yenko's Stinger program, in which anyone, not just diehard racers, could purchase them. This boosted Harrell's popularity, as supercars bearing his name were being sold through factory dealerships, packing full dealer warranties. He moved on from his relationship with Fred Gibb Chevrolet, connecting with dealers on the West Coast, including Courtesy Chevrolet dealerships in San Diego, San Jose, Thousand Oaks, Los Angeles, and Phoenix.

Taking a page from Don Yenko's playbook, Dick assembled a lineup of participating Chevy dealerships that signed up to distribute his products. With his "Mr. Chevrolet" name recognition and red-hot racing career, it seemed like a perfect fit. The majority of the locations were on the West Coast.

This Nova was run hard at dragstrips, then put away in 1973 with a blown engine. The original owner added Mickey Thompson scavenger headers and the Dick Harrell rear spring clamps. It was purchased by longtime Gibb Nova enthusiast Rich Thayer in 2010, who made sure it was restored to its former glory.

Gibb Nova Recap

While the Camaro was stealing the majority of the limelight in 1968, that's not to say that it was the only hot performer in Chevrolet's stable. Engine builders and race teams, such as Bill "Grumpy" Jenkins, gravitated to the Chevy II, finding the compact car a formidable foe on the starting line. Wanting to win in even more race classes, Chevrolet insiders, such as Vince Piggins, saw a great opportunity and partnered with a strong ally in Fred Gibb. Keeping with the theme of "stock" vehicles, Piggins's engineers' R&D

paid off. Once Fred Gibb Chevrolet got the special Novas (with their new and robust transmissions) distributed, and they started winning races, it was proof of concept; the new Turbo 400 automatic transmission was a perfect mate for big-block engines. No harm, no foul was committed as Piggins had found a way to keep Chevrolet in first without breaking the rules.

While Piggins worked with Don Yenko down in Canonsburg to begin crafting Camaros to rule the streets, he and Fred went off in a different direction. They, along with Dick Harrell, set their sights on building a new COPO Camaro that would do nothing but dominate the drag strip.

CHAPTER 5

THE ZL1 CAMARO

THE ULTIMATE CAMARO

High on the success of the COPO L78 automatic Novas, which were still proving potent on drag strips, Vince Piggins was ready to up the ante. Once again, he set his sights on dominating drag racing. This time around, the plan was to assemble a big-block Camaro to compete in the NHRA's Super Stock race class. The regulations stated that vehicles were, for the most part, stock, but there was some wiggle room for a few modifications.

Using the Central Office, General Motors was able to take something that only existed in flights of fancy and make it a tire-smoking reality. The resulting ZL1 took the Camaro to new heights, equipping the pony car with enough horsepower to properly mix it up with the best of them.

This ZL1 number 23 lived the kind of life Fred Gibb and Vince Piggins had envisioned. It was sold new by Lafferty Chevrolet in Warminster, Pennsylvania, on June 23, 1970, and was exclusively raced heavily for the next seven years. It featured twin stripes, done up in lace paint, holes drilled in the doors for lightening, and a custom sticker placed front in center between the gauges that read "THINK WIN."

The decision wasn't by chance. Drag racing's popularity continued to explode in the late 1960s, with 1969 being the fifth straight consecutive year of whopping gains in attendance, participants, and supervised racing for both the NHRA and the AHRA. In 1968, the AHRA marked its first year of 5 million in attendance at its nationwide events. A lot of eyeballs were watching what played out on the tracks and, more importantly, what cars came in first. In 1967 and 1968, the winners were consistently Chrysler race cars. They were crushing those heads-up Super Stock classes, which is where many deemed the real action to be. The heads-up format meant there weren't any handicap start privileges for weaker cars, no separate classes for 4-speed and automatic transmission cars, and no collection of elapsed time brackets. In other words, there were no gimmicks or excuses to hide behind if your car wasn't competitive. It was man and machine with the winner being the quickest, not the one who could skillfully apply the brakes in the timing traps to avoid running quicker than the bracket allowed. It was racing in its purest form.

Chrysler was cleaning up, taking the lead with such teams as "Dandy" Dick Landy and the Sox & Martin duo at the big events around the country. The brand had charged back into all-out support of competition, and the funding and support was paying off. Sox & Martin's red-hot success in the 1968 season earned driver Ronnie Sox the AHRA's Driver of the Year Award, who accepted it "surrounded by Chrysler Corporation bigwigs" who no doubt wore big grins on their faces.

Both Mopar superstars stayed busy off the track, putting on and hosting Super Car Clinics. Dick Landy pioneered the concept in 1967, conducting more than 70 safety-performance clinics in 29 states, playing to an audience of more than 50,000 enthusiasts. In 1968, he would do more than 100 events in even more locations throughout the nation. The sessions were free to attend and "conducted for enthusiasts interested in gaining maximum performance from their cars in sanctioned drag racing." Landy revealed inside race secrets, talked about safety measures, gave tuning tips, and showed slides and movies from past competitions. Audiences gobbled it up. Naturally, he displayed his race cars too; showing off his Charger RT Hemi and Coronet RT. These wildly popular events were held in, you guessed it, Dodge dealerships. "Our clinics emphasize the type of car that can be purchased from a dealer's stock at a realistic price, and then be prepared with all safety and performance features and done so inexpensively," said Landy.

It made for a genius marketing ploy and one that didn't sit well with Piggins. It didn't take long to devise a simple formula that would pump the brakes on Mopars' runaway success. Step one: Get Chevy's COPO process to build an incredible car. Step two: Sell just enough to the public to qualify for those stock race classes and do it through a dealer already willing to play ball. Step three: Throw in a world-class driver to market and race the product. Step four: Unleash the cars in Super Stock Classes. Step five: Win. From there, it was just a matter of repeating steps four and five as many times as possible.

It seemed like a sure-fire plan to Piggins. The dealer would be Fred Gibb Chevrolet, who was already a big supporter of the racing gig and, of course, the driver was none other than "Mr. Chevrolet" himself, Dick Harrell. As for the car, that would be one special piece. GM engineers would start with a Camaro but what was underhood was something truly exotic.

Connecting with Chaparral

The special engine's origins stemmed from the Chaparral Cars race team, helmed by Jim Hall of Midland, Texas. Hall, who had come from wealth, was a talented designer with a degree in mechanical engineering and was the United States road-racing title holder. He was forward-thinking and innovative. He pioneered race car aerodynamics at his own 2-mile paved track in Midland, Texas, called Rattlesnake Raceway. There, he also had access to a skid pad, the latest in electronic and recording equipment, and a machine shop.

All through the 1960s, Hall had been using Chevrolet engines for his race cars, and he was, at the time, the only successful racer to use an automatic transmission in a competition sports car. His forte was creating road course cruisers, not straight-line missiles, but he provided great cover. It was common knowledge that although the company policy was still no racing, General Motors kept a hand in auto racing. Its ties to Hall were heavily speculated, although nothing concrete could be proven.

The automatic transmission that the Chaparral team raced was rumored to have been a direct product of Chevy engineering that "slipped out the back door since the front entrance had been officially barred to the racing crowd." Hall's refusal to say anything about the box other than admitting it is an automatic tended to make the speculation more believable. However it came about, there was no denying of the close connection between Chevrolet and Hall. His car was often referred to as the Chaparral-Chevrolet, even though he designed and built it. It was well publicized that in spite of the no-racing rule, General Motors, especially the Chevrolet division, had its hand in auto racing, company policy or not, through those behind the scene efforts.

Jim Hall was talented behind the wheel and had quite the string of victories, winning such events as the US Road Racing Championship in 1964; the Road America 500 in 1962 and 1965; the 1,000-km race at Nürburgring, Germany, in 1966; and the 12-hour race at Sebring, Florida, in 1965. He also pioneered new technology. As early as 1965 he was using an engine cast in aluminum (a 377-ci V-8) by Alcoa. In 1967, he began campaigning a race car with an aluminum 427 V-8 called the Chaparral 2F, and in 1968 he added fuel injection to it.

This whole scenario was perfect for Piggins and his crew. Sure, on paper General Motors wasn't in the race-car business, making the Chaparral team the perfect scapegoat. If any higher-ups came asking how an engine like the one GM engineers were cooking up for the Camaro ZL1 (from a company that officially was *not* building stuff like this), Piggins could easily throw up his hands and say the whiz-bang tech came from an outside racer. Problem solved.

As for the choice in construction, while the upcoming secret dream car wouldn't be mixing it up on curves like Hall's racers, blasting down quarter miles generates a lot of heat. An aluminum powerplant would do wonders to dissipate it all away. Besides that, no matter if you're going straight or back and forth, lighter weight means faster times. Faster times mean better chances of coming in first. The engine is the heaviest part of a race car and having it shed pounds is a huge plus.

ZL1 Engine Development

Vince Piggins and the engineering crew at General Motors began working on the project in the summer of 1968. It took massive amounts of research to make it all work. Just prior to production, on November 9, the *National Speedsport News* ran an article about Ford's hot new Mustang. Piggins couldn't help but feel a little smug as they prepped what would soon be unleashed. The piece detailed how "despite the performance emphasis in the GM new car ads appearing" that the "folks at FoMoCo" were feeling confident with what they had in the works for 1969.

Ford was planning to move fast in 1969, cranking out a full lineup of performance modifications and engine offerings for its Mustang. Little did Ford know, Chevrolet wasn't sitting idle. Instead, it was gearing up to unleash the company's flagship ZL1. Its exotic big-block 427 engine weighed just slightly more than a cast-iron small-block.

Ford's new president, Bunkie Knudsen, was insistent that Ford would have the hottest line of compacts and intermediates, and he wanted customers to have the perception that they were top dog in the field. The Mustang Mach 1 with the Super 429 racing engine was going to be a major image booster. "When you rev your motor at the red light and a Mach I is alongside, [you] better be prepared to go when the green blinks," wrote the magazine. Another weapon in its upcoming arsenal was the all-new 302 engine, aimed at being a "response vehicle to the Z28 Camaro" that will "blow the Camaro off the road."

Other proof that Ford would be on top in 1969 was the new modifications made to the Cobra Jet 428 engine, the fastback-body style Mustang, and Shelby's new GT, as well as the boost in their dealer networks, growing from 128 to nearly 200. Shelby was also bumping its production from 4,500 vehicles to 5,100 for the 1969 year. After reading the article, Piggins couldn't help but send an internal memo to some of his staff, confident that what they were working on behind closed doors would knock some of the wind from the pesky Ford sails. Below a copy of the story, he simply wrote, "Our ZL1 Camaro will be quite timely and perhaps a bit surprising to Mr. Knudsen and the Mach 1 Mustang."

In December, one of the Chevrolet engineers assigned to the ZL1 project sent a letter to top brass, stating some concerns. After stating that he had learned the special test engine he was working on was being released as a COPO for the Camaro, he said, "Several features of this engine make it highly unsuitable for street use." He cited the open plenum manifold, the lack of exhaust heat for the inlet manifold, the lack of a choke, and the ham-pered power output because of the exhaust back pressure. He concluded the engine should be modified to incorporate the L72 camshaft, inlet manifold, and induction system components. His other suggestion was to "find some method of restricting sales of the COPO so that its purchase for street use, either intentional or inadvertent is impossible" recognizing "our previous experience with this type of release has been very poor in that some jobs will find their way into the wrong hands and drivability complaints are inevitable."

Someone up the chain got the letter and tipped off Vince Piggins about the issues raised, citing they "can be resolved easily." His suggestion was to "modify as much as possible within the framework of competition rules to eliminate undesirable operating characteristics for street performance. It is possible that the free items allowed under competition rules may permit use of a mixture of production parts which will result in good street operation and still provide the latitude for maximum performance in racing."

Piggins wrote back a week later on December 27 with the orders to go ahead and build the first 50 COPO Camaros with the present ZL1 engine specs. "The chance of any of these Camaros being used for street transportation is extremely remote," he wrote. "Most have already been sold for exclusive drag strip usage. Having built these first 50 units for NHRA Super Stock 'C' Class, we will have satisfied their minimum quantity requirements for this class and qualified the specifications for which NHRA have factored the power rating (same as L88: 485 hp)." He went on to say that they "could now modify the ZL1 and in effect come up with a new engine" that

The COPO insiders at General Motors knew they'd be walking on thin ice if they attempted to mastermind the ZL1's aluminum engine all by themselves. By looping in Chaparral (in name, mostly), they got the special blocks cast before anyone in management could get cold feet. Note the plain air cleaner lid. To fly under the radar, there were no special call-outs or advertising to tip off what the ZL1 could do.

Topping the ZL1's aluminum powerplant was a Holley 850-cfm carburetor. It was sourced from the Corvette, taken from RPO L88, which featured a 427-ci iron block paired with aluminum heads.

would allow them to have an eligible vehicle for competing in the NHRA Super Stock D Class. Some of the modifications he suggested were using the engineer's idea: going with the L72 camshaft, manifold, and carburetor. This would make the engine "highly suitable for street use as well as a potent performance vehicle."

Gibb's Order: COPO 9560

Knowing a dealer would need to get involved to funnel out the completed cars, Piggins looped in Fred Gibb and, to a certain extent, Dick Harrell. They collaborated and, in August 1968, Fred requested an order of 50 Camaros, meeting the NHRA minimum production requirements.

The vision of everyone involved was to have these vehicles be minimally optioned cars, with the ultimate goal being all-out, straight-line speed. The first 2 engines were cast in November, while the remaining 48 were cast from January 1969 through March 1969. The vehicles were built at the Norwood, Ohio, plant from December 1968 through early June 1969. They started off as big-block L78-equipped Super Sport cars and then given COPO 9560. This would swap the 396-ci V-8 drivetrain for the ZL1 427-ci V-8, as well as make other tweaks along the way. Common accessories, such as heaters, cast-iron exhaust manifolds, emissions equipment, dual exhaust, 14x7 wheels, and special F41 suspension components were installed.

Additional Super Sport items were deleted and substituted for other special parts. Transmission options were either the M21 close-ratio manual transmission or the heavy-duty Turbo-Hydramatic 400 automatic transmission, similar to ones that had worked so well in Gibb's Novas. The Muncie featured an aluminum case that weighed around 70 pounds. By contrast, Ford's 4-speed tipped the scales at closer to 120 pounds. The Camaro ZL1s that got the 4-speed had an engine stamping of ML while the automatic equipped cars got a stamping of MM.

Tech Insight: ZL1 427 Versus L72 427 Versus L88 427

The aluminum blocks, cylinder heads, and intakes were made at the Winters Aluminum foundry, located in Canton, Ohio. As such, each component was stamped with a snowflake logo; one on the front of the block, one on the driver's side of the manifold, and the one on the driver-side cylinder head. While much of the legwork and real-world testing was done by the Chaparall race engines, the ZL1 engine would have more in common with the L88 block. The biggest difference being the aluminum block and the higher lift camshaft. "The all-aluminum ZL1 engine is a big improvement over the L88, which has only aluminum heads," Harrell said. "This one disperses the heat so evenly that it never runs at over 180 degrees. Five minutes after a run you can lay your hand on it. And it weighs about 25 pounds less than the old 327."

Besides the difference in material, the aluminum 427 received some major differences from the L72 iron-block 427 engine. Overall, the block was beefed up with more metal in all areas, especially the main bearing bulkheads. To strengthen the combustion cylinders, 1/16-inch-thick steel sleeves were used, held in place by a machined groove that locked in a lip on top of the sleeve. Water circulated all around the sleeves to aid in cooling.

The block bolt threads had Heli-Coil steel wire inserts installed into extra deep holes. This would help combat metal fatigue and stripped threads. All the large bolts that were used to mount the cylinder heads and intake manifold utilized flat washers, which prevented galling [when metal seizes up due to high heat and friction] and made for more accurate torque readings. The rods were strengthened and four-bolt main bearing caps were used along with a forged and hardened steel crankshaft. A special heavy-duty oil pump was incorporated into the package along with an 8-quart oil pan. The cylinder heads were also heavily worked over for maximum performance. The exhaust ports, made out of aluminum, were enlarged and rounded (instead of square) at the gasket face to increase airflow by 10 percent. The exhaust valves had a diameter of 1.88 inches across.

By contrast, the steel heads' valves were 1.84 inches in diameter. The intake valves remained the same size as the ones used on the L88 engine (2.19 inches in diameter) but were given steel insert valve seats; marking the first time in a production engine. The intake port contour was smoothed, and the pocket behind the valve guide was nearly eliminated, along with turbulence and blocked airflow. The result was more of a venturi shape with a broader torque range. Other changes included increasing the valve lift from the L88's .560 inch to .600 inch. When paired to an automatic transmission, the rough idle caused many drivers to think the beast was going to stall out. The engine's combustion chambers were modified with the quench area below the spark plug being opened up. Besides this nearly resembling an open Hemi chamber, it also gave a freer flow of fuel vapors into the chamber, improved flame travel, and reduced shrouding effect around the valves.

Compression for the engine dropped from 12.5:1 to 12.0:1, but it helped the powerplant breathe better. The valvetrain, intake manifold, 850-cfm Holley carburetor, and electronic transistor ignition were the same as those found on the L88.

The newly created ZL2 cowl induction hood flowed more air to the ZL1s' engines. Hidden behind the grilles was a heavy-duty, four-core radiator as well as the ignition's amplifier, which is mounted on the hood catch reinforcement. It's needed to get the big powerplant to fire up.

The engine's total weight (with accessories but not flywheel or clutch) was around 520 pounds. The savings between the iron-block and aluminum-block motors was 160 pounds, making the ZL1's 3,300-pound weight roughly the same as a small-block 302-ci V-8 Z28 Camaro. The front rear weight distribution also matched, with about 56 percent of the weight on the front wheels. Output was advertised by General Motors as being around 430 hp, when in reality the engine, when equipped with open headers, produced 575 hp and 515 ft-lbs of torque.

The Winters Foundry stamped its unique insignia on all the parts it created and, as such, the ZL1's aluminum engine features a flurry of flakes. In total, you'll find four of them. One is on the front of the engine block on the driver's side, another one is on the driver's side of the intake manifold, and there are two on both cylinder heads, toward the front of the vehicle.

Around back, the ZL1s featured a special COPO-built Positraction 12-bolt differential with a heat-treated ring and pinion. Chevy knew one of the first things owners would do with their new rides was rip off any factory exhaust system, preferring aftermarket setups. That's what happened with this car, ZL1 number 12. The original owner installed glasspack mufflers and now, Eddie, the current owner, has installed three-cambered mufflers.

Besides the engine, the cars also got a heavy-duty Harrison four-core radiator (RPO V01), a special cowl induction hood (RPO ZL2 and the first-time Camaro had a hood with cowl induction), and an electronic transistor ignition system that featured a distributor with special weights and springs unique to the ZL1 (RPO K66). It required a special amplifier, which was mounted behind the grille, as well as new ignition wiring. The cars also got a heavy-duty suspension featuring a 12-bolt, special COPO-built Positraction differential with heat treated ring and pinion, five leaf springs, and heavy-duty shocks and springs (RPO F41). They all received power front disc brakes and radios were left out to save weight.

The cars came in five colors in sets of 10: Hugger Orange, Cortez Silver, Fathom Green, Lemans Blue, and Dusk Blue. Within each set of 10, 6 were manual M21 transmission–equipped cars and 4 were automatics.

ZL1 Delivery and Debut

Despite numerous delays, General Motors had promised delivery of final cars by the end of the year. As the months dragged on, Fred became increasingly anxious. He and Harrell had plans to debut a new ZL1 in the Super Stock classes at the AHRA's Fifth Annual Winter National event. It was held at the Beeline Dragway in Phoenix, Arizona, from January 23–26. An extra day was added, and even then, the event was swelling at the seams. Entries were limited to 1,000 spots in the various classes and prize money was posted at more than $100,000.

Here it was getting into December and no cars had been dropped off to LaHarpe and, unbeknownst to Fred, they hadn't even been built. Finally, at the eleventh hour, Chevrolet assembled the first two ZL1 Camaros in the last week of December. As soon as they were completed, they were loaded up and trucked out to LaHarpe. The pair, both painted in Dusk Blue, arrived just before midnight on December 31, 1968. "Late that night, we got a call from one of the town cops," said Nancy Gibb. "Dad woke up to the cop telling him, 'You got a pretty angry transport guy that needs to unload two cars.' I went with him to the dealership and boy, was the guy ticked off. Dad got our wrecker out to help get the cars off the trucks since it was so cold they wouldn't start."

Not long after, one car was rushed to Harrell's shop in Missouri for further track prepping. They got everything squared away and it was present for the big race out in Phoenix. With Herb Fox mostly behind the wheel

Either a M21 close-ratio manual transmission or the heavy-duty Turbo-Hydromatic 400 automatics could be installed in the ZL1s. The handle was from Hurst, the same as found on SS and Z/28 Camaros.

(Harrell was busy driving his Funny Car), the ZL1 beat the top two qualifiers before finally losing to Arlen Vanke's Barracuda in the semifinal. While not an all-out thrashing to finish line glory, the display showed what was to come from Chevy racers. An added bonus? Ronnie Sox was one of the contestants knocked out.

48 More ZL1s

No ZL1s were built in January and production wouldn't resume again until the fourth week of February. It continued through the end of April, with the remaining 48 ZL1s on Fred's order form trickling in from February to the end of March. Sadly, they didn't arrive with too much fanfare. Sometime during this period, General Motors switched how these special COPO vehicles' costs were processed. With high-performance vehicles of years gone by, whenever a request came in and was approved, the R&D costs were absorbed and spread out internally in the budget. Sometime after Fred's order and delivery, Chevrolet got serious about making sure every project was profitable and tacked on the R&D cost to the price of the vehicle.

When Fred Gibbs and Vince Piggins began talking about the ZL1 Camaro, Fred was under the impression that final pricing would be around $5,000. But as the final cars rolled in his dealership, he was shocked to see bills tallying at $7,200, as set by Chevrolet. The exotic engine option cost $4,160; way more than the base price of the car, which rang up at $2,700. Word had gotten out that Gibb's rural store was the place

Rollie Paulsgrove bought himself a 1968 COPO Nova from Gibb Chevrolet in the fall of 1968 and came back frequently, resolving a couple minor issues. On one of his return trips in the spring of 1969, he snapped these pictures. That's Dick Harrell's ZL1 race car on the trailer, sponsored by the dealership. The background gives you a sense of how rural the area was surrounding Gibb Chevrolet. (Photo Courtesy Rollie Paulsgrove)

This first car, or any other ZL1, wasn't delivered with a black tail panel, but since a lot of the big-block Camaros had them as part of the X66 SS396 body code, it was applied on the race car for visual impact. (Photo Courtesy Rollie Paulsgrove)

While the car was delivered in Dusk Blue paint, it was repainted in this groovy red shade, complete with lace accenting. Note the resemblance of the shield on the door to that of the one used by Don Yenko and also Dick Harrell. It's unclear who came up with it first but they all used similar designs. Behind the car are two more ZL1s awaiting new owners. (Photo Courtesy Rollie Paulsgrove)

Berger's ZL1

An interesting wrinkle in the ZL1 story is the tale of the third ZL1. While Fred received ZL1 one and two, the third car, a Daytona Yellow one, didn't go to LaHarpe or even to Fred Gibb. It was shipped to Berger Chevrolet in Grand Rapids for the high-performance–oriented dealership to sell.

"We had a big high-performance parts department that generated a lot of business for us and car sales," said Dale Berger Jr., who was general manager of Berger Chevrolet. "One of our young salesmen, Mike Wawee, was young, single, and able to hit all the right places at night to tap into the youth car movement. He was quite a talker and brought in a lot of business. Mike connected with a young clerk in the Central Office who'd tell us whenever a COPO or something else special came out. Mike was on the phone one day with Vince Piggins, who we talked to regularly. He told us about the ZL1 and I said I wanted one. While Fred ordered them, we were selling 1,800 to 2,000 new Chevys a year, much larger and much closer to Detroit, so we found out more."

Berger's ZL1 was the first car built after Fred's two and, surprisingly, was equipped with a whole lot more. Fred wanted his cars to be track terrors, while Berger wanted its ZL1 to be better optioned. The car had floor mats in the front and rear, the D80 front and rear spoiler, an AM push-button radio, and a painted front bumper. Most surprisingly of all, it was equipped with COPO 9737, the Sports Car Conversion. Not only did the Berger staff know what Fred Gibb was up to, somehow they had been alerted to Don Yenko's dealings with the COPO process. Just as with the sYc vehicles, the 9737 equipped the ZL1 with E70x15 tires, Rally Wheels (instead of steelies and dog dish hubcaps), a 13/16-inch stabilizer bar, and the 140-mph speedometer. The pricey car took a long time to sell. Kevin DeWitte headed to Berger Chevrolet on December 24, 1969, nearly a full year after the car was built, to pick up his L72-equipped COPO Camaro and clearly remembers seeing it on display.

"We had that car forever," recalls Dale Berger Jr. "Thank goodness we didn't ask for more. We wintered it, bringing it inside our service department so it wasn't outside in the snow. It took up a stall and was always available to show. I was at luncheon at the Detroit Athletic Club in May 1970 and ran into Joe Pike. I said to him, 'Jeez, I'm still stuck with this ZL1.' He was surprised, saying all the other dealers had sold theirs after they got $1,500 GM kicked in as a credit. That was the first I heard of

While Berger's Daytona Yellow ZL1 packed some fancy dress-up features, it was no paper tiger. Quite the opposite, as this was the only ZL1 to receive COPO 9737, giving it different wheels and tires and a bigger sway bar. When unleashed in a straight line, it would really fly.

A highly potent ZL1 fit nicely into Berger's high-octane image. "We would sponsor a lot of the local guys who were out racing," recalls Dale Berger Jr. "Those were the guys coming back to our high-performance department. They'd race on Saturday and be at our store on Monday buying new stuff." While parked in the show-room, the ZL1 turned heads but didn't change hands, sitting for quite a while before a new buyer became interested.

that and told him I *never* got a check. Joe told me that's because the car was filed as being sold. My team had processed it that way so the rest of them could race. The NHRA needed to see 50 built *and* marked as sold. After telling Joe that, two weeks later, I got my check."

Cockpit amenities included an AM radio and floor mats. The car received RPO Z23, bringing additional items such as the passenger-side grab handle and wood accents on the steering wheel, radio, and light switch. Stewart Warner water-temperature and oil-pressure gauges help with engine monitoring.

Berger's Camaro was the only one in the first set of 51 cars to receive Yenko's COPO 9737, giving it the special speedometer. When drivers gave the 427 maximum thrust, more than likely the ZL1 could approach and exceed the 140-mph mark.

After months of sitting, the high-priced ride finally sold in the spring of 1970 to a young man in Saginaw, Michigan. As Berger recalls, it didn't take him long to blow up the engine, but for one reason or another, Chevy wouldn't warranty it.

This ZL1 (number 35) and about 12 other cars were delivered to Gibb Chevrolet but were sent back to Chevrolet after Fred learned of the new (and very high) price. It found a new home at Sutliff Chevrolet in Harrisburg, Pennsylvania, but not a new owner. To spark interest, Rallye wheels and a decklid spoiler were added by the dealership. Someone finally bought it in February 1971.

for fast cars Fred knew he'd never be able to sell 50 cars at that price, let alone carry that much inventory, which totaled more than $350,000 (nearly $2.4 million dollars today). Fred called General Motors; after lengthy discussions, in an unprecedented move, he was allowed to send most of the vehicles back to the plant.

On May 24, 37 vehicles headed back to Norwood, with Fred requesting his name be removed from the paperwork to avoid finance charges. "Dad was devastated with the price," recalls Nancy Gibb. "When he said something, he always followed through. I remember him on the phone many times asking his contacts at GM what was going on."

At the dealership, it didn't take long for hoodlums to figure out it was quite easy to sneak over after hours, pop the hoods, and steal the 780 carburetors. In order for Fred to continue to have the cars insured, his agency mandated a fence be installed. One was put up around the parking lot behind the store, complete with barbed wire along the top, which provided a decent level of protection.

Fred ended up selling eight ZL1s and transferring five more to other Chevrolet dealers. The task of dispersing the returned ZL1s fell to Joe Pike, Jim Mattison's boss in the Central Office. He started by calling the well-performing Corvette dealers. At first, the requirement was that two

ZL1s had to be taken at a time, which would help lower freight costs. As time wore on and new homes became harder to find, Chevy dropped this policy and allowed one ZL1 to be purchased by interested dealers. "It took him some time," recalls Mattison. "Joe had to sell them one at a time. When it got really hard to generate interest, he'd allocate an extra Corvette if they took one of those ZL1s." Because they were factory, the race-ready ZL1 received a full 5-year/50,000-mile warranty.

19 More ZL1s

Fred went years thinking he was the only dealer to sell the ZL1 but word had gotten out. Other dealers found out about the COPO and 19 more ZL1 Camaros were built and sold. They were assembled in April and May, with the last car, number 69 in the sequence, being built in the fifth week of May.

Two were thoroughly optioned out as Rally Sports (RPO Z22 Rally Sport package) making for a very rare package. Unlike the other 67 stripped-down track missiles, these 2 (ZL1 number-55, painted Lemans Blue, and ZL1 number 68, painted Cortez Silver) had luxury options. The RS package included a blacked-out grille with hideaway headlights and bright accents around the wheel arches, drip rails, and taillights. Each got additional features on top of that too. Car number 55 had tinted glass, a center console, the D80 spoilers, an AM radio, and a rear seat speaker. Car number 68 didn't get the tinted glass or rear speaker but was equipped with front accent striping, the D80 spoilers, and an AM radio.

NHRA Race Class

That spring, the NHRA classified the car in SS/C, citing a pounds-per-hp factor of 6.50 for the car. According to them, the output was cited at being 430 to 480 hp, allowing drivers to cut the racing weight to 3,120 pounds. By contrast, Hemi Barracudas and Darts were rated at 525 hp and forced to run in SS/B class. ZL1 prototypes had tested with ETs in the low 10-second range at 130 mph with blueprinted and modified engines.

May 1969 Media Drive

Super Stock and Drag Illustrated (*SSDI*) scored the opportunity to be the first media outlet to have one of its journalists come out and see what all the ZL1 fuss was about. *SSDI* received a call from Dick Harrell "with an invitation to gaze at, fondle, and drive Chevrolet's most super of all street machines." Writer Roland McGonegal was surprised when he arrived to find Harrell had not one but two ZL1s for testing. The first was a Dusk Blue street car, equipped with mag wheels, Super Stock tires, and a set of headers. A scant 50 miles showed on the odometer. The other was Harrell's modified race car. Besides, Harrell, Fred Gibb and Herb Fox were present. Both cars headed to Kansas City International Raceway for some proper thrashing. Harrell did most of the driving, starting by running his race car to a best of 10.41 at 128.10 mph.

The street car was rolled up to the starting line and a couple of runs were made with the exhaust headers closed. After a smoky start, it ran a best of 12.28 seconds at 118.10 mph. Two more runs and it was still at 12.50 seconds at 117 mph. Since the tires "just couldn't handle the engine all at once when the secondaries cut in," the decision was made to swap out the manual secondary carburetor for a vacuum one. This gave the tires some time to recover before the rear barrels belted them again. An 850 cfm was also installed. The result was a dip into the 11-second range, with times posted of 11.98 at 118.92, 11.90 at 118.92, and 11.85 at 119.06. Harrell knew the car had more in it and adjusted the valves for less low-end torque, dropped the tire pressure to 16 psi, and uncapped the headers. That allowed for a run at 11.78 seconds at 120.84, and then finally Dick roared off a best time of the day of 11.64 seconds at 122.15 mph, shifting the transmission manually. Overall, the magazine was impressed with the times with both ZL1s. "The Turbo trans shifted like it wanted to break your neck," wrote McGonegal, "and the front discs hauled the 3,300-pound monster down in more than enough time."

Harrell informed McGonegal that the blue tester they had been using had a special purpose; it was being set up for a certain young lady from Texas with a heavy right foot. Her name was Shay Nichols.

July 1969 Media Drive

Popular Hot Rodding (*PHR*) tested a ZL1 in its July 1969 edition, comparing it to the "wild super stock or modified production cars you see on the drag strip." The magazine shared how the car's hefty price tag earned it the nickname the "Gold-plated Camaro" but the "Chevy Copa [a typo or period slang for COPO] order reads ZL1." Despite the secrecy, General Motors couldn't keep the lid on how this special vehicle got built. "Without

Once other dealers learned of the ZL1 program, several ordered cars for themselves. This ZL1 (number 62) was sold new on July 10, 1969, at Colonial Chevrolet in Virginia Beach, Virginia. Johnny Tripp bought it on his birthday and covered his hefty monthly loan payments through his race winnings. His consistent first places earned his wicked ride the nickname, the **Red Devil***.*

Super Street and Drag Illustrated*'s tester was Dusk Blue, like this one here, but had been installed with mag wheels and headers. Even then the magazine knew the engine would be a limited-production option and something special. It particularly liked the "reverse scoop" on the hood, claiming it was the only indication something was unique about the car.*

trying to imply that this car is really wild," the magazine feature read, "let us say that it should be delivered with a book of instructions that begins: In case of rain or slick streets, leave car in garage. Honestly, even with sand on the street, the combination of the free-breathing aluminum 427-ci engine and either a 4-speed trans or Turbo-Hydramatic gives you doubts about your ability to maintain control."

The test crew had ample time to compare the ZL1 to a L72 427 Camaro, and it found with the latter, it "took only minutes behind the wheel of a 427 Camaro to realize that nailing the throttle was somewhat like unleashing a wild animal, and you'd better be quick to take command. It didn't take long, though, before that ominous power began to feel really good and easy to get along with. Using this Camaro as daily transportation for several days despite the lack of a radio, brought to mind the question; how could the 427-ci ZL1 engine be much greater?" They set to find out and headed to Dick Harrell's Kansas City performance center. Harrell joined them at the Kansas City International Raceway for some test runs. *PHR* found "the results were pretty amazing."

At first, they ran a ZL1 tester equipped with 8x14 M&H Racemaster tires and a Holley 850-cfm carb with manually operated secondaries and closed headers. The best they could squeeze out was quarter-mile time of 12.14 seconds at 117.80 mph. The S&S headers were opened, a set of N3 Champion spark plugs were installed, and the car was run again, this time producing a 12.11 ET time and a 119.34 mph speed. More tweaks came by way of switching to vacuum-operated secondaries on the same model carb, resetting valves, boosting the timing to 42 degrees, and adding richer secondary carb jets. The result was a 11.78 ET at 122.50 mph.

Still not satisfied, a tall Weiand manifold and a pair of Holley 660-cfm carbs were installed, turning in a best run of 10.28 seconds at 133.05 mph. Finally, the tire pressures were dropped to 6 pounds and a little powdered rosin [a traction compound] was sprinkled on the track. The ZL1 was unleashed once again for the best run of the day: a 10.21 ET at 133.80 mph.

The magazine test crew summed up its impressions like this: "What you have with the ZL1 is something wild for the street, great for stock racing, and adaptable, with available bolt-ons, to highly competition super stock racing. Besides a thrilling performance improvement in the ZL1 over a stock 427 Camaro, the ride is noticeably different. The 160-pound front end weight saving makes handling somewhat easier, and despite a firm suspension, the ride is easy. The comparison of rides would be very similar to driving the same Camaro with a 427, then with a 327 until you step on it and lose rear vision to tire smoke."

August 1969 Media Drive

While most outlets that tested the ZL1s were all about cranking out maximum performance by any means possible, *Cars* magazine had a dif-

ferent approach. The editors "thought it might be interesting to see what the thing would do just the way it comes off the factory assembly line, with street tires, street exhaust, and no more tuning than a check of spark. After all, a few well-heeled guys are bound to buy these cars for the street."

For the test, they headed to the US-131 drag strip in Martin, Michigan. Berger Chevrolet in Grand Rapids, Michigan, had agreed to let them use their yellow number 3 ZL1 just prior to shipping it to a customer in Virginia. The $7,800 test car had the Z28 heavy-duty suspension front disc brakes and 6-inch wheel rims with E70-15 Goodyear Wide Tread GT tires (not belted Polygas tires, which would have offered better traction). It also had 4.10:1 rear end gears with Positraction and the Muncie M22 shifter. The car came equipped with the showroom exhaust system, which was the standard Z28 setup. It had small resonators ahead of the rear axle and one large cross muffler behind the axle with dual inlets and dual outlets. There was concern about it hampering the ZL1's power.

The feature stated: "I'm not condemning Chevrolet for putting this exhaust system on the car. They intend the car strictly for racing. They know the buyer will immediately whip off the complete factory exhaust system and stick on a set of tuned tubing headers. Why worry about spending thousands to develop an efficient factory system? This is a new side of Detroit performance engineering. Up to a point the factory boys are concerned with the ultimate in street performance, and they give you their best. But when the model gets so hairy that it's strictly for the racetrack, you'd be surprised how many little details the factory leaves up to you and the California hot rod industry!" That's exactly what happened as the Berger mechanics replaced the dual pipe/muffler system with street-legal dual chambered pipes, which were an option on Chevelles, Camaros, and Corvettes.

For the theme of the test, it was considered "fair" since the setup was a factory-installed option on the Camaro. When it was unleashed on the

Berger Chevrolet loaned its yellow ZL1 for the Hi-Performance Cars *magazine test, heading about 30 miles south from Grand Rapids to the US-131 drag strip in Martin, Michigan. There, the writers got some time behind the wheel of the impressive machine.*

The magazine crew knew that one of the first things buyers would do to their new ZL1s was to remove the stock exhaust system. Chevrolet engineers knew that too and didn't waste time devising a new system. The standard Z28 setup was used.

track, the best run was a 13.16 ET at 110.21 mph. In total, they ran six passes, all between 13.20 and 13.40 seconds and 108 to 110 mph. The best technique came from burning lightly out of the hole, feathering the throttle for the first 30 to 40 feet, then on it hard and shifting at 6,500 to 6,800 rpm. There were some limitations with the Z28 hood, and its cowl flap that opened by an electric solenoid when the throttle was closed and manifold vacuum goes up. The feathering technique at the line fluttered the valve open and closed, not allowing the engine to fully breathe. In normal street driving, the 850-cfm Holley carb return a paltry 5 to 7 mpg, but "when you jump on that loud pedal, all is forgiven!"

COPO 9567: Going for Gold

Before the first 50 ZL1s had even been delivered, Vince Piggins was planning another phase for the program. Just like he had referenced in his December 27 letter, he had devised a ZL1 engine combination "suitable for street use as well as a potent performance machine," and he had the engineering team get serious about making that vision a reality. What the crew came up with was an over-the-top, flashy head turner, with the goal of having it be way more docile for regular use. Piggins wanted to modify the ZL1 to "come up with a new engine" that could run in NHRA Super Stock D (a class where they didn't have an eligible vehicle). Modifications like using an L72 camshaft, manifold, and carburetor helped tone down the engine's snarly nature.

On March 24, the request to build a pilot car was processed, and it was scheduled to be completed by April 4 for management to review. The vehicle started out as a big-block L78 (396-ci 375 hp) SS Camaro. From there, a detuned aluminum 427 was installed with compression dialed back to a more road-friendly 11:1 instead of 12:1. The car received the Z22 Rally Sport package, M21 4-speed manual transmission, J52 power disc brakes, N40 power steering, D55 center console, U16 tachometer, F41 special performance suspension, ZN2 COPO 9567 springs, and G80 Positraction. It was painted black with a black interior. The rally sport emblems were removed from the front fenders, and the holes left behind were filled in. The bright wheel lip moldings and drip gutter moldings were removed along with the simulated louvers and any other RS badging.

Now with a clean slate, loads of dress-up items were installed. The car got the hidden headlight option and the doors were painted black. A front lower spoiler was installed, painted black, and given metallic gold striping. Gold metallic Z28 stripes were painted on the ZL2 cowl hood, along with gold stripes on the sides that wrapped around the wheel openings. Tires, with the raised white lettering painted gold, were mounted over Z28 15x7 wheels with the dish painted black and a bright trim ring partially painted gold metallic. The side marker light bezels were painted out. ZL1 decals were applied to the rear panel and hood blister along with a ZL1 badge in the grille on the driver's side in place of the RS. Rubber wheel lip stone guards were installed on the front and rear. Inside, the biggest change was a Corvette steering wheel.

The plan was to build 100 vehicles and get them distributed, with 55 getting the M40 transmission and the other 45 receiving the M22 transmission. Chevy management had a target date to get all 100 built in April.

While the ZL1 was superb for the track, it lacked a certain civilization for regular street use. The final product of COPO 9567 was going to change that. Here the test mule sits in a Chevrolet design studio getting final touches.(Photo Courtesy the General Motors Heritage Center)

Going 140 on 696

Central Office employee Jim Mattison fondly remembers one summer night with a special Camaro that almost cost him his job. One week in August, he happened to be driving a hand-built preproduction prototype Camaro with the mighty ZL1 engine. He got a call from the engineering center one morning. "He was trying to track down a particular car and asked if I had it," recalls Mattison. "I reached in my pocket and pulled out the key fob and, sure enough, I had the car. He said he had done some work to it and wanted to talk to me a little more about it." Later that day, Mattison drove down to the engineering building and met up with the caller. "He told me how engineers from Chevy, Ford, and Chrysler, and even some local dealers would get together on a weekly basis and bring out their hottest stuff for a little competition. Seeing as though they couldn't officially do it on GM property or over at Ford or at Chrysler, they were running down a stretch of Interstate 696 that had just been completed. It was arrow straight but not yet fully opened."

After work that night, Mattison, driving his prototype ZL1-powered Camaro, met the engineer and followed his Caprice wagon, which had been stacked with drag slicks. "My group in the Central Office would do zone police cars, which would be vehicles done up as law enforcement. We'd give them out as demonstrators to get business from police departments. They looked like real police cars, complete with a light bar and badges on the doors, that looked official but really said nothing. Some of the staff had brought those out and were using them to keep traffic away from the area.

"We showed up and it was all well-orchestrated. The whole activity was every bit of exciting as going to the Winter Nationals for NHRA. There were cars and engineering trucks from Chrysler, Ford, and GM, and race teams like the Royal Pontiacs and Ramchargers. Apparently, everyone would show up for these events. I remember a couple cars pulling up to the line and running before lights and flashers came out of everywhere. The Southfield and Farmington Hills police departments stormed in, thinking they had come across a bunch of kids street racing. That changed once they started collecting registration slips and seeing the vehicles belonged to Chevrolet Motor Division and the like. All the vehicles were impounded that night, including my one-off Camaro."

A few days later, Mattison came into work and saw a note on his desk to go see his boss, Joe Pike, immediately. "I went into his office and his first question was if I had my company car, and if not, if I could care to tell him where it was," said Mattison. "I told him either at the Southfield or Farmington Hills impound lot. Joe had a copy of the *Detroit Free Press* on his desk and spun it around so I could read the headlines. It said '140 Miles an Hour on I-696, Auto Engineers at Drag Race.'" Joe sent Jim on up to the 14th floor, which is where the top brass offices were. "I wasn't alone and fortunately in good company; there was a bunch of us. GM wanted to fire the whole bunch of us for embarrassing the company and giving it a black eye as we were still operating under a no-racing ban. I'm sure similar stories were transpiring at Ford and Chrysler. Luckily for us, Lucy Seaton went to bat for us. His son was Pete Seaton and a successful racer running Chevys. Lucy was in charge of Corporate PR and, with his help, we were all put on 'special assignments,' which was basically a slap on the wrist for six months. Miraculously, he got all those impounded cars back too."

The *Detroit Free Press* piece reported that on these late-night drag sessions, more than 60 cars would show up and close down 3-mile-long stretches of the expressway for 140-mph drag races. The action would start around 11 p.m. and go until after 2 a.m. The most popular stretch was on an unlit westbound stretch between Northwestern Highway and Orchard Lake Road. While most of the participants were teenagers, sources within the auto industry said it was common knowledge that the races were frequented by car enthusiasts who are also engineers at Ford, Chrysler, General Motors, and American Motors. As it turns out, the racers even used the Southfield City Hall and police station as a staging area. One police officer was quoted as saying he thought the cars gathered weekly for "some sort of reliance or reliability run." State police who would have been responsible for patrolling the 25-mile stretch of I-96 and I-696 were unaware of the racing and said they only have one car assigned to cover that area.

The newspaper reporter wrote that one of the cars seen both in the staging lot and on the expressway was registered to one of Detroit's leading high-performance Chevrolet dealership. He went on to say that cars were "generally late factory performance models, and most had large racing tires and jacked-up rear ends. The gathering also included several sports cars, station wagons, and a few vintage hot rods." After 11 p.m., the cars "roar out of the parking lot" in a long convoy that passed right by the Southfield police station and then onto westbound I-696. From there, they'd pull over to the shoulder and median of the expressway, strung out for about a mile on both sides of the two westbound lanes. When regular traffic slowed, the cars would pull out, blocking traffic for as long as five minutes, to let the two lead cars compete from a standing start. "As soon as they took off, the lines of cars behind them also shot forward in a confusing mass that saw cars skidding, swerving, and bouncing down the shoulder and median of the expressway to avoid hitting each other."

The whole pack would follow the racers, take an exit ramp to get off, and then head back to the staging lot to do the whole thing all over again. The newspaper article concluded with "the meetings were initiated by some of the original proponents of performance cars. Many of those persons are now auto performance engineers and executives with the Detroit's automakers, according to several industry sources."

The design concept called for the Camaro to be painted in a stealthy black and metallic gold scheme. Even the raised white lettering on the tires and the wheels' trim rings were painted gold to match. (Photo Courtesy the General Motors Heritage Center)

The 69 ZL1s were devoid of any sort of call-outs or badging and intended to fly under the radar. The 9567 went in a totally different direction and showcased major ZL1 branding. Up front in the grille on the driver's side, a new ZL1 badge was mounted. (Photo Courtesy the General Motors Heritage Center)

Somewhere along the line that spring, Berger Chevrolet (the recipient of the yellow number 3 ZL1) caught wind of the program. It reached out to the corporate offices at Chevrolet, saying it wanted in and went so far as to place two orders for COPO 9567 Camaros (possibly separate orders for manual- and automatic-equipped vehicles). Joe Pike talked with the dealership, saying the order couldn't be honored as the 9567 hadn't even been released. Another sticking point was with how the cars were optioned. Pike wanted the cars to be ordered all the same, like the initial batch of 50 ZL1s. While this new 9567 would surely stack on tons of options, he didn't want deviations from the approved list. In its request, Berger had made all kinds of swaps and departures. On April 15, 1969, a baffled Joe Pike wrote an interoffice letter to a colleague addressing the situation. Clearly Berger had an inside track on the pulse of what Chevy was up to, as a bewildered Pike closed with: "It is amazing how this dealer gets his information."

COPO 9567 Pricing

While the 69 ZL1s were retailing for around a staggering $7,000, these COPO 9567 Camaros were slated to be even higher. Pricing sheets reveal a manual transmission–equipped vehicle was going to cost $8,581.60, while an automatic would set buyers back $8,676.60. The cosmetic prototype went over well, but with the new and astronomically higher pricing for these special projects, the plug was pulled. The air still hadn't been cleared on the forced buyback and top executives weren't happy. Berger Chevrolet's

request for its two orders came in before that hefty pricing was fully known.

Finally, Don McPherson wrote an internal letter on June 16, 1969, stopping all ZL1 activities. Citing the Deproliferation Committee and in particular Joe Pike, who had been very busy trying to move the returned inventory, the "ZL1 is an unsaleable option because of its current cost to the customer." McPherson went on, "Would you please let me know how this option should be released and where it should be released, if anywhere, to make it legal for racing? If there are any areas, either COPO or RPO, that are not required and are not being sold to the customer because of cost, I would like to cancel."

That didn't squelch ZL1 news entirely. A month later, Vince Piggins sent an interoffice letter informing his colleague that as of July 3, 1969, 69 Camaro ZL1 COPO 9560 had been built and distributed to dealers and that they were legal to run in the NHRA. Another interesting note included in the memo was that Joe Pike was still receiving additional inquiries from other dealers interested in obtaining their own ZL1 Camaro COPO.

The black and gold prototype has never been located and best guesses are that it crushed. "The 9567 Camaro was to be something special, but when the exorbitant costs hit the books, the program was killed," recalls Jim Mattison. "I liked the concept of what they were going to do but then I had to look at the business case of it. It was to be a serious traffic builder for dealers and serious contender for D Stock in the NHRA. Vince was always looking for the competitive edge. As much of an enthusiast as I was, I had to side with the bean counters. Both cars were crushed. It was a very unique

Original Owner Spotlight: Ken Barnhart, ZL1 Number 16

Ken Barnhart started drag racing in 1955 and wheeled everything from a 1951 Mercury to a 1939 Cadillac coupe to a 1955 Chevy station wagon down quarter-mile strips. That 1955 packed an engine that Ken built himself, and in 1961, he won the nationals, outrunning a factory-backed 1961 Pontiac.

In 1968, Barnhart was browsing through a magazine story that detailed how Bill Jenkins was getting a ZL1 Camaro that he was going to race. "It was my thought that Jenkins was king of the strip but I was out to dethrone him," said Barnhart. He went to every dealer in the northwest suburbs of Chicago but "no one knew anything about those cars." Undeterred, Barnhart picked up the phone and dialed Vince Piggins. "He gave me a whole bunch of information, of which I had no clue what he was talking about," said Barnhart. "I wrote down the COPO number but still

no Chevy dealers had any idea about getting one."

Puzzled, but not one to sit idle, Barnhart went to Biggers Chevrolet in Elgin, Illinois, and ordered a 396 375-hp orange with black vinyl top 1969 Camaro. "Right after I ordered it, what do I see but an ad in *Drag News* for Fred Gibb saying he had 50 ZL1s for sale," said Barnhart. "I got on the phone and talked to Fred in person for nearly two hours. It wasn't a discussion; he interrogated me to make sure I was a bona fide racer. He was adamant these cars went to racers and would go down the track. Finally, we agreed on a car and I went down on April 8, 1969, with a check in hand. The lot behind the dealership was full of them but up front were three cars cleaned up. Two were in Hugger Orange and one with a 4-speed, which I told Fred I wanted."

The saying on the front lower spoiler came about at the 1970 NHRA Nationals in Indianapolis, Indiana. "I was taking my time in the burnout box and Buster Couch, the official starter, motioned for me to hurry up," recalls Ken Barnhart. "I yelled back, 'Just a second, I'm comin'!'" After Barnhart's run, he encountered a painter in the pits, who he asked to paint it on the car.

Shortly after Barnhart bought the car in the spring of 1969, he had a little custom shop in Elgin, Illinois, paint the black shadowing on the car and to his helmet. The lettering on the doors and fenders was applied by one of Barnhart's part-time employees, Jerry, who moonlighted as a sign painter.

After trailering it home, Barnhart unloaded the car, drove it around the block twice, and then pulled it into his service station and pulled and blueprinted the engine. "I set up the car right and was ready to go racing," said Barnhart. The problem was he wasn't. Appendicitis and a stint in the hospital put a wrench in his plans to head to the 1969 Indianapolis Labor Day weekend national championship and unleash it on the two cars Jenkins had competing. "My goal was to go there and beat him," said Ken. "I was under strict orders from my doctor to stay put. I asked what about if I drove down just to watch. They said no. I said, 'What if I fly?' Again, they said no. I went anyway and watched the races."

After healing, Barnhart charged back for the 1970 season, competing his ZL1 in Super Stock B and winning the class. "That year, all the cars were ZL1s in SS/B," said Barnhart. In 1971, he was the runner-up, losing to a 1965 Dodge Hemi driven by Greg Charney. "I broke a rocker stud, but I ran the whole stretch on seven cylinders. The whole time we were neck and neck. We didn't know who won until we picked up the time slips. When the car ran good, I was never beat. In 1971, when the class was loaded with Hemi cars, I was the only Camaro in the field. After each run, when I was coming down the return stretch, it was like a wave as the crowd stood up and was whooping and hollering. They were so excited when the Camaro won another run. Even back then, people knew it was a rarity.

Born and raised on his family's farm, Barnhart couldn't leave the homestead fast enough, always wanting to have his own auto business. After working in several garages, he got a Standard Oil station, operating it from 1959 through 2010. It worked out well, fueling funds to acquire and race toys like his ZL1.

Barnhart competed all over, taking his ZL1 to events and meets in Pennsylvania; Columbus, Ohio; and Dallas, Texas. After swapping in a Turbo-Hydramatic transmission, Barnhart started bracket racing the Camaro. He hated every minute of it and went back to a manual 4-speed, rowing his own gears.

"Eventually into the mid-1970s, I got into bracket racing, but I hated every minute of it. I was used to running in stock classes where man and machine had to be the utmost unit. You had to have the fastest car and be the best driver. That combination was going to put you ahead of everyone else. I had a reputation as being a quick driver and shifting through the gears. Other races always came up and would ask what automatic transmission I was running. I was so quick."

In 1973, Barnhart had Dick Arons Race Engines, located just outside of Detroit, Michigan, build not one but two engines for his car. "Dick convinced me that everyone running iron blocks was running faster," said Barnhart. He also had an aluminum engine built, which is in the car now, wisely not wanting to bore out the original block. The valve covers were made in 1966 for a 1967 Chevelle that he raced.

It's just a happy coincidence that Barnhart ended up with ZL1 number 16 and his birthday is March 16. Not long after he got it, Barnhart opened up the rear quarter panels to accommodate bigger tires. Reconsidering, he bought replacement panels in the late 1980s, with plans to restore the car back to stock. After giving it more thought, he changed his mind, wanting the Camaro to retain its track-ready personality.

Personal Reflection: Jim Mattison, Central Office Employee, 1968–1972

Jim Mattison was working for the Central Office in the Fleet and Special Order department, which handled the COPO paperwork. As he explains it, he was a pencil pusher there from 1968 to 1972. "I lived in the greater Detroit area my whole life," recalls Mattison. "I was a motorhead through and through. The department's main thrust was not to build factory hot rods, but when something hot came in, since I was a young guy and into it, the other guys in the office would say 'Give it to Mattison, he likes this kind of stuff.' Soon all these COPOs were coming across my desk to process. Since I was in my early 20s, I was in hog heaven. I had Corvettes, Z28s, and all the COPO cars that I could take home at will. It was paradise. We never had budgets. If we left a meeting talking about something new and all the heads were nodding in agreement, we went for it. No one asked how much it would cost; we just did things."

time back then. I feel very fortunate to have been a part of the golden era of General Motors."

ZL1 Zenith

Without a doubt, the 1969 Camaro ZL1 stands head and shoulders above the rest of its COPO-created counterparts. The 69 special vehicles created represent the zenith of how a Central Office Production Order could be used to surreptitiously build something that, by all accounts, should have never passed anything more than a water cooler conversation in the halls of General Motors, let alone get a full greenlight for production.

The rule-breaking car was brash, obnoxious, and purpose-built, designed and destined to be an all-out drag strip demon. From its dog dish hubcaps and lack of badging to its race-bred aluminum motor, it should have, as Shay Nichols told us, fallen off the delivery trucks and gone right to work destroying any and all drag strip records. As she, Ken Barnhart,

and many other racers discovered, it wasn't as simple as pointing and shooting when the lights turned green, roaring to glorious victory. As with any potent performer, there was a learning curve to be mastered; once it was, the ZL1s simply screamed, winning many NHRA and AHRA national events.

Even more extreme than the car's performance is the fact that these cars ended up in the hands of drivers who used them regularly on public streets. These covert COPOs left Chevrolet dealerships bearing a full 5-year/50,000-mile factory warranty and were used for everything from cruising to commuting.

Not only was it a car that came in first, it was a car of firsts. It was the first time Chevrolet used (in a production car) an aluminum engine block, a double pumper carburetor, and open chamber cylinder heads. It was also the first and only time an option package cost more than the base price of the car. Everything about the mighty 1969 ZL1, from its creation to its dominance on the track, has become the stuff of legend, living on in the hearts of enthusiasts the world over.

There's no smoke and mirrors to this trick; big burnouts come easily to the ZL1's ground-shaking 427-ci V-8 and only require a heavy right foot. It's feats like this, and the clandestine development story, that make these cars so desirable and dreamworthy.

CHAPTER 6

THE CAMARO (1969)

COPO Super Car Production Ramps Up

1969 Camaro

Total Production: 1,300
estimated (198 Yenko)
Total Left: 800 estimated
(~100 Yenko)

Don Yenko had big dreams for his Camaro program, and he was always thinking bigger. Not in engine size, as the final product was spot on; 427 power in the lightweight Camaro body was a wonderful combination, and enthusiasts everywhere loved it. What Don had in mind was with scalability.

Don was really hoping his 427 Camaro program would take off in 1969. It was quite a stunt he managed to pull off, getting Chevrolet to mount in the bigger engines right on the factory floor. It was all looking good until other dealers found the secret out and started ordering their own.

Not all of his competitors saw the same need. For example, Nickey Chevrolet, the largest Chevrolet dealership in the United States, was located near downtown Chicago and saw tremendous value in upselling its aftermarket performance business. The concept of the Camaro engine swaps fit quite nicely into its upselling business model. Because of that, never once did the dealership order a COPO performance vehicle, as the top staff never saw the need, though they certainly had the clout to get it done.

To Nickey management, the hassle of contacting GM's brass, filing the required paperwork, making numerous phone calls back and forth hammering out details, then waiting for approval, not to mention the build time, just wasn't worth it. They much preferred a different scenario: a customer wants to go fast and walks into the Nickey showroom with a pocket full of cash. They want a hot 427-powered Camaro. Nickey was set up as a one-stop shop with all the resources and staff to get the job done in a matter of hours. In no time, the hood, battery, radiator, and old engine are yanked and the new powerplant was put in, no doubt with a bunch of other upsold parts added on. Everything is reassembled and the transaction is done. The happy customer is peeling out of the lot and many more are pulling in, wanting similar results.

It was a similar case in New York. The crew at Baldwin Auto and Motion Performance didn't even learn about the COPO program until years after it had ended. As such, they stayed the course, modifying their 427-cars on a case-by-case basis and getting them distributed.

Don's case down in Canonsburg was different. To be clear, his technicians had the exact same know-how on removing smaller V-8s and bolting in mighty 427s. The process, no matter who was doing it, went like clockwork and even used the same engine mounts. In 1967, the very earliest conversions were swapping out 350s for complete 427s. With the debut of the 396 big-block, the process became simpler, as it only the bottom end (block) was

Even though the COPO was going to equip the Camaros with a special powertrain, many owners couldn't resist further tweaking to get even more out of it. Lots of cars, like this one here, had such things as exhaust headers and traction bars installed shortly after leaving the dealership. Larry Christensen owns this one.

exchanged, reusing the intake, heads, and accessories. In 1968, the process was the same, but it intensified. Beside the powertrain, now cosmetic changes were introduced, resulting in leftover parts such as stock hoods and wheels. While Don and his team worked hard to resell all these discarded items through the local Pittsburgh-area newspaper, it quickly became a nuisance.

That caused Don to opt for a different path from his competitors, choosing a business model that leveraged something he had that no one else did: a robust dealer network. He had been working on and perfecting it since his race-ready Stingers in 1966, so he had close working relationships with a collection of dealers around the country. They were willing and ready to stock some hot Yenko-crafted machines. Equally important was their ability to advertise in their respective markets, further getting the word out about Don's Camaros. When listing their inventory of Yenko Camaros for sale, it sure didn't hurt the Yenko brand by describing them with such lofty phrases as the "427 Boss of the Road," a "custom modified super sportscar," and "the great Yenko High Performance Cars."

Additional ads even mentioned Don by name, describing him as the designer of some of the cars' features. With the growing popularity of the cars, the dealers in turn capitalized on the draw, declaring they were the exclusive Yenko dealer in their area. All this fed itself, perpetuating Don's ultimate goal: get finished, modified Camaros not just out to his lot but to all those other nationwide dealer lots as well. The growing demand was way more than what his team could handle. The solution Don found to match his lofty goals was to delegate the heavy lifting (in this case, quite literally) back to Chevrolet. He realized if he could get the factory to install not only the upgraded suspension and accessory components found in COPO 9737 but also mount in a 427 right on the assembly line floor (presumably through a yet to be identified COPO build request), he could get a whole lot more Yenko Camaros out into buyers' eager hands.

In early 1968, Don was on the phone with Vince Piggins, asking what could be done. As the appeal wore on, Don kept pushing for his pay dirt of an idea, and finally in November, Piggins approved the request. Don wasted no time, quickly placing an order for 50 Camaro coupes. He ordered 100 more coupes later that month, with additional orders placed throughout the following months. Finally completed, 427-equipped Camaros began arriving to the Canonsburg lot in early winter of 1969, all ready for final Yenko cosmetic tweaks. From there, it wouldn't take long to get them shipped and distributed around the country. It was a game changer with loads of promise.

COPO 9561 and 9737

Under a newly created COPO 9561, all cars had their RPO L78 375-hp 396-ci V-8 engine deleted and an RPO L72 added. This equipped them with a 427-ci V-8 engine with 11:1 compression. The motor had been available on full-size Chevrolets, such as the Caprice, Impala, Bel Air, and Corvette

Finally, enthusiasts got what they had been expecting and wanting for years: a factory-installed 427-ci V-8 in the Camaro. Don did all he could to keep the COPO deal a secret, knowing that if he did, he could massively scale his 427-power inventory.

Anthony and Bertha Mandella of North Versailles, Pennsylvania, purchased this Daytona Yellow Camaro at Yenko Chevrolet on July 11, 1969, for $4,637.60. Note the special hood and front spoiler; two unique accessories that made the cars stand out.

since 1966. It wasn't slated to be installed in Camaro since Chevy was still standing by its internal edict of no engines bigger than 400 ci in the intermediate (Chevelle) and pony cars (Camaro). The COPO gave Don a loophole, permitting Chevy to build something that officially was never meant to be.

The powerplant incorporated cast-iron cylinder heads and engine block, which had four bolt mains for increased strength. It also had forged aluminum pistons, mechanical camshafts, and a forged-steel crankshaft. Other add-ons included a Holley 780 vacuum secondary carburetor, an aluminum intake featuring split plenums, chrome valve covers, and a single-point aluminum distributor showing a stamped part number of 1111499 on the housing. As set up, the L72 was rated at 425 hp at 5,000 rpm. Engines paired to the 4-speed transmission were stamped MN while the automatic L72s were stamped MO. All of these engines were built at the Tonawanda plant in New York; had orange painted blocks, oil pans, and cylinder heads; and weighed around 660 pounds. The valve covers, water pump, air cleaner, balancer, exhaust manifolds, dual exhausts, fan, and timing chain and cover were shared with the Camaro ZL1's 427-ci aluminum V-8 engine.

Keeping the L72 cool was a newly added Harrison heavy-duty four-core radiator (RPO V48). A ZL2 special ducted hood (the same as what was installed on the ZL1 Camaro) was created and listed on the car's windows stickers as an "air breathing hood with built in sealed plenum chamber and throttle operated solenoid valve." It allowed for cowl induction, based on throttle position, offering an opening at the base of the windshield that channeled air back into the air cleaner, where a circular rubber boot mated

The Mandellas encountered a problem with their M21 transmission, taking it back to Yenko Chevrolet on March 4, 1970, for the area service manager to inspect. He found the issue couldn't be warrantied. The couple then reached out to Joel Rosen at Motion Performance, who suggested an M22 4-speed be installed, which is what happened.

Down the street and around the corner from Yenko Chevrolet, on Strabane Avenue, was this muddy dirt and gravel overflow lot. Don rented it to hold extra inventory. Scattered throughout the rows are COPO Camaros and Chevelles, waiting to be transformed into Yenko Super-cars. (Photo Courtesy the Barr Collection)

Parked side by side, COPO Camaros sit out in the open. The wire fence encircling the property did little to protect the valuable inventory. Numerous former employees remember frequent incidents with hoodlums hopping over and making off with stolen parts. (Photo Courtesy the Barr Collection)

With the conversion complete, Yenko super cars are loaded up onto a Yenko transport truck and shipped out. The Rally Wheel center caps would be snapped on once the vehicles were unloaded at their destination. (Photo Courtesy the Barr Collection)

with the hood to prevent any fresh air from leaking out. The hood and setup were so popular that beginning in January 1969 it became an available RPO on Super Sport and Z28 Camaros as well as the Indianapolis 500 pace cars and subsequent festival replicas. To help Don's vehicles get their power to the ground, a high-performance front and rear suspension pieces (springs and shock absorbers, RPO F41) was installed.

That wasn't the only COPO these cars got. As part of 9737, the Sports Car Conversion, 15x7 Rally Wheels wrapped with E70x15 wide tread tires were installed along with a 140-mph speedometer (the standard unit topped out at 120 mph) and a 13/16-inch front sway bar.

The cars also received a 12-bolt differential housing with 4.10 Postraction and a heat-treated ring and pinion, special shocks, and the five leaf springs as found on the SS big-block Camaros. The rear end was stamped with BE for these COPO cars. Because of 9561 and 9737 tacked on together, these Camaros are often referred to as Double COPOs.

Power front brakes (RPO J50) with discs up front (RPO J52) were mandatory options per Chevrolet engineers who were felt they were needed to help drivers control and manage the abundance of newfound power. Two transmissions were made available: a M21 4-speed manual or a M40 Turbo 400 automatic. The manuals were stamped with a B in the sixth digit (example P9xxxB) and automatics would have an X in the third position (69Xxxx). Autos also had a CX code on a tag on the passenger's side of the unit. In total, 171 Camaros were equipped with the manual while 30 were automatics.

When it came to exterior paint, six colors were available: Daytona Yellow (code 76, 34 examples produced), Rally Green (code 79, 21 examples produced), Olympic Gold (code 65, 10 examples produced), Fathom Green code 57, 34 examples produced, none of which received vinyl tops), Lemans Blue (code 71, 51 examples produced), and Hugger Orange (code 72, 51 examples produced). All of the cars had the optional front and rear spoilers (RPO D80) installed. The front spoiler came in black and was mounted under the front clip. The rear spoiler was body color and was mounted on the rear edge of the trunklid. The Yenko side body striping wrapped up onto its corners for an integrated look. Interior trim only came in Code 711 black standard.

Don had his pick from a variety of options to further enhance his new crop of rides. To dress up the outside, some were equipped with black vinyl roofs (RPO C08) and an Endura body color bumper (RPO VE3) while options inside included power steering (RPO N40) and the Special interior group (RPO Z23), which included woodgrain accents in the steering wheel, an assist grip, and bright pedal trim. Don equipped all his Camaros with an AM radio (RPO U63).

The first 50 cars had a body code of X66, indicating the cars were built on a Super Sport 396 platform with chrome accents on the simulated rear quarter panel and a blacked-out tail panel surrounding the taillights. While the black body sill was a component of X66, it's hit and miss whether or not the Camaros received it. The other early cars had a body code of X11, indicating they got the Z21 Style Trim group with vertical chrome bars on the taillamps, chrome roof drip rails, chrome headlight rings, wheelwell moldings, a blacked-out rocker sill, and front fender and quarter panel pinstripes. Cars painted in Fathom Green did not receive black rocker panels.

Starting in April, the rest of the Camaros, the largest group, were built. They were base cars that didn't get the Style Trim so they were devoid of all chrome trim and the blacked-out tail panel. The grilles on all of the Camaros Don ordered were painted Argent Silver with a blue Chevy bowtie mounted in the center.

The Camaro's gauge cluster was redesigned for the 1969 model, and the pod grew from two to three gauges. The center section protruded so it was even easier for Don's techs to mount the aftermarket Stewart Warner tachs. After July, the COPO cars would get an optional tach in the right pod as part of RPO U16.

Canonsburg Changes

The cars showed up to Don's lot in mid-January with the 427-ci engine already installed. The process of getting them finalized as Yenko Supercars and out on dealer lots was heavily streamlined. All cars produced through May had Stewart Warner 970 Custom Series tachs screwed right into the center section of the gauge cluster on the driver's left side and blocking the speedometer. They required a special sending unit, which was mounted on the firewall next to the power brake booster. Starting in June, cars wouldn't need this add-on, as they came from the factory equipped with the optional RPO U16 in-dash 6,000-rpm redline tach in the right pod of the gauge cluster. As part of U16, the fuel gauge was moved to the center pod.

To de-emphasize the Chevrolet connection, most of the Chevy bowtie emblems mounted in the middle of the grille were removed. The rear bowtie was also plucked off, leaving two staggered mounting holes in the rear panel. Left with no option to cover them, Yenko's team drilled two additional holes on either side of them and added two more badges. On the driver's side, a Yenko red, white, and blue crest was added while the passenger's side got another 427 badge. Visually, the final product leaves

This Olympic Gold Camaro parked in front of the downtown Chicago skyline is the vehicle **Super Stock** *magazine tested at York Dragway for its July 1969 feature. Note the one-off 427 badge placement ahead of the front wheels instead of on the hood's cowl. (Photo Courtesy the Barr Collection)*

It's got a neat but somewhat off-kilter look to it. The rear panel placement of the two badges was purely function following form. It was faster for techs to remove the factory-installed bowtie and drill an additional hole on either side of its mounting holes than to get them aligned as on the 1968 Camaros.

The red, white, and blue Yenko crest, which debuted in 1968, was used again and mounted to the front fenders underneath the Camaro script badge.

The standard installation of the hood stripes had some variations. Sometimes techs installed them farther up the hood cowl, closer to the windshield, trimming the excess. The sYc arrowhead would then be mounted farther up too, draping over the cowl. Holz Chevrolet in Madison, Wisconsin, installed the hood pins on this car because parts were being stolen while it sat on the lot.

The side stripes were shared across all of Don's 1969 supercars and, as such, he wanted to make them universal. The rear fender section came in two sections, allowing overlap. This allowed the stripe to be lengthened or shortened as well as made the stickers easier to ship. As evidenced by the black vinyl top, this Camaro received RPO C08.

The three individual headrest stickers came printed on one 3M sheet. Technicians would do the best they could to center them, sticking all three on at once and then removing the surrounding backing. The final product was stark and easily recognizable.

Don was quite the creative doodler, and he was always sketching new designs for his cars. Here's a concept he had for the 1969 stripe kit. Underneath the car's shadows reads DY '68. (Photo Courtesy Brian Henderson)

After decades, the stickers in this unrestored Yenko Camaro are beginning to finally come loose. Applying them was as simple task but one that made the cabins of Yenko's Supercars stand out.

two unevenly placed badges that are not aesthetically pleasing, especially when compared to the 1968 Yenko. The earlier Camaro merely had a circular gas cap in the center with no holes drilled in to the rear panel. Given a blank slate, Yenko placed his two badges (Yenko crest and 427 medallion) on the same level, drilling holes on the same plane. For 1969, it wasn't his choice but a matter of convenience and quick thinking. In a one-off case, the *Super Stock and Drag Illustrated* test Olympic Gold test car retained the bowtie but had Corvette 427 single digit emblems tacked on. Yenko crests were also installed on each front fender, directly below the factory Camaro script.

Technicians added distinct 427 badges that Don commissioned himself to the sides of the raised cowl on the hood as well a single 427 badge applied to the rear panel. Side stripes and a center hood stripe graphic were available in both white and black and added. While the front fender and door section were one section, the stripe covering the rear quarter panel

Other than the sending unit for the tach, which was mounted on the firewall, next to the power brake booster, Don's techs didn't do any mechanical work under the hood. Given the meager shop area with a single chain hoist, they couldn't be more thrilled. Their only touch was the red and white sticker on the radiator shroud.

was two. The stripes were the same as what was used on 1969 Yenko Chevelles and 1969 Yenko Novas. They were also advertised in Yenko's catalogs, urging buyers to give their cars "the Yenko Style." The two-piece design allowed the sections to be lengthened or shortened to accommodate varying lengths of vehicles. On the Camaros, the slit where the two were joined is noticeable just ahead of the lettering, toward the front of the vehicle. In rare instances, a few examples were ordered without the striping.

Mark Gillespie worked at Yenko and recalls the cars had the stripes put on as the final touch in a separate building, across the creek from the dealership. He also recalls a humorous recollection when Donna Mae put an ad in the local paper seeking "stripers" to help with the massive influx of work. Soon the phone was ringing with young ladies calling in asking about work, misreading the posting as an ad for "strippers."

Don was quite the imaginative doodler and always coming up with design sketches. In one of his early renderings, he had considered a red and blue motif for this striping and also considered moving the Yenko lettering to the front fender. In the end, he opted for the lettering to be inside the stripe on the rear quarter panel.

Interior

Inside the cabin, simple white sYc stickers were applied to both headrests. Underhood, a white and red "Yenko SC 427" sticker was stuck on the top of the plastic radiator shroud. Other options included additional Stewart Warner gauging, a Hurst dual-gate shifter for automatic transmission–equipped cars, and the special Atlas-created aluminum wheels with the Yenko crest on a white sticker covering the Atlas logo on the center cap.

Ed Hedrick

Ed Hedrick was a Yenko-sponsored driver who spent lots of time behind the wheel of 427 Camaro. The leadfoot grew up in New York and has been racing since he got out of high school. He worked his way up from a 1939 Ford two-door to a 1960 Pontiac to a 1962 fuelie Corvette. Early in 1966, he purchased a Shelby Cobra and competed the rest of the year and into 1967, winning the Northeast street eliminator and NHRA World Points championship.

"The way Shelby listed the car," said Hedrick, "it could run in three different classes. I set the record in C Sports and was competing in B when Jere Stahl cautioned me, saying if I won all three classes the NHRA would put me out of business and change the rules. It was kind of pitiful; during races I could let the light change and sit there, then run down whatever was in the next lane for the win." Hedrick had quite a bit of money sunk into the wonder car and, needing some extra cash, decided to sell it.

In 1968, he started driving for Bill "Grumpy" Jenkins, who was competing a Camaro and Nova. For 1969, Jenkins decided to only run one vehicle, of which he would pilot. Stahl had close connections with Don and connected Ed, who purchased a yellow COPO Camaro from him. "I knew the car was built with a COPO, as that's the only way it would run Super Stock," said Hedrick. "The car I bought had been used to tow another COPO to Harrisburg in the rain," recalls Hedrick. "Somewhere along the way, the pair jackknifed and bent the rear fender. I picked it up at the dealership but didn't test drive it until I got home. I was under a time constraint to get it apart and ready for track use. I blueprinted the motor, added headers, Lakewood traction bars, and slicks. The class required the stock carb and I couldn't modify the wheelwells. It was without question the fastest Super Stock E in the country."

Ed Hedrick was quite talented behind the wheel of his Yenko Camaro, and in October 1969 won the Manufacturers Cup for Chevrolet, winning the Super Stock Eliminator top spot in the NHRA's Division I. "Stahl had just built prototype headers for the 427 and they put a set on my car," recalls Hedrick. "I'd pull up to the line, hit the gas, and boom, it was gone." (Photo Courtesy the Barr Collection)

Dealer Distribution

Once completed, the cars were quickly distributed to the Yenko dealer network. In no time, they were gobbled up by racers who put them to use. The *Daily Notes*, based in Canonsburg, Pennsylvania, bragged about its hometown hero, writing a feature in May 1969 stating that Don's special cars "have come through with astounding wins." They reported that on April 19, a 427 Yenko Camaro competed at York Dragway and the vehicle "ran so fast that the drag officials had to stop the clocks for a check." The car was a demonstrator borrowed straight from Don's lot, showing 8,000 miles on the odometer. It wore 8-inch slicks and a hastily installed set of headers. At the track, it turned in a time of 11.94 seconds at 114.5 miles per hour. Ed Hedrick was behind the wheel and commented, "I'm sure we could have gone a lot of faster but the clutch was so rough I couldn't make any power shifts." Later in May, Hedrick set Super Stock E record in a Daytona Yellow Yenko-sponsored Camaro, running at York Dragstrip and blasting to 125.7 mph. Don's vision had come to fruition and the gamble was paying off.

When young pilots climbed out of their jets, they were quick to want to jump into a brand-new Yenko Supercar. High-powered cars such as this were all the rage for military servicemembers.

A full load of Yenko Camaros and Chevelles are unloaded at Colonial Chevrolet, located on Virginia Beach Boulevard in Norfolk, Virginia. With the dealership's close proximity to the bustling Norfolk naval station and its constant influx of young sailors and gearheads, hot cars like this didn't sit for long. (Photo Courtesy the Barr Collection)

Super Stock July 1969 Media Drive

Super Stock magazine got its hands on a gold and white Yenko Camaro, which was plucked from the Canonsburg lot and driven straight to the York US-30 Dragway for some proper thrashing. The magazine crew had just tested a ZL1 and felt "that anything else along this line would be less than anticlimactic" but found they couldn't have been more wrong, saying "everything about this package appealed to them." They liked the price and the performance, finding it in the "same league as the lightweight" ZL1. An added bonus was in the styling and appearance department, which, with the Yenko add-ons, they deemed to be boss. They titled their feature "Yenkoamaro Z/427/28/SS" and said "what all that means is that Yenko Sports Cars has taken the best of the Z28, added 427 power, their own trim, and created an 11-second street bomb that works!"

Super Stock's tester was an L72-equipped Camaro with the only extras being an out-of-the-box Doug Thorley headers. The crew at Yenko hadn't performed any fancy head work or upgrades to the carb. The car did have spring clips on the rear, since their runs would be made with both street tires and slicks. Professional Super Stock drag racer Ed Hedrick was on hand to wheel the muscle machine on the cold, rainy afternoon test session. With the headers closed, he eased into a run, feeling the car out, and returned a 14.05 at 102.50 mph time. The next run he was more serious. The tires were filled to 28 psi, earning a 12.59 at 108.17 times. Now ready to drop that further, the slicks were bolted on, the headers were uncorked, and a 6-inch extension was added to the exhaust. The spark plugs, carb, and jets were all the same from the factory. Hedrick slid behind the wheel and, after a couple burnouts, blasted the Camaro for a best run of 11.94 seconds

at 114.50. The *Super Stock* crew was impressed, with the added bonus being the car "will pull 10 mpg on a trip" and could come with the Turbo-Hydramatic transmission and air-conditioning. "It's not just a brute horsepower maker that won't do anything but go straight," they said in closing. "It's a crossbreed with thoroughbred characteristics."

As a young man, Kevin DeWitte frequented Berger Chevrolet, checking out its hot rides. In October 1969, he went in thinking he'd buy an L78 Nova. But after seeing this 427 Camaro, he had to have it. In recent years, Berger has continued its tradition of making and selling special Camaros. DeWitte bought this supercharged 2010 Camaro SS to pair with his original.

Berger Chevrolet: Dale Berger Jr. (1938–2018)

One dealership involved heavily with performance was Berger Chevrolet in Grand Rapids, Michigan. After Yenko Chevrolet, it ordered the second largest order of L72 Camaros, processing nearly 50 vehicles. The cars were dressed up even more than the ones ordered by Yenko, many coming with the Super Sport fender stripes and a few with the Rally Sport option (RPO Z22). Dale Berger Jr. was general manager of the dealership and ordered each and every one himself.

"Our high-performance parts department was so large and busy," recalls Berger. "We had customers all over. We even had one customer in South Africa who we'd regularly ship large containers of speed parts. A young salesman, Mike Wawee, was really into the fast cars and selling them like crazy. He was real promoter." He said, "It was nothing for us to stock 10 or 12 Z28s or tons of Chevelle SSs."

"Our insider at the Central Office tipped us off about the COPO Camaros for 1969. We placed an order for the first run of about 20 cars in early winter of 1968. We delivered 9 the first day they came in since Mike had already presold them. The rest went quick and I said, 'Shoot, we better get more.' Plus, they weren't much money. About two weeks later, we ordered another 20. If you were a dealer and had the COPO number, which we did, Chevy couldn't tell you no; they were fair to all the dealerships. It also helped that we were so large and selling 15 to

Dale Berger Jr. came up with the dealership's performance logo and tagline, drawing inspiration from a druggist's mortar and pestle. Just as they'd be concocting remedies to help patients feel better, Berger sought to be known for prescribing ways to make drivers go faster. Continental Decal in Sparta, Michigan, started making them in 1968 and still makes them today.

20 Camaros a month. All our COPO Camaros had Rally Wheels and the Style Trim group, while some had vinyl roofs and the RS package. I also ordered 10 of the COPO Chevelles. Seven had 4-speeds and three had automatics. They went quick too. Chevrolet never did figure out how we got our cars and knew about the COPO numbers."

This Burnished Brown Camaro was heavily bracket raced when new. Grady Burch owns it today and restored it to how it was run back in the day, equipped with plenty of aftermarket mods.

Looking Ahead

On October 25, Yenko issued a press release stating a "significant milestone in the history of Yenko Sportscars, Inc." The momentous occasion was the announcement that Colonial Chevrolet, a key Yenko Sportscar network dealer located in Norfolk, Virginia, had taken delivery of Yenko unit number 350 for 1969. The release closed with a tease of what Don and Donna Mae had in mind for 1970: further expansion. Their vision for the new year was to establish a coast-to-coast network of high-performance Chevrolet dealers for the purpose of merchandising "Safe Super Cars." They were going to work with these dealers to help them maintain themselves as high-performance centers using "national sportscar and drag racing programs coupled with national advertising, promotion, and dealership training."

The training program consists of sales, parts, and service seminars designed to keep the "dealer personnel abreast of this ever-changing, youth-oriented specialty field." The plan was similar to what Dick Landy and the Sox & Martin race teams were doing with Mopar: hosting their own Super Car Clinics in Dodge dealerships. Don was forward thinking and wanted to get his name out there as the go-to for the best in Chevrolet performance and safety. In April 1969, he wrote to Ed Cole, informing him nearly 50 of these centers had been set up. He closed his letter by saying that "if Chevrolet isn't going to build the Chevelle and the Camaro with hi-po 427 mills next year, I'd like to order 500 COPO cars."

Word Gets Out

Don had stumbled into a real honey of a deal with his iron-block 427-equipped Camaros, and he did everything he could to not let the cat out of the bag about how, or more importantly where, they got built. Don had dreams of being the Carroll Shelby of the Chevrolet world, with his name synonymous with his high-performance Camaro. Initially, he was to be the single source for these L72 COPO cars, but that all changed because of a young love romance.

Jim Mattison was working in the Central Office and was heavily involved with the special COPO cars that came through. "In 1968, I was dating the daughter of a local Detroit Chevy dealership [Emmert Chevrolet]. Every time I'd go over to the family home to pick up my girlfriend to take her out, Stan [her dad and the dealer's owner] would ask me what was new at Chevy. I told him about the COPO program and he was quite interested. Being a good businessman, he wanted in on it. He asked me what it took to get some. I told him they were all supposed to go to Yenko but I'd look into it. The next week I found out if he ordered 10, he'd get the go-ahead for the approval. I came back and told him what I found. He said for me to stop in and see his sales manager at the dealership to get some order forms. I not only ordered the cars at the dealership, I received the orders at my desk and processed them on to the factory." That paved the

It wasn't just in the United States where these COPO Camaros were sold. Haney Garage, Ltd., in Haney, British Columbia (about 25 miles east of Vancouver), ordered this Daytona Yellow example. Jack Ueda bought it new, with intentions of ruling the streets of Kelowna, his hometown. He did just that for two years, even installing a roll cage for additional safety. Haney sold two others COPOs: another Camaro and a Chevelle.

way for other dealers, who placed orders themselves for COPO L72 Camaros to follow suit. While the minimum order for the vehicles was 10, many dealers ended up selling far fewer COPOs than that. Jim reports finding it quite common for one dealer to order 10 and then parcel them out in dealer trades.

COPO Circulation

On July 25, 1969, an internal memo was sent by Chevrolet to dealers on how to properly warranty this new crop of COPO Camaros. By now, it was painfully obvious that Don Yenko's dreams of being the token COPO Camaro dealer were dashed. When listing all the parts that made these cars special, the memo clearly stated that "This COPO option is 9737 Sports Car Conversion/Yenko and contrary to the implication in the COPO option name shown, it is also applicable to other Chevrolet dealers firm orders as well as 'Yenko Sports Cars, Inc.'" Chevrolet cited in a memo that 700 L72 COPOs were in process for the model year, but production continued until November 1969.

RS COPO Camaros

In rare instances, some of the subsequently ordered COPO Camaros, like some of the cars Dale Berger Jr. ordered, came equipped with the Rally Sport Option. This equipped the cars with the RPO Z22 package, which included a black molded grille with the sliding door hidden headlight feature, headlight washers, and an RS emblem mounted in the center of the grille in place of the blue Chevy bowtie.

Additional exterior add-ons were black body sills, simulated rear fender louvers, front and rear wheel opening moldings, and bright roof drip moldings. Around back, the reverse lights were moved from the center of the rear lenses to their own housings below the bumper. The taillights had bright accents, too, and there was an RS emblem mounted in the center of the tail panel. Inside there was an RS emblem on the steering wheel. Typically, Rally Sport badging was mounted on the front fenders, but some COPOS had Camaro script emblems installed.

Some RS COPO Camaros were equipped with the rare and one-year-only RPO V75 Liquid Tire Chain ($23.25). This vacuum-operated

RS Camaros are easy to identify, thanks to their hidden headlight grilles. This Lemans Blue example was sold new by British American Chevrolet Oldsmobile in Toronto, Ontario, to a wide-eyed college student. Trying to juggle school bills and the hefty car loan proved too much, prompting him sell it to Johnny Zamit. Zamit competed regularly at area quarter-mile strips. After porting the cylinder heads, the leadfoot got the COPO into the high 11 seconds.

This RS was dressed to the nines, getting additional upgrades inside, including a Custom Interior, as part of RPO Z87 (costing about $110). This package added woodgrain to the dash and center console, chrome around the pedals, a glove box light, and a passenger grab handle. This car also has a sport-styled steering wheel (RPO N34, costing around $35) and center electric clock and tachometer in the right gauge pod.

Whoever ordered this car wanted all the bells and whistles, checking the box for RPO U17 ($94.80), which added these lower gauges to the center console. This option package for Special Instrumentation also added the clock and tach to the center gauge cluster.

As part of the RS package, brightwork was installed around the taillight lenses, the simulated fender vents were placed ahead of the rear wheels, and the reverse lights were moved down to underneath the bumper. Frost Chevrolet in Mechanicsburg, Ohio, sold this Tuxedo Black RS to original owner Larry Bostick, who was known for keeping the car immaculate. Tim Schell now owns it and the other two featured cars.

While Don didn't succeed in being the sole provider of factory 427-powered Camaros, he did succeed in creating some of the most iconic muscle machines of the 1960s. Today, the Yenko Camaro is highly sought after and known the world over. David Boland owns this example.

system was meant to increase traction on icy or snowy roads by deicing the rear tires. It worked by using upside down aerosol can applicators mounted in the trunk above the rear wheels. If the wheels began to spin, pressing a button on the underside of the dash for a few seconds sprayed liquid in front of the rear tires. Fewer than 200 Camaros (COPOs and not) had this option. When the aerosol cans were depleted, drivers could access them through the trunk and replace them.

Camaro Conclusion

Don Yenko deserves a lot of credit for his contribution to the COPO muscle cars of the 1960s, with some arguing 1969 was his crowning achievement. His steps leading up to the L72-equipped Camaro (his charging ahead with his Stinger program, then changing gears to modify his 1968 Camaros) led him to dream bigger, eventually culminating in the cars of 1969. Enthusiasts were wanting a 427-equipped Camaro, but Chevrolet wasn't

officially going to build and sell one. Cunning Don picked up on the laws of basic supply and demand, recognizing that interest was through the roof, and through the Central Office paperwork he could boost supply by having the 427s installed at the factory, then get them sold through his special dealer network. Going beyond that, his imagination and his determination to become the Carroll Shelby of the Chevrolet world drove him to build out his sYc brand, developing a proper look and feel for his COPO creations that are still recognizable and iconic today.

It was a move of brilliance, and had he been able to contain the secret, the sky would have been the limit to his ingenuity and the program's profitability. Much to his dismay, but to past and present enthusiasts' great delight, other dealerships did find out about COPO 9561, ordering their own non-Yenko Central Office creations. These 427 Camaros helped changed the tide in the street-and-strip battles taking place around the nation, putting Chevrolet back on the map in the minds of performance enthusiasts and paving the way for the brand's future muscle car achievements.

CHAPTER 7

1969 COPO CHEVELLE

A Giant Leap Beyond the Common Chevelle

Looking to expand his offerings to his dealer network in 1969, Don Yenko included not only the Camaro but also the Chevelle as part of his tuned-up lineup. Just as with the Camaro, the mid-sized Chevelle had its engine offerings severely limited in RPO form. When the second generation of the car came out in 1968, the biggest powerplant was the L78 396-ci, 375-hp Turbo-Jet V-8, and that would be true for 1969 versions too. Just as enthusiasts and shops were swapping out the L78 for bigger and better engines in Camaro engine bays, the same thing was happening with the mid-size Chevelle. Baldwin-Motion, for example, had been transplanting 427s in Chevelles since 1967 and including them in their Fantastic Five lineup of 427-equipped Chevys.

Dave Riffle, from Washington, Pennsylvania, purchased this Chevelle brand new from the Yenko dealership. He bought it on August 15, 1969. It's one of 28 equipped with an automatic transmission. The rest of the 99 ordered by Don had 4-speed manuals.

Another engine swapper was Don's former partner and driver, Dick Harrell. Harrell and his team, based in Kansas City, stayed busy bolting 427s into their Super Camaros and Super Chevelles. By 1968, Harrell had distributed nearly 100 of those vehicles through his dealer network. Besides swapping in a 427 short-block to the factory-installed 396 and going through it to maximize performance, Harrell's team also installed a complete Hays blowproof clutch assembly. In the looks department, the 1968 Chevelles were fitted with a special dual-scoop A&A Engineering fiberglass hood and special accent striping. Customers could choose between Appliance Plating or Cragar wheels, and any 396 badges were swapped for 427 plaques. Harrell advertised they pumped out 450 hp and offered a 500-hp version, complete with dual Daytona-type AFB carbs on a lightweight manifold. If that wasn't enough, there were plans for a 550-hp engine package. Harrell's cars cost $4,395 and could be purchased through his dealer network, which included Chevrolet stores in California, Arizona, Illinois, and Kansas City. *Super Stock* magazine did a couple hot passes in a midnight blue example at the Kansas City International Raceway, where it turned in times as low as 12.84 seconds at 107.14 mph.

After hearing about what those other road rivals were up to, Don came to like the concept too, knowing his own 427-equipped Chevelle would be the perfect addition to his line of sYc street dominators. He was going to like it a whole lot after working the COPO paperwork charm. So much time and energy would be saved by having the cars delivered to his door and dropped off the transport truck with the L72 427-ci V-8 engine already installed. His plan was to get them in, slap on a few stickers, and then get them out and distributed through his extensive network. Just as with Camaro, if he had kept a lid on it, the idea would have been ingenious. But fate stepped in and other dealers found out. Soon COPO Chevelles were being ordered by more than just Yenko Chevrolet.

COPO 9562

Beginning in the early spring of 1969, Don made an initial order 50 Chevelles, with the majority of those being sold in April. Two subsequent batches of 25 cars were requested in early summer. All told, Don ordered and sold 99 COPO Chevelles. The cars were specified to be Malibu sport coupes, but in the same way the 1968 and 1969 COPO Camaros started off life as Super Sports, the COPO process started with the RPO Z25 Super Sport option and then eliminated SS identification when possible. More than likely, these removals came at the request of Chevrolet, which didn't want Don's creation conflicting or confusing shoppers about its top dog SS offering.

Prior to 1969, the SS package was a stand-alone model for the Chevelle, but in 1969 it became a special trim and engine package available to any two-door Chevelle model. Besides dress-up items, it included a 396-ci V-8 in three different horsepower ratings. COPO 9562 specified the

Just as with Camaro, the L72 427 ci had no trouble mounting in the Chevelle's large engine bay. When Chevrolet installed the engines at the factory, Don and his technicians saved so much time and energy.

375-hp version, as the L78 was near identical to the L72 in terms of dimensions, water pump pulley location, distributor, and any other components that were bolted externally to it. The L78 was then substituted with the High-Performance Unit, an L72 427-ci V-8 stamped with a special engine suffix. The engines were all built at the Tonawanda, New York, factory and were shipped to assembly plants for installation, saving Don and his team time and giving them something no one else had. The majority of the COPO Chevelles were built at the Baltimore, Maryland, facility (B) with two additional vehicles built at the Kansas City, Missouri, facility (K), and one more was built at the Freemont, California, plant (Z). All the Chevelles got a 12-bolt, 4.10:1 rear axle, stamped KQ on the passenger-side tube. It included a special heat-treated ring and pinion and a special Positraction unit.

The Super Sport option package brought cosmetic upgrades too. Up front, a blacked-out grille with bright center bar was installed. Typically, an SS badge with smaller 396 font underneath would be installed in the middle, but on these COPO Chevelles, the standard blue Chevy bowtie as found on the Malibu was mounted. A Super Sport hood, with twin domes and simulated air intake grilles at the rear, was retained. The cars also got hideaway windshield wipers and molding at the rear edge of the hood, around the windshield, on the roof rails, and around the wheelwells.

On the side, the Chevelles, as part of the Super Sport, had items deleted in regard to the marker lights. Up front on the fender, the vehicles kept the Super Sport side marker lights but without any engine identification. On

The COPO Chevelles got the Super Sport's blacked out grille and chrome center bar, but instead of the distinct SS center badging, they were given the blue bow tie, found on lower trims. The hood, with its twin power bulges, was also a Super Sport part.

These publicity photos show a newly converted Yenko Chevelle. While ads showed the sticker arrowhead and stripes running down to the leading edge of the hood, sometimes they'd be mounted much shorter, as seen here. (Photo Courtesy the Barr Collection)

the rear quarter panel, just in front of the rear marker light, the "Malibu" script was deleted too. While a wide paint stripe running down the profile beltline (available under RPO D96) could be had as an SS option, Don chose to leave it off as his team would add stripes once the cars arrived at the dealership.

At the rear, SS cars had a blackened area instead of the Malibu silver paint mounted between the taillights. COPO Chevelles would have another SS badge with smaller 396 font underneath deleted and left off.

Inside the cabin, the SS badging on the center of the steering wheel, the door panels, and on the trim bar nameplate mounted to the dashboard above the glove box were deleted and standard Malibu badging went in their place.

Besides the looks, the SS package brought performance upgrades too. Power disc front brakes were installed along with dual exhaust complete with chrome tips and a heavy-duty suspension. Typically, special 14-inch wheels, with decorative SS emblems on the hub, wrapped in F70x14 white-lettered tires would be installed but under COPO 9737, F70x15-inch tires on 7-inch Rally Wheels (Code YH) were mounted on Yenko's Chevelles.

Under COPO 9562, the Chevelles would get special chassis and suspension, heavy-duty 4.10:1 Positraction axle, and special turbo 400 or M21 4-speed transmissions. Cars equipped with the automatic transmission were stamped MP while 4-speed cars were stamped MQ on the engine pad.

In general, Don ordered the cars with RPOs such as vinyl or cloth bench or vinyl bucket seats, 4-speed transmissions, and standard steering. Variations were made and, as such, cars with automatic transmissions, radios, vinyl roofs, power steering, or rear antennas were built.

Changes in Canonsburg

Once the vehicles were delivered, additional tweaks were made by Yenko's technicians to brand the vehicles. Side stripe graphics (the same as found on the Camaros) were applied along with twin hood stripes, ending in the "sYc" arrowhead near the front edge. Yenko crests were applied on the front fenders, behind the wheels.

Also on the front fenders, Don's specially crafted 427 badges were applied in front of the marker lights. These pieces were custom made with three individual numerals of four, two, seven, connected by a wide, solid bar underneath. They were the same badges Don used on his 1969 COPO Camaro but placed in a different location. While Yenko techs applied them to the Camaro's raised ZL2 hood cowl, on the Chevelle they mounted them on the front fender ahead of the marker light. Space was tight given the Chevelle's front styling, which included a sharp cut back on the fender. Some techs actually cut the badge's lower bar to mimic the angle, thinking the badge jutted up against the chrome line. Some owners also took it upon themselves to color the numbers black, but as they left the dealership, they were all silver.

This Chevelle had the same custom-made thin number badge that was applied to 1968 Camaros. More than likely, Don wanted to use up whatever inventory was left over before moving to his newly rolled out thick-bar 1969 style. (Photo Courtesy the Barr Collection)

With no rear spoiler for the Yenko side stripe to end on as with the 1969 Camaro, technicians trimmed it to match the cut of the rear fender. On lighter colored cars, such as yellow and orange, the stripe would be black. For darker cars, such as red or blue, it would be white. (Photo Courtesy the Barr Collection)

A Yenko crest and 427 badging would be mounted on the Chevelle's rear black trim bar, mounted on either side of center. (Photo Courtesy the Barr Collection)

While it's tight, the new 1969 badge did fit on the front fender. Badges have surfaced that had the front corners trimmed off, matching the cut-back chrome molding of the headlight surrounds. These could be a result of a technician mounting the badge too far forward or perhaps thinking it would be more aesthetically pleasing.

Dave, the original owner, bought this muscle machine to cruise around looking for a street race and an opportunity to beat up on some Mopars. The car was built on July 23, 1969, and sold a few weeks later. Johnny Griffin owns it today.

THE YENKO 427 S/C SUPER CARS

You've waited long enough to tame your kind of town and your kind of road—on your kind of terms. Here are the Yenko 427 Super Cars! And they're all GUTS!

SPECIFICATIONS:

. . . 427 CID 450-hp engine with hi-lift cam and solid valve lifters.
. . . Hi-rise manifold with 800 CFM Holley four-barrel carburetor
. . . Four-speed close-radio Muncie transmission with special Hurst shift linkage (dual gate floor-mounted linkage with Turbo Hydramatics)*
. . . Power disc front brakes/15x7 wheels (14x6 on Novas) WT GT tires
. . . 4.10:1 positraction rear axle with special heavy duty ring, pinion and axle shafts
. . . Reversed air-breathing hood scoop with built-in sealed plenum chamber and throttle operated solenoid valve*
. . . Computer tuned heavy duty suspension including special shocks, springs and extra H.D. stabilizer bar
. . . Front under-grille spoiler
. . . 450 hp @ 5000 with standard exhaust configuration
. . . One piece Aluminum cast Mag Wheels optional at extra cost with Yenko emblem

STANDARD APPEARANCE FEATURES:

. . . Custom YENKO side and hood striping . . . Unique headrest styling . . . Distinctive 427 & YENKO emblems . . . Transistorized tachometer . . . 140 mph speedometer* . . . Rear deck spoiler*

*Yenko Camaro 427 Only   SPECIFICATIONS SUBJECT TO CHANGE WITHOUT NOTICE

MEET THE MEAN ONES!

Given his artistic abilities, Don may have very well sketched out this eye-catching ad, showing off his trio of Supercars for 1969, including the Chevelle. These renderings differed slightly from the final products. Note the Chevelle doesn't have the chrome cross bar in the grille or the blue bowtie and is lacking any side badging. The Camaro's rear section close-up still has the factory bowtie mounted as well. (Photo Courtesy the Henderson Collection)

The hood stripe and sYc arrowhead design was simple but strong and matched the other two 1969 Yenko Supercars: Camaro and Nova. While Camaro hoods would get the newly created thick bar 427 badges, they were left off the Chevelles' hoods.

Dealer Network

Once the cars were completed, they were sent to participating dealers in the Yenko Supercar dealer network. In 1969, Don had nearly all of the East Coast and into the Midwest covered. Dealers carrying his cars were in Alabama, Connecticut, Florida, Georgia, Illinois, Indiana, Iowa, Kansas, Kentucky, Massachusetts, Missouri, Minnesota, New Jersey, New York, Ohio, Pennsylvania, Tennessee, Virginia, and Wisconsin.

Symmetry came back into play on the Chevelles' rear when it came time to mount the two badges. Because the black panel was blank and had no SS badge or a bowtie like on the Camaro, when it came time to drill the badges' holes, technicians placed them on either side of center.

Don was only able to get the 140-mph speedometer on his Camaro through the Central Office. The Chevelle would be left with the standard 120-mph unit. Super Sport Chevelles normally would get an SS badge in the middle of the steering wheel. The COPOs had bowties there instead.

While the Yenko crest remained the red, white, and blue style, the 427 badge could be either this thin-number 1968 style or the 1969 thick-bar design. No matter which one a car got, it certainly broadcast the right message: something special is under the hood.

Just as with the Novas and Camaros, a Stewart Warner tach was mounted to the dash in front of the stock gauge cluster. With his racing background, Don certainly knew the value of a smooth and confident start off a line and wanted his customers to nail their shift points.

For around $210, customers could have a Hurst dual gate shifter installed on their automatic-equipped Chevelles. This relocated the shifter from the steering column to a floor-mounted console setup. Keeping the shifter in the gate's left channel would have the transmission shift normally, but for more control, drivers could slide it to the right. There, they could manually control the gears, helping prevent missed shifts.

Don stands next to his loaded-up tractor trailer, stacked three high with completed Yenko Chevelles. Both styles of 427 badging were used; the middle one has the 1968-style thin number badge while the top Chevelle has the 1969 thick-bar style. (Photo Courtesy the Barr Collection)

Jim Spencer, of SPAN, Inc., was the one responsible for securing the Yenko transport truck. It was lettered with "Hi-Performance Sports Cars" and the Yenko crest to alert passing motorists of its precious cargo. Spencer also helped get the cars distributed to the sYc dealerships. (Photo Courtesy the Barr Collection)

Don was big on branding, which is probably why his products are the most well-known of the COPO-created cars today. Just as back then, people see them and instantly recognize them.

Other COPO Chevelles

When other dealers found out about the advantageous setup Don had with Chevrolet, they quickly joined in on requesting their own COPO 427-equipped Chevelles. Known quantities of cars sold include 6 from Berger Chevrolet in Grand Rapids, Michigan; 6 from Jack Douglas Chevrolet in Hinsdale, Illinois; 4 from Queens Chevrolet in Ohio; and 20 that were shipped to Canada. Many dealers ordered additional options such as the D96 side stripe, which was a large stripe surrounded by a thin pinstripe that was painted on the beltline of the vehicle, tapering at each end.

This other batch of Chevelles generally received COPO 9566, which was very similar to COPO 9562, the High-Performance Unit that brought on the 427-ci V-8. The 9566 included the motor swap, plus SS 14x7 wheels with PL5 RWL tires, whereas Yenko's Chevelles were equipped with 15x7 Rally Wheels. There were some other variations, based on how the Chevelle was ordered. For example, they would get COPO 9562 AA if it was equipped with a 4-speed manual transmission and Positraction rear axle. COPO 9562 BA was used for 3-speed automatic transmissions and Positraction rear axle car. COPO 9694 CA was for cars with a 4-speed manual transmission and the Sports Car Conversion (COPO 9737) and

Lucky Leon Noble received this ultra-cool car as a graduation present from his parents. The young man drove it around his hometown of Jackson, Kentucky, as a daily driver, racing it on the street every chance he got. On occasion, he did get out to Mountain Park Dragway, in Clay City, Kentucky, for a few quarter-mile blasts. With slicks and 4.56 gears, he dipped into low 12-second times.

Brewer's Chevrolet in Campton, Kentucky, got on board with the COPO action, ordering this Lemans Blue Chevelle. The dealership was heavily involved in NASCAR and a major player in their local high-performance scene, selling several COPO Camaros and Chevelles. These high-powered cars were right on track for the dealership's leadfoot customers.

Original Owner Spotlight: Roger Day, 1969 Dick Harrell Chevelle

Three days after graduating high school in 1966, Roger Day went to work for the Ford Motor Company. He was on the assembly line in Claycomo, Missouri, working on special projects, buffing and detailing the 1967 show cars. After a few weeks, he wanted to get himself a brand-new, discounted car.

"I was leaning toward the Fairlane GT," said Day. The dream fizzled when he chatted with his foreman. "He informed me I had to be there 90 days to get the company rate." Not willing to wait, Day went out and found a great deal on a burgundy 1966 Chevelle SS396 at Parrish Chevrolet in Liberty, Missouri. He happily wheeled it into work much to the dismay of his foreman. "He wasn't too happy seeing me pull up in it," laughs Day. He wouldn't see it for long; Day left the company and after a couple of fill-in jobs, started working for the Whitaker Cable Corp in Kansas City. There, he managed quotes for wiring harnesses for the Big Three. He drove the Chevelle back and forth to work for three years. "I wanted to upgrade the car, especially the motor," recalls Day. He had already logged more than 100,000 miles on it and returned to the dealership. He headed to the parts counter to price out a crate 427 block. The sales

associate suggested some other speed parts and, as the dollars added up, Day decided it wasn't cost-effective.

As it turns out, he just had to wait for his desired Chevelle-427 combo to come his way. A month later, Day cruised by Bill Allen Chevrolet (one of Dick Harrell's participating dealers) a little before 8 a.m. "They were pushing three cars out to the front of the lot and this bright orange coupe caught my eye," said Day. "I had to pull in and check it out." Knowing he'd be a while, he called his boss and told him he'd be late to work.

As part of the new shipment, the dealership had not only a Dick Harrell Chevelle but also a Nova and Camaro from Harrell's shop. Day wasn't distracted; he wanted the Chevelle. Despite his interest, the salespeople wouldn't let the young man drive the car until he had made a deal. Day put his money where his mouth was and purchased the car.

"I walked around the car and spotted the Harrell Performance Center MSRP with details on mods made at his shop." Harrell's place was just down the road and, in 1969, he put his name on a handful of Chevelles. He removed SMOG components, installed a degreed harmonic balancer, and adjusted timing. A Sun tach, hood locks, and black hood stripes were

Roger Day was working six blocks away from Bill Allen Chevrolet and always had a good look at its new inventory. His COPO Chevelle was one of three built at GM's Kansas City plant. His was put together in the third week of July, near the end of the 1969 model year. The 1970 SS style hood stripes were painted on at Dick Harrell's shop as a unique touch.

In a departure from his normal ways of branding, in 1969, Harrell created these three-dimensional, multicolor crests, installing them on the decklid. This was a big departure from the simple and straightforward plaques mounted on the 1968 COPO Novas he modified. He also added the 1967 Impala 427 V flags on the Chevelles' front fenders.

Harrell's shop tweaked the 427 to improve performance by modifying the distributor advance curve and timing and by removing the A.I.R. SMOG equipment. Total output was bumped from 425 hp to 450. Power was good, but frustrations with reliability caused Day to eventually trade the car in to Sharp Chevrolet.

installed along with emblems on the decklid and Chevy V-8 flags on the front fenders. The price tag of $4,430.05 didn't bother Day; he was making $2.75 an hour at Whitaker.

"The '66 ran well, but the 427, on the other hand, had lower gears and would jump in the air when I hit the throttle," said Day. Bill Allen even came out and chatted with Day about his new purchase. "He congratulated me on buying the 'Dick Harrell Super Car.'" Day drove the new ride to work later that day and continued to commute in the COPO.

Besides the daily grind, he also used the car for the occasional street romp. His first race was in December 1969 on Highway 33 near Plattsburg, Missouri. He was up against a high school classmate in his metallic green 396/350 Chevy Nova. "John smoked his tires at the start line while I screamed to the turnaround," recalls Day. "In the end, it was a hollow victory." The lively sprint had scuffed a cylinder wall. Because it was still under warranty, Day headed to Bill Allen's and dropped off the car for repairs. He got a call later that day from the service manager, who told him they needed him to come to the dealership to meet with the zone manager.

"The first question he asked me when I came in was had I been racing the car," said Roger. "The zone rep turned to the service manager, disgusted, and said GM should have never put these big motors in these cars. Kids were just going to mess them up," recalls Day. Despite the grilling, General Motors replaced the Chevelle's short-block.

In May 1970, Day drove his car to a friend's house for a Memorial Day barbecue. There in the back pasture, he met a pretty young lady over the flicker of a glowing bonfire. The gal's name was Karen, and right away, they hit it off. It got late and not wanting to stop their conversation, Day offered to give her a ride home. "We ended up talking the night away on the drive," recalls Day. As he got within a block of her apartment in the wee hours of the morning, the Chevelle's alternator light came on. "The fan belt had slipped off and was shredded. She loaned me her car and I drove to a relative's nearby to stay the rest of the night," said Day. Early the next morning, he got up, headed to the local parts store, and installed a new belt. The hiccup couldn't ruin the wonderful night before; the lovebirds saw each other every day for the next two weeks, after which they were engaged. "All summer long we dated in the Chevelle," said Day. "It was a summer romance that turned into nearly 50 years of marriage."

The only thing that brought Day more joy than stoplight showoffs was when his honey rode along. One memorable race was on a July evening when he and Karen came across one of Karen's high school classmate in

The Sun Super gauge on the steering column was just one add-on Dick Harrell's shop mounted to the COPO Chevelle, tacking on an additional $68 for the accessory. The door panels, steering wheel, and trim bar above the glove box all read "Malibu," not giving off any hints above the vehicle's true performance capabilities.

No doubt to protect the identity of the 427, Harrell installed hood locks on the Chevelle. The Hugger Orange paint was available only with the SS option but could be specially ordered on cars like this, which was ordered as a Malibu sport coupe.

While the Yenko Chevelles all got black interiors, other dealers ordered their COPOs with variations, like this white cabin. The radio was an option, costing $61. In August 1969, Harrell brought over two other cars besides Day's: a modified Camaro and a Nova.

Roger and Karen Day's first date took place in the COPO Chevelle on Memorial Day weekend, May 30, 1970. The lovebirds were engaged two weeks later. Today, they are still together and still have their special car.

his strong-running Challenger 440 Six-Pack. "We set it up on Highway 13 between Gallatin and Hamilton," recalls Day. "They flagged us off and he really got into it. I eased off the starting line, then punched it, having no trouble pulling away from him. Flashing red and blue lights heading our way on Highway 13 prevented a rematch!"

Those happy memories slowed that fall when the oil light came on. Day took the car to Sharp Chevrolet in Hamilton, Missouri, where Karen's stepfather was sales manager. The engine was taken apart and it was diagnosed as a faulty oil pickup tube, which had fallen off in the oil pan. The odometer showed 35,000 miles and, as such, the dealership offered to repair the engine under warranty. Day was set on getting a new engine, and when that offer was turned down, he traded the car in for a charcoal grey 1970 Camaro RS.

Fast-forward to the late 1990s and Day began tracking down his old car. He and Karen had moved to Texas but still visited family in Kansas City. "I once saw the Chevelle parked near my brother's house and would drive through the neighborhood, hopeful I might spot it again," said Day.

He lost track of it for more than 38 years. In 2008, a renewed search led him to an earlier owner's daughter, who said the family had sold the Chevelle for scrap. Despite the letdown, Day never lost hope. He picked up the hunt again in 2009 and, after much persistence, tracked his car down in Ottawa, Illinois. Within hours, he was on a flight to Chicago and driving to the storage unit where his Chevelle sat. He's since had the car fully restored back to its former glory.

The Bill Allen staff wouldn't let Day take the Chevelle off the lot for a test drive until he had made a deal, not that the young man needed much convincing that he wanted the hot car. This wasn't the first Chevelle modification for Harrell; in 1968, he and his team hopped-up a handful of 396 cars, installing 427 short-blocks under their hoods.

Super Stock & Drag Illustrated August 1969 Media Drive

Super Stock & Drag Illustrated tested one of Yenko's 427 Camaros for its July 1969 magazine and wasn't going to stop there. For its August publication, it grabbed a yellow with black vinyl roof Yenko Chevelle for a proper track test. The car, showing 4,500 miles on the odometer, had come from Marshall Chevrolet in Reading, Pennsylvania; everything was in stock form, save for a lifter adjustment. The magazine crew headed straight for the US-30 Dragway. There wasn't time for any road course numbers, but they did some "prerace playing on the backroads." The goal was to "make the test as relative to the prospective buyer and enthusiast as possible" and all the runs were made the same way as anybody else would at their local dragstrip.

After a couple smoky burnouts, they pulled up to the line, clicking off 13.85 seconds at 103.68 mph in their first pass. More runs were made, coming out at near idle and punching it about 50 feet out. They found the tires still broke loose "very badly and continued to do so into second gear."

Realizing the car would perform better with proper race slicks, the best they could eek out was a 13.87 at 103.92 mph. They dropped the tire pressure in the rear to 20 psi and boosted the front to 45 psi, which helped claim a 13.70 seconds at 104.01. One of Yenko's associates, Dick Williams, removed the air filter element, and after a couple smokier burnouts, managed to blast to 13.63 seconds at 104.16 mph. Part of his technique was shifting gears around 6,000 rpm. More passes were made with all settling in the 13.60s. The magazine crew decided to hang around until the sun went down and wait for cooler air. The decision paid off as three runs made after 10 p.m. were below those recorded in the sun. The first clocked in at 13.40 seconds at 106.25 mph, the second run ticked by at 13.36 seconds at 106.89 mph, and the last pass was the fastest, coming at 13.31 seconds at 108.04 mph.

The magazine wrapped up its feature by suggesting the car, which was quite heavy, pegging the scales at 3,635 pounds, would behave better with headers, tires, and a proper tuning and could get into the 12 second range with no trouble. Overall, they found Yenko's creation to be a good package and "well worth the loot." They liked the Chevelle's "mellow but authoritative sound" and were quite happy everything ran consistently during their entire time with it. "If you want the roominess of a larger car," the maga-

Unlike the batch of Chevelles Don ordered, this one has the RPO D96 side stripe. Boasting its own side stripe, this Duncan Hines dining car, built in the early 1940s, is on display at the Historic Railpark and Train Museum in Bowling Green, Kentucky.

the vacuum-power brakes (RPO J50). The COPO 9737 option included 15x7-inch Rally Wheels with trim rings and center caps. Also included were F70x15 raised white letter tires. A speedometer gear drive adapter and heavy-duty radiator rounded out the option.

One interesting note about the COPO Chevelles is their anomalies. Whereas the Camaro program had been in effect for some time before 1969, the ordering process for the Chevelle was a bit more haphazard, with more assembly line mistakes occurring. Cars were built that retained their steering wheel SS emblems while others had the holes drilled in their rear quarter panel, anticipating Malibu script. Others left the factory wearing lower Malibu body molding.

Around 1984, Ray Hurst heard Noble was selling the car and purchased it. He made the tired machine road worthy, but with the focus on his young family, Hurst sold the car in 1989. His son, Van, fulfilled a lifelong dream and purchased it in 2014 and owns it today, living less than 2 miles from Brewer's Chevrolet, where it was sold new.

zine feature closed, "the scat of a much smaller one, and the distinction of a Grand Touring class, the Yenko 427 Chevelle may just be your thing."

Don's Bluff Called

While Don worked hard to get his Chevelles approved for racing in the NHRA, the rules committee finally had enough of some of the shenanigans. They asked him for sales history of the Yenko Chevelles to see if enough had been sold to warrant being placed in Production classes. A nervous Don, knowing he didn't have enough units moved, reached out to his dealer network, asking for sales info, complete with purchaser information. When the forms came back in, Don and his dealers padded the data and listed dealership owner spouses, magazine writers, and other "buyers" as proud owners of Yenko Chevelles. Don was creative, but often that imagination of his would wind up driving him to think of ways to bend the rules to accomplish his purpose. Whether or not the NHRA caught on, the Yenko Chevelle was not approved for racing in production classes.

Chevelle Closing

The Yenko COPO Chevelle represented just another way Don Yenko saw possibilities and swung for fences. Knowing there was a market for big-engined Chevelles, just like Camaro, made clear after seeing competitors perform more than a few motor swaps, Don figured he'd join the fray.

But if he was going to do it, he was going to work smart, not hard. Not only would a 427-equipped Chevelle be a wonderful addition to his sYc lineup of vehicles, if he didn't have to have his technicians perform any kind of major modification, he'd save time, money, and had the ability to rapidly scale inventory. It was a total win-win-win for the Yenko brand. While that plan didn't come to a screeching halt, it was slowed down when Don's veil of exclusivity was pierced and other dealers found out they, too, could order their own COPO'd 427 Chevelles.

Whether of the Yenko variety or not, these big, comfy, and powerful cruisers helped establish the Chevrolet brand as a formidable foe at stoplight romps and late-night drags.

Don wanted to keep the COPO Chevelle ordering process to himself, but, alas, once other dealers caught wind of the special deal, they swooped in and stole his thunder, building and selling their own. However, there was a silver lining. Don learned bigger wasn't always better, especially with what lay ahead in the years to come.

CHAPTER 8

THE 1970 YENKO DEUCE NOVA

MINI MUSCLE TO THE RESCUE

1970 Yenko Deuce Nova

Total Production: 175
Total Still Out There: 103

Other COPO Novas
Canadian Novas: 2
Total Still Out There: 1

"You've seen them before. They're the boys at the stoplights with their heads out the windows, watching for the red to turn green, revving up the loud engines on their super-header . . . specials. The rear ends of the bright red, canary yellow, striped hot rods may be jacked up on high springs with exhaust pipes hanging below, almost touching the pavement. They're the boys who drive the muscle cars." That's the way a June 27, 1971, *Tampa Tribune* article introduced a piece on the muscle car phase, where all through the 1960s those young guys and gals were out cruising in force. But as the decade drew to a close, stirring winds of change were beginning to blow.

Yenko Deuces were the stuff of dreams to leadfoots including Mike Miller. In 1970, he was 17 and lusting after the hot car, but being a high school senior, he was strapped for cash and couldn't afford one. He settled on a used Nova SS, lining up regularly to street race a buddy whose parents had bought him a new Fathom Blue Deuce from Dale Chevrolet in Milwaukee, Wisconsin. "I never had any luck beating him," said Miller. "Upgrading to a Deuce was always on my to-do list." He finally crossed it off in 1986 when he purchased this Cranberry Red example.

The high-octane days of the ever-escalating race to produce cars that were bigger, faster, and more powerful were numbered. Insurance companies were taking closer note of the rise of performance vehicles and set the big bruisers squarely in their crosshairs. Young drivers were getting behind the wheels of high-powered cars and finding themselves in over their heads. In 1970, 20.9 percent of the nation's motoring population was under 25, yet drivers 24 and under were involved in 34.6 percent of collisions. Younger drivers, drawn to the high-horsepower machines, were getting in more frequent and more serious accidents, running up larger claim costs for the insurance companies.

All those wrecks brought up another issue: repairs. According to insurance agents, muscle cars and pony cars designed to appeal to the young male were deemed extremely vulnerable to damage and costly to repair. They cited bumpers that don't bump, grilles that collapse into the radiator, and protruding design elements such as aluminum noses as major gripes.

On January 1, 1970, a group representing 120 insurance companies was called before Congress to defend the dramatic increase in premiums. The explanation was that skyrocketing auto repair costs, not to mention muscle cars being more prone to theft and vandalism, was the culprit. The Senate subcommittee on antitrust and monopoly had spent nearly two years looking into the cost of auto insurance, eyeing the steep rise in premiums. Now, armed with data, it was ready to take action, turning its attention to automakers.

Hot Cars in Hot Water

In late January 1970, transportation secretary John A. Volpe warned the National Automobile Dealers Association that automotive advertising had reached an inflammatory level in its emphasis on speed. Citing ads that encouraged youthful drivers to speed and research showing that auto accidents were the leading cause of death in the 16- to 25-year-old age group, he didn't mince words. "At the present time," said Volpe, "I have no authority to control advertising. But if the situation continues I won't be afraid to ask for it."

Another strong critic of muscle cars was Dr. William Haddon Jr., president of the Insurance Institute for Highway Safety. "Muscle cars with lots of horsepower are fine on the race track, but it's almost criminal irresponsibility to use these on public roads," he said. "Because of advertising techniques, the image that is being sold at great expense to the American public is that you don't have safe transportation, you have thrills on the American highway." One perceptive writer in the *Corsicana Daily Sun* summed it up well, stating: "The chickens that Detroit hatched with its long campaign emphasizing speed and performance are coming home to roost."

In February and March, insurance companies began shifting the emphasis from the driver group to the car itself. They began re-evaluating the relationship between insurance rates and the kind of risk the insured represented. For the first time, high-performance cars fell into a special insurance rate category.

Muscle Car Defined

According to insurance company guidelines, "muscle" or "performance" cars were classified as any 1970 model with at least a 350-hp engine or more and a manual transmission or any 1970 car with a ratio of vehicle weight to horsepower of less than 10.5:1. Another rule of thumb used by the insurance industry was flagging cars that accelerated from 0–60 mph in less than 8 seconds. Meeting any of those three criteria would land you

With the dawn of a new decade, insurance companies and government officials were on the warpath in 1970, working to stamp out Detroit's ever-growing horsepower race. Don Yenko remained determined and resilient, pivoting deftly from his crop of Chevelles and Camaros to craft a new batch of road-going rockets.

Left alone, it was hard to consider Chevy's Nova a serious muscle machine. Unless you stepped up to the factory's hottest version, the SS, which came equipped with an L48 350-ci V-8 boasting 300 hp, the car was seen as nothing more than a gentle grocery getter. Don's ruse was brilliant, substituting in the Corvette and Camaro Z28's LT1 350-ci V-8. That, paired with his racy design touches and performance add-ons, was going to make the Nova fly, both on the street and under the radar of insurance companies. Mark Pieloch owns this one.

a muscle car designation. About 7 to 10 percent of all 1970 cars fell within this definition.

A three-year study of 400,000 cars in 20 states revealed that losses suffered by high-performance cars in accidents were 56 percent higher than for standard vehicles. Collision claims for these muscle cars were 50 percent higher and comprehensive claims 117 percent higher than the average standard-car claim, presumably due to the high rates of theft.

Nationwide Mutual added a 50-percent surcharge on high-powered cars, Allstate Insurance increased rates 20 percent on hot cars, and State Farm Mutual (the nation's largest insurer) added a 25-percent surcharge on polices of 1970 model high-performance and muscle cars. A dry one-liner in a *Chicago Tribune* joke section read a fictional "Jed Smoot has sold his car to raise money to pay the premiums on his auto insurance."

One proponent of the hikes was Ed Daniels, Insurance Exchange general manager of the Michigan Auto Club, who called the muscle machines "motorized missiles." He added, "All law-abiding, safety-minded drivers have at some time been challenged at traffic lights to race with one of them." He went on to say that "when a car has an engine which can attain speeds of 120 or more miles an hour on the road and can accelerate from a standing start to 60 miles an hour in less than eight seconds, it contains elements of danger not possessed by ordinary cars. Combine this with racing stripes; four-on-the-floor gearshifts; big, bulging racing tires; air scoops; spoilers to

hold down the back end; and you have more than transportation. You have an invitation to race to use the street for a drag strip and to forget about safety."

"The only alternative to penalizing performance cars is for the 90 percent of insured club members who don't buy these cars to subsidize insurance costs for the hot car buyer, and we don't think that is fair," wrote Daniels. "These cars are powered far too strongly for the needs of any motorist in any foreseeable circumstance, and far above the capacity of present streets and roads."

In time, insurers would refuse to write new polices on muscle cars, even from already contracted customers, except on an assigned risk, high-cost basis. Money lenders got tough too, becoming more and more reluctant to lend money for muscle car purchases. If they did, they demanded higher down payments.

Muscle Market

Despite these wallet-hitting measures and the strong talk, demand for high-performance cars remained high, or at least as the year started out. Analysts expected the market to continue its trend of growing every year. In 1967, muscle car sales had totaled 350,000 units. By 1970's year end, the market was expected to move 750,000 units. Those high-revving, big-tired wild rides continued to appeal to the youth market, which was a big force. At the time, there were 1.2 million licensed drivers in the United States and 40 percent of them were under 35 years old. The median age of the driver was 28, and by 1973 this would drop to 26.8. Car enthusiasts were on average spending $400 a year on special goodies for their cars, while 17.7 million were attending drag races each year. More than 287,000 competitor entries were filled for drag races, and 43 million tickets were sold to stock, drag, Indy, Trans Am, Can Am, midget, and sprint car races.

Carmakers in Detroit weren't going to change gears and slow down with their offerings, at least not yet. Ford's marketing manager estimated at the beginning of 1970 that 600,000 buyers were ready to "plunk down the price for a true muscle car." The model year boasted a full crop of all-out performers from all of the Big Three. Options abounded from all makes in Detroit. Buyers could select such rumbling examples as the Cougar Eliminator, Mustang Mach 1 and Boss 302, Torino Cobra, Mercury Cyclone, Olds 4-4-2, Chevelle SS396, Camaro SS and Z28, Chargers, Challengers, and Barracudas.

Despite the optimism and marketing spin, the fact remained that buying trends were shifting toward small, compact cars. In time, it would be clear that the muscle car market had dried up. "Once the fastest expanding segment of the automotive market," wrote a *Des Moines Register* October 1971 article, "the muscle car is going the way of fins, foam dice dangling from rearview mirrors, baby moons, and antenna foxtails." Small was in in a big way with 1970 import car sales racing ahead of their 1969 pace. In the

With its massive naval base and constant flow of sailors itching to go fast, Norfolk, Virginia, was one town where hot rods were hotly sought after. This Forest Green Deuce was sold new there, at Colonial Chevrolet. All through the 1970s, it stayed near the port in the Virginia Beach area, passing through the hands of several Navy men. It now belongs to Yenko historian Joe Barr.

first nine months of 1970, 903,143 imported cars had been sold, breaking the old 1969 mark of 753,647 from January 1 to October 1. Volkswagen was leading the charge, dominating the growing market with 430,340 vehicles sold in the United States which was up from a year prior, with 368,715 sold in 1969. Their advertising message was even "Think small" and it was clearly resonating with shoppers.

Designing the Deuce

It was a precarious time for high-power cars, but determined Don Yenko was still willing to wade out into the waters of uncertainty to build something new. Knowing driver's wallets were being pinched, if not emptied, with the new insurance mandates and watching market trends, Don stopped going down his usual route of stuffing big-block engines into his COPO cars. That play wouldn't work anymore, as Chevrolet began offering their LS6 454-ci V-8 in the Chevelle, and it was slated to be installed in the Camaro too but never made it to production.

Don had his work cut out for him with this new vehicle, but to do it right, it'd have to be a careful balanc-

ing act. On the one hand, he had to create something hot and high-spirited, catching the eye of the octane-fueled band of youngsters still prowling the streets looking for a race. On the other, it'd have to be sedate enough to be overlooked by eagle-eyed insurance agents and wary money lenders everywhere. To pull off this feat, he looked to Chevrolet's compact-sized Nova.

The Super Nova

Don wasn't new to modifying the model. In 1969, he built a handful of Super Novas, going the exact opposite direction in his approach. Things had changed drastically in just 12 months. Back then, he kept up with his Camaro and Chevelle theme, stuffing a L72 427-ci V-8 under the hood. While he wanted a trifecta of COPO-created cars, Chevrolet balked at his third request. There's debate as to why, but for one reason or another, Chevrolet turned him down on allowing the L72 427-ci V-8 to be installed in the Novas on the factory floor.

That didn't stop Don. Just as he had in 1968 with his Camaros, he took 28 Nova Super Sports equipped with the 396-ci L78 big-block and swapped in 427 short-blocks. Like the other 1969 cars, the Novas then received side striping, hood graphics, and Yenko badging. Inside, sYc stickers were

The third time wasn't the charm for Don, who just couldn't get Chevrolet to comply with his wishes to process his 1969 Nova through the Central Office. Still, when Don was through with them, the road-going rockets would clean the clock of any stoplight contender. To separate the modified cars from Chevy's own performance package, the center SS badge in the grille was removed.

The modified Novas fit in nicely with Don's lineup for 1969, matching their Chevelle and Camaro sYc counterparts. The factory-installed, center SS badging was removed and exchanged for a Yenko crest and 427 badge.

No one knows for sure why Chevrolet turned down Don's request to have an L72 427-ci V-8 installed on the assembly line at the factory. That rejection wasn't going to slow him down and, upon hearing the news, Don had his techs do what they already had been doing on Camaro: swap in 427 short-blocks into the L78 big-block. Two have been confirmed as receiving the treatment, with evidence to suggest perhaps a couple more also received the 427s.

The formula for the interior remained simple and straightforward: screw in a tach on the dash and mount a lower gauge cluster and call it a day.

The only form of Yenko branding inside the cabin came in the form of the white sYc stickers applied to both headrests on the front bench seat.

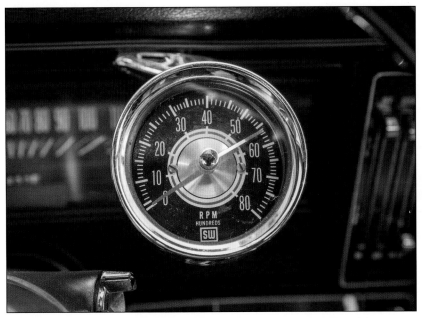

The Stewart Warner tach was a great add-on, especially for drivers who liked to mash the gas. With a ground-shaking 427 under the hood, more than likely that was every single driver. When it came time to craft his 1970 Nova, Don designed a way to raise it a few inches, making it even easier for leadfoots to read.

The Nova's sYc hood stickers required an extra step not needed on the 1969 Camaro or Chevelle. While the center of those hoods was flat, the SS came with a special hood, complete with twin simulated air-intakes. Yenko technicians had to carefully affix the stickers around these dress-up chrome rectangles that added no go but were just for show.

A 1969 Yenko Nova is strapped to the top deck of the Yenko transport truck, along with other prepared Camaros and Chevelles, and is ready for delivery. (Photo Courtesy the Barr Collection)

confused the two cars, he gave this 1970 Nova a different name, calling it the Deuce. When asked why, Don claimed he was just being hip and keeping with the times. "We're just using the name that the kids have been calling it [the Nova model] all along," said Don, referring to how the Nova came from the moniker of the Chevy II.

Frankly, his move didn't catch anyone off guard. When he debuted the car early in the summer of 1970, the *Wausau Daily Herald* acknowledged Don was "yielding to the insurance company squeeze on large engines," seeing right away what he was up to. The mainstream move away from big muscle cars got so dire, Don even canceled an order of 1969 COPO Camaros due to slowing sales and fading interest.

Creating the COPO

For 1970, Chevrolet offered the Nova in three different flavors: coupe, sedan, and the performance-oriented Nova SS package, which was only available on the coupe body style. Being an economy car, Chevrolet didn't offer a lot of preset trims, choosing instead to have buyers pick out assorted options that they wanted on their ride. "Isn't that better than our trying to second-guess what you like?" Chevy asked in an ad.

That worked for Don, who was going to pick out what he wanted on his Novas either way. In a departure from his normal protocol, when he ordered his batch of cars, he didn't order them as Super Sports like he did with his Camaros and Chevelles. Instead, he marked them to be standard coupes, stripped down and lightweight; then, using his COPO connections, he had them equipped with the go-fast goodies from RPO Z26 (the Super Sport package) but with none of the badging or dress-up items. Besides a host of cosmetic upgrades, such as a blacked-out grille with SS badging, black-accentuated rear panel, simulated hood air-intakes, and fender louvers with bright accents, the SS package brought disc brakes and a host of suspension upgrades (RPO F40 and F41). They consisted of stiffer spring rates, a larger front sway bar, performance-oriented shocks, and a rear sway bar.

applied on the headrests and some extra gauging was installed. The cars came with a full factory drivetrain warranty for 90 days or 4,000 miles. An additional eight Nova SSs were sold with factory-installed L78 396s and Yenko cosmetic tweaks.

Whether you picked a Nova with 427 or 396 power, both were downright fast, but with this new Nova venture, Don wisely tried a different tactic that was tailored to the current economic climate. To make sure no one

Somewhere around a couple dozen of 1969 Novas didn't get the 427-ci engine installed by Don's team, being sold with the factory 396/375 engine left under the hood. The COPO ordering process wasn't being used this year en masse on the Novas, but a few did have some Central Office tweaks. This example was special ordered through a COPO so it could be painted Nutmeg Brown Firemist, a Cadillac color. It also had the rear end swapped to 4.10:1 under a COPO. Mark Pieloch owns this one.

COPO 9010

Don's batch of vehicles was equipped with stiffer front coil springs (coded EL) and rear five-leaf springs (coded BK) under RPO F62 and RPO G32. Front disc brakes (RPO JL2) were installed, which were vacuum powered (RPO J50). Underhood, the cars marked on the build sheet as getting the RPO L65 350-ci V-8 engine with a 2-barrel carburetor. Farther down on the

The Nova's engine bay had no trouble accepting the high-output LT1 engine. The engine's factory-installed valve covers had a semi-dull aluminum finish, just like these, whereas over-the-counter GM replacements and current reproductions are highly polished and shiny.

All Yenko Deuces received Hurst one-piece black knobs atop the handles. As part of their Day Two modifications, many drivers soon swapped them out for the classic cue-ball white knobs or T-handles. Don threw folks for a loop using the Hurst AutoStick and relocating the shifter to the floorboard. Automatic-equipped Novas with the bench seat were only available with a column shift. Anyone walking by who peeked in would automatically think the car had a manual and was set up to go.

list, however, COPO 9010 sneakily exchanged it for an LT1 350-ci V-8, good for 360 hp. The small-block engine was new for 1970 and used in Camaro Z28s and Corvettes. It was built for high performance, featuring solid lifters, forged pistons, four-bolt main caps, a steel crank, and an aluminum high-rise manifold. Its 360-hp output was the highest horsepower rating available in a Chevy small-block. When equipped with a 4-speed, the engine was stamped CTB. Paired to the TH400, it was stamped CTC.

The cars came equipped with dual-exhaust (RPO N10) and a heavy-duty cooling system that was comprised of a three-core radiator and a clutch fan, which was used on the Novas with an air conditioner. Vehicles equipped with the automatic transmission, which had provision for transmission cooling lines, had a stamped tag on the radiator showing VR while VK was used for the radiators on the 4-speed transmission–equipped cars. Either tag can be found on a stamped metal plate affixed on the passenger's side of the radiator.

Available transmissions included a close-ratio 4-speed M21 manual that was stamped B. It came with a special curved Hurst shifter, bent to wrap up and around the seat for easy access, topped off with a black ball knob with white lettering. The handle was borrowed from the Pontiac parts bin, where it was installed on bench-seat equipped Pontiac GTOs. The other transmission was the TH400 3-speed automatic transmission, which was shipped to Yenko with the gear selector on the column. These received a stamping of CW.

COPO 9737

The Novas also received COPO 9737 for the Sports Car Chassis Conversion Package, which Don advertised as being a "custom-designed Trans Am Suspension." It added upgraded, heavy-duty suspension components. As part of RPO F41, which was only available in the SS package, the cars got a front 13/16-inch sway bar and a three-piece 5/8-inch rear anti-sway bar and specially valved AC Delco shock absorbers. The rear differential (stamped CBW) got a heat-treated 4.10:1 heavy-duty, 12-bolt Positraction rear axle, which was a feature not found in any other Nova than a Deuce. It was the same unit found on the COPO 1969 Camaros and Chevelles. At each corner, E-70x14 whitestripe tires were fitted to body-color painted XT steel wheels with hubcaps.

Inside the cabin, all the COPO Novas were ordered the same. They all got black interiors, an AM pushbutton radio (RPO U63), a windshield antenna (RPO U76), and the special interior group package (RPO ZJ3). This included bright trim on the brake, accelerator, and parking brake pedals; additional bright framing on the instrument cluster; a glove box light; a right front doorjamb dome switch; satin finish on the rearview mirror; and bright dome lamp bezel. The Deuces, being standard cars, didn't receive carpeting, instead they received a rubber floor covering.

"(It's) sort of a stroked Trans Am power," said Yenko, adding, "and it's not just an engine dropped in a standard car. The Deuce is engineered for high performance from the radiator to the rear suspension."

Ordering the Novas

This all-original interior shows just how the COPO Novas would have left the Chevrolet factory before the various Yenko accessories were installed. The Spartan cabin is utilitarian and all-business, built for straight-line speed. There's no frills or creature comforts, apart from the AM radio. With the tach moved up to the hood and more in the driver's line of sight, leadfoots had an easier time monitoring the road and their engine's RPM.

Don ordered his Novas in two different batches, together totaling 175 vehicles. The first order for 125 cars was placed on December 16, 1969. All of the cars were built in three consecutive weeks but not until the fourth week of May and the first and second weeks of June. The multi-month delay could most likely be attributed to a GM labor strike.

This initial run came in five sets of 25. Each set received a different exterior paint color from Chevy's pallet of factory colors; there was Cortez Silver, Gobi Beige, Forest Green, Fathom Blue, and Cranberry Red. Each color had the same transmission and power steering option breakdown within each set of 25: 15 were 4-speeds, 2 were 4-speeds with power steering, 4 were automatics, and 4 were automatics with power steering. The cars were received at Yenko Chevrolet on June 8, 1970, and were then shipped out to participating dealers on June 15, 1970.

The exact date when Don ordered the second batch of 50 Novas isn't known. It was late enough in the year for him to be able to incorporate the new spring colors that had become available in early 1970 for the Nova. This next set of 50 vehicles came in equal sets of 10 for the 5 colors that were available: Cranberry Red, Fathom Blue, Sunflower Yellow, Citrus Green, and Hugger Orange. The latter three were the new spring colors. The transmission and power steering options weren't as clear cut and neat. All of the color sets received roughly the same distributed amount: six or seven were

Don ordered 35 COPO Novas painted in Cranberry Red. After getting converted to Deuce form in Canonsburg, this one and several others were shipped to V. V. Cooke Chevrolet in Louisville, Kentucky, which was well known for its speed offerings. The dealership would do such promotions as hosting a "High-Performance Week" in December 1970. Spectators could come in and see the store's championship-sponsored oval track and road race cars, as well as attend a free racing clinic with "Mr. Chevrolet" Dick Harrell.

Chevrolet offered these exact wheels on the Nova SS, calling them Sport Wheels. Even though General Motors had worked with Don on the Deuce's COPO, he couldn't help but circumvent their relationship to seek out a cheaper deal. By directly calling Motor Wheel, the wheel supplier, directly, he was able to negotiate a lower price on his order of 175 sets. The font of the center cap Y matches the font of the interior door panel and side stripes.

built with 4-speeds, one was a 4-speed with power steering, and either two or three were automatics with power steering.

Canonsburg Changes

As with all his products, once the cars were delivered to Canonsburg, Don and his team went to work, performing additional modifications and adding on customer-requested options.

Magnum Wheels

One visual change to the Deuce was with the wheels. The vehicles arrived from the factory with body-color painted two-piece stamped-steel 14x7 Code XT wheels. Prior to the cars coming, Don ordered new sets of wheels for all incoming 175 Novas. He went with 14 x 7 Magnum 500 Custom Super Sport style wheels in a magnesium gray finish with blackout pockets, buying them directly from the Motor Wheel Corporation in Lansing, Michigan.

The company advertised that a set of four rang up at $79.95, but no doubt Don got a deal, given the large quantity purchased. These same wheels could be optioned on Nova SS coupes, but in Chevy literature, they were listed as 14x7 Sport Wheels. In reality, they're the exact same wheels as

the 500s. One difference is that when ordered as an option from Chevrolet, they included deep inset trim rings. Some original owners liked that look so much they ordered the rings from the dealership's parts department to put on and dress up their Deuces themselves. Motor Wheel stamped all the wheels whether as Sport Wheels on Nova SS cars or Magnums on Deuces with Code AO.

Because of the abundance of work, Don hired a local repair shop across the street from the dealership to do all the wheel and tire swapping. To save costs, Don only ordered four wheels per car from Motor Wheel; choosing to leave the painted XT spare inside the trunk, complete with its original whitestripe tire. The quickly growing stack of leftover painted XT wheels was thrown in a pile behind the dealership and nicknamed the "rainbow," as they had the bright Nova colors of yellow, green, red, blue, and orange. It's not clear how Don got rid of them, but it's likely many of them were mounted with snow tires and sold to customers for winter driving.

The new wheels had a center cap bearing a red circle behind crossed flags, wrapped with the text "Magnum 500." Don had foil Y decals made that his team fitted directly over the factory decals. The design was different than previous wheel caps, such as the one used on the 1968 Yenko Camaro. For the Deuce, it was a silver Mylar Y with serifs on a simple black background. Because the Magnum's logo was embossed, on original Deuce wheels you can still see it under the thin foil Yenko decal. Lastly, the XT's open-ended steel nuts were swapped for chrome lugnuts to dress up the Magnum 500s. On pricing sheets, Don listed the wheels as being "SS," saying they included Yenko hubs. The wheels would have retained the factory whitestripe tires, but in the spirit of Day Two modification, many enthusiasts swapped them out soon after buying their Deuces.

Wheel Options

Deuce buyers could select two optional wheel designs, readily seen on page 18 in the Stinger*Stuff HI-PO parts catalog that Don rolled out in 1971. There was his Yenko Atlas, available in both 14x6 and 15x8 sizes, and cast-in aluminum, which Don had been offering since 1968. The Atlas center cap, with "Aa" font above crossed checkered racing flags, would still be covered up by a white sticker showing a Yenko crest. Atlas wheels ended up being a rare option, with few Deuces receiving them.

The Motor Wheel's unique Spyder wheel was the other option, and it had a polished and etched aluminum center cap with a triple-plated steel rim and a chrome-plated bullet cap surrounded by a black recessed wheel center. The choice of including the wheel in the Yenko catalog as an option for sYc cars was quite peculiar. With all of the dozens of aftermarket wheel companies that existed, Don certainly had his pick of wheel design to include. More well-known styles, such as Cragar's S/S or Keystone Klassics, would have been more popular with enthusiasts. While its certainly possible Don liked the unique Spyders, it's more likely that because

The automotive aftermarket industry was booming in 1970, with speed parts of all kinds being made available to hot rodders. Despite a clever ad campaign involving a provocative Miss Muffet playing off the nursery rhyme about arachnids, these Motor Wheel Spyders weren't the most popular choice. Don still offered them in his catalog, probably because of a discount deal worked out after the large quantity of Magnums he ordered.

The hood-mounted tach was a departure for the Yenko team. Up to that point, Don had his team mount an aftermarket tach behind the steering wheel, screwing it directly into the dash. On the Deuce, it was moved out onto the hood, which was becoming all the rage for race-ready muscle cars. Naturally, brand-minded Don made sure the Yenko crest made its way onto the face of the gauge.

of his large purchase of Motor Wheel's Magnum, some kind of backdoor deal or discount was worked out for him to offer them. Few buyers ended up purchasing them.

Dixco Hood Tach

On the Deuce's hood, a Dixco HT/x hood tach in a glossy black housing was installed. Dixco advertised it mounted in minutes, only requiring one 3/4-inch hole to be drilled into a car's hood. However, some Deuces left with three holes drilled through their hoods. The tachs came with a "unique locking method" for theft protection, which amounted to two additional pins on either side of the center stud. This prevented dubious passersby from twisting off the piece. If a Yenko tech decided to use them, two more 1/8-inch holes had to be drilled into the hood for them to drop in to.

The tach's face was internally illuminated, and there was an adjustable set pointer for RPM control. Switching to the Dixco brand was a departure for Don, who had typically sourced the gauges for his car creations from Stewart Warner. The Deuce's hood tach was made by Dixson Inc. an aftermarket parts supplier out of Grand Junction, Colorado. It was offered as an over-the-counter upgrade for high-performance Fords and Chrysler vehicles. For each respective customer, Dixco embossed company logos in the center of the housing on the front, facing the driver. They did Ford's oval

and Chrysler's Pentastar and, for the Deuces, they did the same, embossing the Yenko crest on the front.

Deuce Dress-Up Items

Automatic-equipped Deuces with the column-mounted selector had it removed. Technicians would pop a pin in the column to remove the lever, leaving the hole gaping and exposed. Next, they would install the floor-mounted Hurst AutoStick and bezel. The unit mimics a 4-speed, boasting a chrome bezel; rubber boot; curved, polished handle; and black shift knob with white lettering. To the casual passerby, it would appear to be a manual transmission; the only two giveaways being two pedals in the driver's footwell instead of three and the automatic shift pattern on the knob.

Ever the marketer, Don dressed up the Deuce to attract attention while cruising the streets and pounding the strips. Red, white, and blue Yenko crest emblems were installed on the front fenders, but instead of requiring drilling and guide pins, they were adhered with double-sided tape. Around back, the factory Nova badge on the right rear corner of the trunklid was removed and its two mounting holes were covered by another colored Yenko crest, also held on by double-sided tape.

The exterior body stripe stickers with YENKO Deuce lettering cut out on the rear quarter panels were applied by area body shops and sometimes

In typical fashion, Don had any kind of factory model designation removed so buyers would consider the car his creation. On the trunklid, the factory Nova badge was removed and its two mounting holes were covered by a red, white, and blue Yenko crest. This one shows some wear and fading, as it should; it's all original.

An easily identifiable aspect of the Deuces was the side stripes, which ran the length of the vehicle before gracefully wrapping up and over the rear fender, widening then narrowing to flow down to the center of the decklid. There's a lot of similarities between the design and the Mustang Boss 302, which featured nearly the same configuration, only they were inverted to flow from the center of the hood and then out and down the front fenders. An ad from Yenko Sportscars for the Deuce featured a one-off Deuce mimicking that. Someone had modified the side stripes to poke fun at Ford's hopped-up pony car.

Even today, the twin hood stripes have a contemporary look and feel. They're aesthetically pleasing, following the hood lines, and the LT1 design has all the makings of a factory performance graphic. That kind of creativity seemed to run out on the center Deuce lettering. Whereas the quarter panels and door panels got groovy, far-out fonts, here it's purely functional. The LT1 lettering was mounted either slanting in toward the cowl as seen in the image to the right, or out, as in this example.

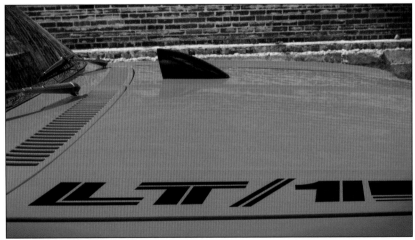

While Don knew the engine's air cleaner "360 horsepower" sticker would be an immediate red flag, he felt fairly confident the massive LT1 callout would fly over the heads of insurance agents and cautious parents everywhere. The theme would have carried nicely over to the front fenders with the custom badges, but ultimately Don decided to leave them off. This Deuce has the LT1 lettering following the line of the rear edge of the cowl, which looks more cohesive but the stickers were stuck on like this or slanted out.

Don tried something new with the interior of the Deuce's cabin, having his technicians adhere Mylar trim bars to both door panels. No sYc lettering was stuck onto the seat headrests and no Yenko crests were added anywhere either.

Don loved his stickers, but on the Deuce he took the time to make sure one was removed. Before the cars were shipped off, techs would take a razor blade and slice off the bottom portion of the factory air cleaner sticker, detaching the part that said "360 Horsepower."

local hired kids. They included a full-length side spear that wrapped up onto the decklid and then met in the middle at the bumper. In profile, they mimic hockey sticks and are sometimes called that. The hood also received twin stripes with LT-1 lettering. The stripes were consistently one color for each paint color. The exception was Citrus Green, which could come in either white or black.

Simple deuce lettering was placed in the middle of the hood, calling out the special muscle machine. Inside the cabin, Mylar trim bars with the wording "Yenko Deuce" were adhered to the inside of both door panels. Unlike prior years, no headrest sYc decals were installed.

While typical protocol for Don's team was to add stickers to his products, the Deuce had one removed. Underhood, the LT1's output rating sticker of 360 hp on the air cleaner was modified. Using a razor blade, workers at the dealership would slice off the lower portion of the sticker to obscure any hint of what the LT1 was truly capable of, fooling any snooping insurance agent or cautious parent. Scratch marks are sometimes evident in the air cleaner covers of unrestored, original vehicles.

Due to the compressed schedule and time-intensive work, the second batch of cars received their Deuce touches by Hurst at their facility in Michigan. These 50 cars had an H prefix attached to their stock numbers. An interesting note; all the Deuces painted in the spring colors were converted by Hurst.

The influx of hot inventory attracted the attention of some shifty characters who would try to nab parts in the wee hours of the morning. The problem became so bad Don hired Jim Buckels to sit in his car with a shotgun across

his lap across the street from the dealership all night, keeping a watchful eye on the Deuces. Those long overnight hours were taxing, and Buckels had the habit of becoming drowsy and falling asleep. To help him in his duties, Don got him a guard dog. One morning, Donna Mae and Don came to work to find a Deuce that had its entire engine removed. Donna recalls finding paw prints on the fender, figuring their K-9 sentry was "apparently intrigued by the engine removal" and had moved in closer to happily watch. On another occasion, she recalls coming into work and finding the dog missing entirely.

The 6-Cylinder Deuce

Wanting to get the word out about his new Nova but not wanting to wait until his first batch of COPOs came in, Don grabbed a single bare-bones Fathom Blue 1970 Nova from the lot and dressed it up in Deuce form sometime in early spring of 1970. Whereas all 175 COPO Novas had black interiors, this mock-up had a light blue interior. Every Nova received badging on the front fenders above the orange marker lights, calling out the engine size. To keep the ruse secret, Don's team removed the "250" numeral badging and actually left it blank, leaving the alignment pin holes visible.

A set of the 14x7 Sport Wheels that were only available on SS coupes were installed on white-lettered tires, which were more in style with the hot rod and Day Two scene. As one original owner who quickly swapped out his original set of tires said, "whitewalls were [for] older folks." Pictures of the 6-cylinder mock-up car in ads threw restorers and enthusi-

A prototype of Dixco's power dome hood accessory was mounted on the promo Nova. It lacked air inlets and, for the most part, was purely dress-up. Note above the marker light, the two holes where the 250 engine call-out badge was mounted. (Photo Courtesy the Barr Collection)

Evident through the windows is the promo Deuce's light blue interior instead of the COPO Nova's black interior. The car also still wears its factory-installed painted 6-inch-wide steel wheels and dog dish hubcaps. These were swapped out for Magnum 500 wheels. (Photo Courtesy the Barr Collection)

The promo Nova was hurriedly transformed into Deuce form and rushed out for this photoshoot before technicians realized they forgot to remove the black and chrome Yenko crest from the left side of the trunklid. It was quickly popped off and the shoot resumed. Just visible through the windshield is the automatic's column shift lever, indicating the car never received the Hurst AutoStick modification. (Photo Courtesy the Barr Collection)

The double Yenko crest gaff was caught and remedied. The Magnum 500 wheels have also been installed along with Goodyear white-lettered tires. The promo car also got the bullet sport mirrors. (Photo Courtesy the Barr Collection)

asts for a loop; they assumed all Deuces were delivered from the factory with white-lettered tires, leading to them becoming accepted as correct on restored cars.

Another anomaly was twin Yenko crest badges on the back at least for a period. On the left, the standard black and chrome crest that most cars Don's team sold wore remained, as this Nova wasn't destined for high-performance purposes. When it was pulled and converted, the technicians also slapped on the traditional Yenko Supercar crest on the trunklid and, for a while, it wore both. It was the same design and badge but painted red, white, and blue. Later ads show pictures with the silver crest removed, matching how the rest of the Deuce lineup looked. The car also had some of the planned options mounted to it, like the boxy hood scoop and the bullet-shaped, Talbot-style rearview mirrors in flat black.

When it was completed, the dressed-up car was used for promotional purposes and photography. It was used in many marketing campaigns, including the often-used "Mini Muscle" ad promotions. Keeping the car's true identify a secret wasn't easy. Yenko technician Warren Dernoshek experienced one awkward trip to a local gas station to refuel. Some local kids saw the car and eagerly approached it, dying to see what was under the hood. Not wanting to give away anything, Dernoshek kept it closed but had to wait until the kids got bored and finally went away before returning to the dealership. Going one step further, he waited until they were out of earshot before starting the vehicle up, knowing the 6-cylinder's sound would give it away.

LT1 Fender Badge

Sometime that summer of 1970, Don had planned on creating and including custom LT1 emblems on the Deuce. The look was simple black rectangles with LT1 sans-serif lettering in the middle, surrounded by a chrome edge. They were to be mounted on the front fenders above the marker lights. Grayard Co. from Brooklyn, New York, was contracted to make the batch.

On September 11, 1970, Donna Mae asked for an update and was told they were to be shipped on September 17. On October 15, 1970, Donna called and completely canceled the order, but it was too late. The badging came into the Yenko dealership but was never put on the vehicles. Here's why: Besides being so late in the year, Don had been thrown for a loop when the COPO Novas arrived in his lot. He was expecting them to mimic his batch of 1969 COPO Camaros and COPO Chevelles that all had the SS trim and badging deleted. Because of the special nature of the COPO order, Don hadn't planned for the factory to include the "350" fender badges. He was expecting nothing to be mounted above the light. This is evidenced on the 6-cylinder mock-up Deuce that, for the publicity photoshoot, had its fender badges removed.

The LT1 badges were simple and straightforward but, ultimately, deemed unnecessary. The factory-installed 350 badge lettering was not only accurate, but also three-dimensional and more attractive with its white and chrome motif. It made the most sense to streamline the Deuce-conversion process and leave them on. Several pairs of the LT1 badges turned up in Deuce glove boxes or were kept by technicians.

Don assumed his COPO Novas would arrive without badging and with no holes drilled into the fenders. He was hoping to have his team in the back shop slap these special LT1 badges on with adhesive tape. When the transport truck dropped the Novas off and he saw the cars' 350 fender badging still on, he made the decision to save time and energy and not remove them. They were accurate after all. Underhood was indeed a 350-ci V-8, just not the one that everyone thought it was. Not sure what to do with the custom-crafted LT1 badging, some technicians threw them into the glove boxes of Deuces for new owners to enjoy while others kept them around the shop or in their toolboxes.

Deuce Pricing and Options

The completed Deuce retailed for $3,993, but Don, always thinking, offered a plethora of options. All told, if a buyer loaded up his or her car, the price would ring up at $4,360.50. Options available included power steering ($90); a pair of trendy bullet-style Sport mirrors so large that they prevented the wing windows from fully opening ($20); a lighted tri-gauge instrument package made by Dixco, like the hood tach, and part of the Hustler series containing water temp, oil pressure, and ammeter gauges ($60); and a special three-spoke sport steering wheel ($59.95). In a June 13, 1970, pricing sheet, the mirrors, gauges, and steering wheel got a special callout, with Don saying they were "an excellent aftermarket for <u>all</u>

The optional, chunky steering wheel reminded Don of his days racing, and he felt that when drivers wrapped their fingers around it, it would give the Deuce a sporty feel. It was significantly larger than the stock steering wheel, which was dainty and thin by comparison.

The most understated of the exterior paint colors offered on the Deuce was Gobi Beige. It was a hard hue to love, especially on something performance-oriented, leading Don to not include it in his second order of COPO Novas.

Novas." The steering wheel was a GM over-the-counter part. It was used as a production piece on the rare 1970 Buick GSX, boasting a chubby foam outer grip. In an age when steering wheels were thin and dainty, the chunky style looked racy and performance-oriented. Don liked the look of it as it was similar to Corvette steering wheels and ordered hundreds of them, initially wanting them to be a standard option on all the Deuces. As the story goes, en route to the dealership, the parts truck delivering the order was involved in a serious collision, damaging a majority of the steering wheels. Don collected what was salvageable and sold the remaining pieces as options to Deuce owners. They didn't take off as well as he wanted, and he had steering wheels in stock through the 1980s. It's rumored he would occasionally give one out to Yenko Supercar owners coming into the dealership for service.

Two other options were initially planned for the Deuce but never fully rolled out. There was a pair of side-by-side rear, adjustable spoilers made by California Custom Accessories, based in Gardena, California. They looked like air flaps and Don advertised it as "an exclusive design that bolted on and was flush fit," even though the company stated they would fit any car and distributed them through speed shops and auto parts dealers for about $15. The second option was a boxy hood scoop/power dome, similar to the ones used on AMC's Rebel Machine and the Jeep Commando Hurst Special Edition. Dixco was going to be manufacturing them for Yenko, but its rumored issues arose, causing them to abandon the project. The unit featured an integrated lighted tach and a prototype was installed on the blue 6-cylinder promo car.

Selling the Deuce

Overall, the Deuce seemed to be just the ticket to fit the current climate. The car came with a full factory five-year warranty and was advertised as being easy to insure and a gas saver that (with slight exaggeration) packed enough room for the whole gang plus all the luggage space in the world.

Ads for the Deuce ran, stating "Tired of outrageous insurance costs on your HI-PO car? See the '70 1/2 Yenko Deuce!" and "Worried about the '71 Horsepower drought? Buy a '70 1/2 Yenko Deuce with an LT-1 high compression engine—and the performance you paid for!" One that must have been penned when Don or Donna must have been feeling particularly poetic read: "The last of the Red Hot Novas! In Seventy-one the 396 is 23 Skiddoo, 350–275 is the best you can do, Hi-Compression is goodie gone goodbye. Seventy-One Prices will be really high, warranty's going down and insurance is sky high!"

The clever rhymes and marketing worked, at least initially. Once the first group of cars were completed, they were sold and shipped off fairly quickly as the model year end drew ever closer. Don's well-established network of participating dealers paid off; by this time, it included a total of 50 Chevy stores spanning the East Coast and Midwest.

A minimum order quantity of three cars was put in place so that the delivery trucks left Yenko's dealership full, even if that meant multiple dealers in the same area had to combine orders. Donna Mae sent out a bulletin to all the Yenko Sports Cars dealers on August 12, 1970, reporting good news about the Deuce. After speaking with several dealers, she found that

Original Owner: Ken and Becky Schoenthaler

Ken Schoenthaler bought himself a brand-new Nova but it wasn't a Deuce, at least not to start with. In April 1970, the young man ordered a Fathom Blue L78 396-ci V-8 Nova from Burhy Chevrolet in Ox, Iowa. It finally arrived in late July, and he enjoyed the heck out of it until it blew up; quite literally. He was living in Davenport and attending an auto body shop course at the Iowa Community College. While he had zero plans to upgrade, swap, or sell the car, there was a night when his curiosity was piqued. He was out on his apartment balcony a few months later when a Fathom Blue Yenko Deuce rumbled through the parking lot below. It was the first one he had ever seen. "As it slowly cruised by, I was thinking, 'That thing is just bad-ass cool,'" remembers Schoenthaler.

That wasn't his first introduction to the Yenko mystique. He certainly knew about them and, more importantly, just what they could do. "The Yenkos were a bit of an urban legend around those parts," recalls Schoenthaler. "They were just that god-awful fast." Schoenthaler remembers hearing rumors of a green Yenko Camaro in Cedar Rapids that was simply "baddest thing that ran the streets." That firsthand balcony experience was reinforced with an ad for the Deuce he saw in the *Cedar Brook Gazette*. Rapids Chevrolet touted they had a new lot of Deuces "HOT off the transport," showing a picture of them being unloaded off the truck.

While the 17-year-old enthusiast wasn't thinking of getting one, that changed a few weeks later in January 1971. While motoring down a

Like a lot of young buyers, original owner Ken Schoenthaler upgraded to his Sunflower Yellow Deuce from an L78-equipped Nova. "The car was okay," said Schoenthaler. "But it wasn't as fast as I thought." An icy road brought an end to the vehicle; the odometer showing fewer than 5,000 miles. The car was totaled, but Schoenthaler escaped the accident unscathed, save for having to get two stitches.

The upgrade from L78 to LT1 paid off for Schoenthaler. "It was fast right out of the box," said Schoenthaler. "I rarely got beat on the street. The power to weight ratio was extremely good. During that time frame, your car was everything and who you were. Although for a long time I never fully knew what the Deuce was or the story behind it."

wintry country road, Schoenthaler came around a small curve, slid, and smacked right into a bridge, totaling the car. "I had studded snow tires on the car and I dropped the right rear wheel off the pavement, onto gravel." A friend in a car behind him saw everything unfold. "He told me the axle shaft dropped out of the housing and the car started sliding." Schoenthaler

escaped the wreckage right before the Nova burst into flames. He was banged up, but thankfully just in need of a couple stitches. In no time, he was thinking of what to do about his ride. "I had no recourse," he said, adding, "I couldn't go back and order another big-block; Chevy had stopped making them." Sitting around his apartment, he kept staring at that Deuce ad, which he had held on to. "I said to my roommate, 'I wonder if the dealership has any left,'" said Schoenthaler.

The next week, he and that buddy were cruising over to Rapids Chevrolet to find out. The dealership had gotten a whole truckload but was down to two remaining models: a Sunflower Yellow and a Gobi Beige example. "They fired up the yellow one, which was manual," said Schoenthaler. "It was real cool, and yellow looked better than beige."

Taking his insurance money and a borrowed sum from his grandmother, Schoenthaler went back the next week with his dad and made

Ken and Becky Schoenthaler have enjoyed and cherished their decades-long ownership of their Deuce. "From the moment I saw it, I knew it was fast," recalls Becky. "I was sure he going to race it." Schoenthaler reached out to Don on several occasions after buying the hot car, writing him letters. He even purchased a Yenko crest patch and had Becky sew it on his trusty jean jacket.

the purchase. The car rang up at $4,650.90, a hefty sum for the young man. "We drove off the dealership and on the first turn out of the lot the car went sideways," recalls Schoenthaler. "It was that much more of a handful [than the L78]," said Schoenthaler. "Out of the box, it was flat out fast." Just like Yenko had envisioned, the car was potent but never raised any flags with the insurance companies. "With the 396 SS I was paying 97 cents a day for insurance," said Ken. "The rates went down with the Yenko."

Back home, his first stop was heading to his girlfriend's house. "I remember looking out the window when he first pulled up," recalls Becky. "It was noisy and I didn't know if I was ready for a boyfriend with a bright yellow with black stripe bumblebee–looking car. But he was happy and that's all that mattered."

While insuring it was a breeze, it wasn't as easy getting all that power to the ground. He did have a lot of time to practice. "Back then, every stoplight was a drag race," recalls Schoenthaler. "Everyone was up for a run. One night, a full family pulled up next to me in a 396 Impala station wagon. The light changed and we were off." Schoenthaler remembers another intersection showdown in downtown Davenport, a favorite hangout for muscle machines. "There was an AMX with dual quads on my left and a Torino Cobra Jet on my right," he said. "The light was getting ready to turn and all hell was going to break loose. Then a sheriff deputy came up behind us and things got real quiet. We all turned off and went home in different directions."

Not all the memories made with Yenko were made running all out. Schoenthaler drove the car to his college classes and through one nasty winter. "Coming home from Cedar Rapids I got caught in a snowstorm," said Schoenthaler. "It was the most useless vehicle in those conditions. If you kicked the clutch, the rear end locked up. I tried everything I could to come home in neutral." Ken and Becky got married on October 9, 1971, and made sure to lock the car away in their garage so no wedding-goers shaving-creamed the car or worse.

Not long after, the couple headed to Schoenthaler's brother's farm, where they installed bright orange Super Mufflers dual side exhaust on the car. On the way home, Schoenthaler couldn't help but get on it for a test run, which caused another unexpected reaction: Becky going into labor. "We were coming up to a bridge where we raced often. We knew it was a quarter-mile stretch," said Becky. "Ken punched the gas and everything inside of me just went down. Our son was born that night."

Another memorable high-octane night was running a 1966 Chevelle painted red with fish scales and packing a 427. The Miller brothers owned the car, and Schoenthaler remembers it stood out with lights on the dash that beat to music. "I had been looking for this guy for a while. I happened to catch him one night at a light. I pop up next to him and he reaches into his glove box for his shifter glove, which he then put on," said Schoenthaler. "We were supposed to have date night," recalls Becky. "But once we saw the other car, Ken told me to make sure I was buckled up. I pulled it tight and closed my eyes." The light changed and the two rumbling cars roared off, racing down past the Col Ballroom. During the run, the dual side exhaust broke, but only under Becky's side. The muffler started smacking the underside of the car, adding to her nerve-wrecking experience. "The Yenko outran him and, boy was he pissed," recalls Becky. "Most people never had a clue about the car. They saw the 350 emblems and figured it was no contest. That changed once we got out there on the open road." The key, though, was traction. "You had to get it on the ground. Otherwise, something with a whole lot less horsepower

Schoenthaler played guitar in a band and met Becky through her roommate, Nancy. One warm afternoon in July 1971, Schoenthaler headed to Becky's home to meet her parents for the first time. Wanting to capture their daughter's blossoming love, they couldn't help but snap this shot of the couple perched atop Ken's rolling pride and joy. (Photo Courtesy the Schoenthalers)

would run all over you. As teens, we all thought we were bulletproof. I had friends who were deployed to Vietnam and the only thing that kept them alive was their high-performance car back home."

The couple purchased an Impala, which Schoenthaler used to get to body school. They moved into a new home in 1973 and one day while Ken was gone, Becky found she needed the Yenko. Her parents came

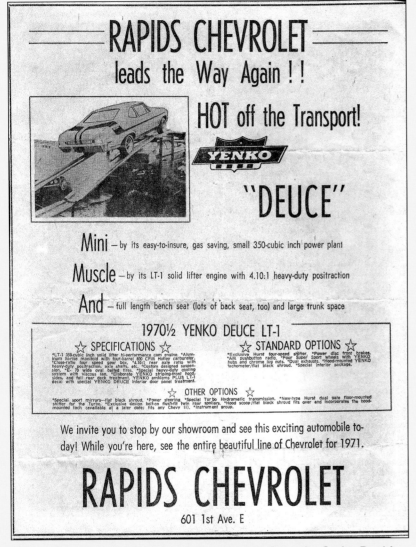

This tattered and faded ad is the exact copy from the **Cedar Rapids Gazette** *that caught Schoenthaler's eye decades ago. Somehow he managed to save and preserve it all these years later. "Considering how I folded it up, stuck it in my pocket, and left it lying around my apartment to use as a coaster," said Schoenthaler, "I'm still surprised I have it."*

to visit and asked what projects around the house they could help with. Becky wanted a clothesline and her dad helped dig the holes. "He told me all we needed was concrete," said Becky. Not wanting to hold up progress or wait for Ken, she grabbed the keys to the Yenko and rumbled down to the local lumberyard. There she loaded two heavy, dusty bags of concrete mix into the trunk. "The construction workers were looking at me with open mouths," recalls Becky. She drove past the corner gas station, a hub for gossip. "All the locals are standing out on the corner watching me drive past," said Becky, adding with a smile; "I knew I was busted."

The couple had more kids and found the Yenko wasn't a great family car. "Occasionally, we'd take our oldest out," recalls Becky, adding, "he'd love to go and power test it, giggling the whole way." It was never taken to the track, which Schoenthaler attests "saved it." The same grandmother who loaned him funds also loaned him space in her barn to store the car, where it sat for many years. Today, only 22,000 miles show on the odometer. "All this came from a bad situation that turned into something that turned into lifelong passion," said Ken. "If I could go back and do it all again, I'd do it in a heartbeat."

"As teens, we all thought we were bulletproof," said Schoenthaler. "We'd run all out at triple digit speeds. I had friends who were deployed to Vietnam and the only thing that kept them alive was their high-performance car back home. It's hard to fully explain it, but there was a strong feeling on the streets, a sense of brotherhood." (Photo Courtesy the Schoenthalers)

Just as when they were new, the Deuces still hold a certain draw for octane-fueled enthusiasts. Purchasing this one was a lifelong dream of Joe Barr, whose favorite color for Yenko cars is green and who also loves a manual transmission in his ride.

they had no problems getting buyers coverage for their Deuces. Two dealers even reported selling them to under-25-year-old drivers, one citing the driver's premium went down from $480 for his traded-in Camaro to $300 for his new Deuce.

As time wore on, it became tough to sell the cars. With a price tag of more than $4,500, interest slowed. The latest sale date for a Deuce is October 1971. To help generate interest, the dealer had to apply massive discounts and remove some of the performance options. The truth was too painful to ignore: shoppers weren't into performance like they had been. New government regulations clamping down on engine compression was coming for 1971 cars, and more drivers were being swayed to swap in their muscle, even mini muscle like the Deuce, for more fuel-efficient rides.

Canadian COPO Novas

Don's 175 Deuces weren't the only COPO Novas built in 1970. Central Chevrolet-Oldsmobile in London, Ontario, received two that summer. By now, the COPO process wasn't a mystery and Central decided to make its own pair of Novas. One was Forest Green and the other Cortez Silver, and both were equipped with M20 4-speed transmissions. The silver Deuce was shipped on June 6, 1970. It listed for $4,350 but was discounted $750 to a St. Thomas, Ontario, buyer on October 2, 1970.

Racing Classifications

Slowing sales weren't helped at all by a lack of progress in getting the Deuce classified for drag racing in the NHRA's stock classes. Just like Fred Gibb and Vince Piggins wanted their COPO 1968 Novas and Camaro ZL1s to

compete in production (not modified) drag race classes, Don wanted his cars to compete there, too. Cars that won in that segment were attractive to wide-eyed spectators who relished the notion of going down to their closest dealership to buy (and drive) whatever won the weekend before. Multiple antsy dealerships in Don's network began reaching out to him, wanting answers.

Don wrote to Wally Parks, the founder and president of the NHRA, on August 5, 1970, alerting him that a somewhat highly inflated figure of 500 Yenko Deuces had been sold to date. Seeking the similar production classes of their other vehicles, Don informed him that it was a Chevrolet Nova equipped with a Z28 engine installed by Chevrolet at the factory under a COPO and was available in either Turbo-Hydramatic and 4-speed configurations. Don went on to state that all other American Manufacturers Specifications remain the same and asked for a prompt classifying, even copying Vince Piggins on the letter.

That request was ignored. On March 4, 1971, Don reached out again, this time to Bill Dismuke, the NHRA's tech director, requesting an immediate classifying of the Deuce in stock categories. He cited the same ultra-high figure of 500 sold. Yenko Sportscars intended to continue marketing limited-quantity specialty rebuilds in the future, and any help he could contribute to streamline the classifying process would be greatly appreciated. Again, Vince Piggins was copied. Dealerships became impatient, reaching out to Don, inquiring as to the delay. More and more customers weren't too happy when they showed up to their local track and couldn't run in the stock classes.

The NHRA simply ignored Don's letters, most likely due to his exaggerated production claims from prior years on other models. Much to Don's dismay, the Deuce was relegated to Modified Production. More than likely, the NHRA's refusal to let the Deuce run in stock classes stemmed from the 1969 Yenko Chevelle. The NHRA had requested a detailed sales history confirming their availability to the public and, more importantly, that their minimum requirement had been met. Don solicited sales info from his network of dealers, asking them to fill in purchaser information on a designated form. The paperwork was submitted but included such bogus names as dealer owners' spouses, magazine writers, and "other" buyers listed in order to pad the numbers and justify the sales. Clearly Don couldn't help but bend the rules in a hurried effort to get the classification, but the NHRA was having none of it.

Some owners shared that sentiment, with one disgruntled racer who had his own share of resentment for not being able to compete in stock classes at tracks around him, removing all Yenko stickers from his ride in protest. He left the shields on the fenders, but only because he thought they were drilled and pinned, not stuck on with adhesive. The owner also begrudgingly left the crest on the trunklid, but only so there wouldn't be vacant holes in his car.

On April 10, 1971, Don reached out to the president of the National Association of Automobile Racing (NAAR) in Oakmont, Pennsylvania, to have the Deuce classified in stock competition. The NAAR wasn't quite the NHRA, but at least it was something. Don got a letter back on April 26 saying the Yenko Deuce would be allowed to run in F/Stock to which he replied that would "keep lots of Yenko Deuce fans happy." The loosely regulated AHRA had no problems with the Deuce either and allowed it to run in E Stock classes.

In the fall of 1970, Central Chevrolet from Cleveland, Ohio, sponsored driver Tom White, who competed in a Citrus Green Yenko Deuce, dubbed the *Draggin' Deuce*, in the AHRA's 3/E Stock Automatic class. In spite of it having the smallest engine in the class and competing against 428 Fords, 440 Wedge Dodges, and 396 Novas, the Deuce clicked off quarter-mile times at 12.68 at 108 mph. The class record was 12.67, set at Norwalk Dragway in Ohio. White summed it up this way: "It's the most fabulous car I've ever raced!"

Deuce Wrap-Up

Showing his versatility and creative, out-of-the-box thinking, Don crafted a special car with his Yenko Deuce. He attentively watched the buying trends, pivoting when the 427s became old news, to create something that, by all accounts, should have done well. It had the right size and looks to draw young customers and the right engine to slip through the cracks of the insurance companies' muscle car crackdown. Where he got tripped up was with the racing classifications. The NHRA was the place to be to compete and they were forcing his customers into modified classes, which had the exact opposite effect Don and his dealer network partners wanted. As in previous years, his cars were intended to be viewed as street-legal, buyable vehicles.

Not that it mattered much. Even if the racing classifications had been worked out, there was another problem that was much bigger: the Environmental Protection Agency (EPA). The EPA was established at the end of 1970 as "a kind of federal gladiator in the war against pollution." It got to work enforcing the National Air Quality Standards Act, passed in September 1970, which, among other things, set national air-quality standards and required 1975 model automobiles to achieve a 90-percent reduction of the 1970 standards for emissions. Detroit automakers angrily pushed back, saying the technology wasn't there to meet that goal, but the EPA wasn't budging nor blowing smoke; cars would have to get cleaner. Surprisingly, Don was ready to attempt one final COPO-built car, and for this swan song, he'd think even smaller.

Despite the forethought and planning, Don's Deuce was a bridge too far for the economic times. The execution was spot-on, and the vehicles came out just like he wanted, but given the clamping down on four-wheeled performance, Don and his dealer network couldn't scale to the levels he had anticipated or desired. While maybe not in sanctioned races, in stoplight romps, customer satisfaction remained high, as these Deuces went wild, beating nearly everything they lined up against.

CHAPTER 9

THE 1970½ COPO CAMARO

WINGING IT: CHASING DOWN A WIN

The 1970½ COPO Camaro

Total Produced: Under 100 (estimated)

Total Still Around: 8 (estimated)

Chevrolet didn't need an outsider partner like Don Yenko or Fred Gibb to build something fast although it certainly helped. Occasionally, unique rides came from within the walls of General Motors. Such is the case of the Camaro Z28, the personal project of Vince Piggins, Chevrolet's performance product manager. Prior to his career at Chevrolet, his work centered around automotive engineering and getting brands such as Hudson out in front in NASCAR championships.

With the 1970 COPO Camaro, Vince Piggins saw a need and stepped in to address a major problem. Once he caught wind that the Camaro race team was having traction issues, he quickly greenlit a COPO to resolve the issue, installing the Firebird's high-back rear spoiler.

Piggins brought that first-place mentality into the Chevrolet brand, drawing on it as early as the mid-1950s when he helmed the underground Chevy racing program, turning black-and-white barebone sedans into what were called Black Widow race cars. When unleashed, they blasted across finish lines and made the brand proud. He kept that passion and know-how with him, as evidenced in his greenlighting multiple COPO orders coming in from Don Yenko and Fred Gibb.

The Dawn of the Z28

While Yenko and Gibb received the majority of the limelight attention for the vehicles they ordered, the track-destined Z28 was Piggins's baby, and for good reason: the Camaro was struggling. One auto writer even stated Camaro sales had bombed, selling just one-fourth of Mustangs. As the writer saw it, "Chevrolet has made almost no effort to convince a more and more savvy buying public that it is doing anything to develop an engineering program similar to Mustang."

The slump wasn't lost on Piggins, who made it his mission to make a change. Faster than any dealer could, in December 1966 he pioneered and pushed through special high-performance equipment as option RPO Z28. This equipped Camaros with a 302-ci V-8 engine with a Holley 4-barrel carburetor, a 4-speed transmission, heavy-duty suspension, dual exhaust, and disc brakes as base equipment. His explicit goal was to get them into the hands of racers, financially backed by outside sources, of course, who would then go tear up and crush the Sports Car Clubs of America's Trans American Challenge Cup Series. The series had just been formed in 1966, and Piggins made sure enough of the track stars were built to be homologated. The trick worked and sure enough, buzz was created with many saying even before the race series had kicked off, the Z28 Camaro was the one to beat.

Sadly, the Z28 didn't zip out of the gate to immediate success in 1967, losing to Ford and its ultra-quick Mustang. But it charged back hard in 1968 and 1969, locking in back-to-back title wins. Behind both of those victories was the Sunoco-backed Camaro race team of Roger Penske, a Philadelphia Chevrolet dealer.

Javelin Jabs in the SCCA

As the 1970 season dawned, things were looking great for Chevrolet, which was ready to take home another victory. Those happy and eager feelings came to a screeching halt when rival American Motors decided to buy its way into racing and hire the best in the business, swiping Penske away to manage its Javelin race team, for a rumored $2.5 million contract for both the 1970 and 1971 seasons. Following Penske was his hot shot driver, Mark Donohue, who had driven the Camaros to victories. It was a staggering blow, especially because Camaro was debuting its second-generation overhaul for the 1970 season.

Piggins had a long history of making Chevrolet cars win and the Z28 was no different. Before letting the Gibb COPO Novas and ZL1 COPO Camaros loose on drag strips, he had slipped a special Z28 package on the Camaro to help it secure top honors in the SCCA's Trans Am race series.

Penske's devotion to Chevy had faded after he inspected preliminary designs of the car and had a strong suspicion it would be uncompetitive right out of the gate, citing some concerns with its aerodynamics. A front spoiler was developed, called the Auxiliary Panel and Valance Lower Bumper Extension, and plans were drawn up for installation on the Camaro but GM executive John DeLorean, with his penchant for Pontiac, was having none of it. He wanted to reserve those parts exclusively for the Firebird, to give it a unique look and performance edge. On October 31, 1969, the plans for its use on Camaros was canceled. Moves like that irritated Penske, making him all the more willing to jump to team Javelin.

Chaparral to the Rescue

Without a team manager, Chevrolet turned to its ace in the hole: Jim Hall. The renowned driver had sustained serious injuries in a 1968 Can-Am event in Las Vegas and was still recovering. After the crash, he suffered additional burns from a motorcycle accident. Still he signed on, confirming what many had been thinking: he and Chevy were tight. "There have always been strong suspicions of Chevrolet factory aid in Hall's Midland, Texas, shops," wrote a *News Journal Sun* article, "and this year the suspicions became even louder when, for the first time in his racing career, the typically wealthy and lanky Texan announced he would race two Camaros in the Trans Am."

Jim Hall, Hap Sharp, and the Chaparral team had many years of race car success and had quite the background in automotive aerodynamics. The team logo was a roadrunner, the same beep-beep bird that inspired Plymouth's iconic logo.

It was a surprising move; Hall typically stuck to racing his own investor-backed, Chaparral race cars. But Chevy needed him, and he agreed. He procured three 1970 Camaros in November 1969 and, in a span of months, built them to compete, testing the trio at Rattlesnake Raceway, his private Midland, Texas, racetrack. Ed Leslie of Monterey, California, signed on to be the team's second driver, while the third vehicle was kept in reserve

The race cars were painted white and featured bold blue highlights in the form of a big bow-tie on the doors and a wide center stripe. They were ready to compete, packing side exhaust, a roll cage, and a gutted interior.

as a spare. The 302-ci V-8 engine was built and dyno tested by Chaparral's chief engineer, Gary Knutson, who reported it put out more than 440 hp at 7,000 rpm. Hall, known for his aerodynamic prowess, wanted to further modify the cars but was restricted with some of the SCCA's class limitations.

Automobiles that raced in the Trans Am series had to be homologated, meaning a specific number of each make of car that raced had to be produced by the manufacturer. For the 1970 race series, the SCCA and American Competitions Committee of the United States FIA (ACCUS) decreed that no less than 2,500 units or 1/250th of last year's production, whichever is larger, must be made before the car is eligible to compete.

Moved Up, NOT Delayed

It's often wrongly assumed that Chevrolet was caught off guard or caught sleeping when it came time to develop a Camaro for 1970. In fact, Chevy was thinking ahead in light of a serious impending regulation. The plan was to carry the 1969 body style into the 1970 model year, launching an all-new second generation in September 1970. However, new government safety regulations were being rolled out in January, forcing them to reconsider. The new protocols mandated improved side impact protection, requiring the 1969 body style to be updated with side impact beams in the doors and rear quarter panels. The expensive venture would have ultimately led to a dead end. Although when equipped with the beams, the vehicle would have met the safety standards, which would only have been useful for six months of vehicle production before the all-new Camaro launched.

After running cost-analysis models and facing the crossroad, the brand found it more cost-effective to advance the schedule of the second-generation Camaro by the required six or seven months than incorporate the beams into the existing and outdated platform. The new car didn't require the impact beams because it incorporated stiffer rocker panels and had a solid roof that wrapped around to the quarter panels. The impact beams would be added beginning in 1973, after growing pressure from Ralph Nader and the Ohio Public Interest Action group, citing missing spot welds on Pontiac Firebirds, among other safety implications.

Production began on February 26, 1970, cutting short the necessary final engineering for the Trans Am–oriented Z28 package. The model launched with an RPO D80 spoiler package as standard equipment, which added a full length, one-piece fiberglass spoiler across the rear edge of the trunklid.

Chevy wanted to get some mileage out of its 1969 Camaro design and had plans to reuse it for the 1970 model year. New safety regulations caused them to rethink that plan, and it was decided it would be more cost-efficient to bump up the forthcoming 1971 design, which had a "slippery new shape." The Z28 package included special wheels with F60x15 white-lettered tires, but these have been swapped out for Minilites, matching the Chaparral race car.

Spoiler Alert: Aero Lift

Preliminary testing by the Hall team revealed the immediate flaw, and pinpointed by Penske, with the low-back design, which was very similar to the one used on the previous-generation Camaro. The 1969 design was more angular and boxy, lending it to be more receptive for downforce through the spoiler. This new car, however, was designed to be European in looks and more of a GT car than a race car. During testing on racetracks, it was found the car drifted on corners, losing traction at speeds above 120 mph.

Hearing of the problem, Piggins stepped in with a solution. It soon became obvious that Hall's Camaros needed the same high-backed rear spoiler that gave downforce to the Firebird teams. To get this done, he'd need to call an audible, but boy was he in a pickle. Equipping the race Camaros was no problem but the SCCA hadn't approved the piece prior to the season starting. In a way, like Don Yenko, he'd have to scramble to get the components made and installed on the needed quantity of street legal cars in order to have them allowed for competition. As a July 17, 1970, *Sheboygan Press* article about the Trans Am series stated, "… in fact, whatever component is added to a Trans Am sedan, it must be available for sale." The SCCA required evidence of 1,000 parts made and mounted to production vehicles.

Originally, the new Camaro body style, referred to as the "Super Hugger" in marketing, had a low-back spoiler design, similar to the one found on the 1969 Camaro, like the Z28 pictured here. It looked attractive but proved ineffective at high speeds. After Chevy's race successes in previous years, all eyes were on the new car and how it would perform.

The Firebird Fix

Piggins asked Jim McDonald, Pontiac's general manager, for permission to use the center section of the Firebird's three-piece spoiler. McDonald readily agreed, but Piggins wasn't out of the woods just yet. While the center sections were interchangeable, the Camaro's rear quarter panels were sharper than the Firebird, necessitating rear end caps to be created. The next step was connecting with A. O. Smith, the supplier who actually built the fiberglass pieces.

The solution to give the race cars traction was to install a taller spoiler sourced from the Firebird, improving downforce. To use it in the Trans Am race, it'd have to be available on production vehicles, necessitating a COPO order. It was a three-piece unit with a center section flanked by two end caps.

The spoiler's rear end caps installed over the rear fenders. While not appearing fully integrated, they were functional and a big improvement.

While it was clearly a rush job, A. O. Smith couldn't agree to get the parts made much before April 1, 1970. It was sent a handful of quarter panels and trunklids and tasked with getting it all to fit. Using temporary tooling, different end caps were cast that ended up being crude, sloppy, and extremely tough to line up. It wasn't a dialed-in operation; to get them to fit properly, the technicians built in some breathing room, expanding the drilled holes in the quarter panels and decklid by as much as .33 inch. The leftover gaps were then filled in with putty. In some cases, the fender holes ended up being elliptical in shape to accept the mounting bolts. Each end cap had two bolts holding it in, while the center section had eight.

Within a span of three weeks, on April 8, A. O. Smith had enough final mock-ups to show engineers and to get approval for production. Soon thereafter, Piggins invited SCCA officials to the Norwood assembly plant for a massive dog and pony show, showing how these high-backed spoilers were well under way and deep into production. He was hoping to get it done before the opening race at Laguna Seca, on April 18–19, but production snags arose with the caps fitting extremely poorly, and the meeting was canceled.

Faced with no better alternative, Jim Hall and Ed Leslie competed in the race without the spoilers on their vehicles. Despite the 1.9-mile, 9-turn track being one of Hall's favorite tracks, Hall and Leslie each had issues and did not finish.

COPO 9796 AA

Back in Ohio, the flaws in the spoilers were worked out as best as they could be and entered production at Norword on April 20, 1970. Piggins approved it as COPO 9796 AA, the Rear Deck Lid Extension. On April 26,

One big difference with the production COPO spoiler was with the gas cap. The race car had a trunk-mounted fuel cell and an extended filler cap with modified bodywork.

The batch of consumer Camaros that received the spoiler had *D80 R DECKLID EX* (for extension) on the build sheet, and a few lines down *9797AA* was listed. The D80 line was crossed off in pen or deleted, and then the COPO number would be circled and "COPO Spoiler" was handwritten in.

1970, a press release went out informing dealers about the upcoming option, which could be had for $36.90. He also hurriedly brought in an SCCA official, eagerly wanting the thumbs-up. John Timanus was sent by the SCCA and toured the factory on April 23. Only a handful of spoilers had been installed on completed vehicles, but somehow Piggins sweet-talked and distracted him, getting a tentative approval for it to be used in racing. Hall's trio of cars had them hastily installed in preparation for the upcoming Dallas, Texas, race, which was slated to be held on April 26, 1970.

Penske Problems

All seemed to be well until a gripe arose from a familiar old friend. After the Laguna Seca race, a jolly Roger Penske was having an "I told you so" moment with some of his Chevrolet pals. His buddies had caught wind of the retrofitting, telling him about what crafty Chevy was cooking up. Penske, a rule-breaker himself, normally would be applauding Chevy's ruse, but with his checks now coming from American Motors, he was motivated to find a way to slow their progress. He filed a complaint with the SCCA, citing that these spoilers were not widely distributed and were only available as an RPO option to buyers.

Word got out about the upcoming modification, as in a May 31 *News Journal* article about the Chaparral Camaros that stated: "Special aerodynamic spoilers were not on the car [at Laguna Seca] because the Chevrolet factory had not yet enough of them for general public use, a requirement of all special Trans Am options."

The Mess in Texas

Negotiations went back and forth as the Dallas event approached, but General Motors was ready to race in spite of the commotion caused by the complaint. It wasn't waiting for the SCCA to say they couldn't race nor was it going to ask for permission. Acting-as-if was the plan for the day, but just in case it failed, Piggins devised a backup plan just in case the SCCA shut them down at the last minute. He brought several dozen completed spoilers to the local Chevrolet dealerships and had them mounted on as many Camaros as he could. He had the cars parked throughout the spectator lot, full of several hundred cars. If any officials balked at the spoiler's availability while in the pits, Piggins's plan was to casually walk out to the parking lots, pointing out the abundance of Camaros that "spectators" had "randomly" shown up in, confirming Chevy's story that the high-back spoiler was out and readily obtainable.

His bluff was never called, and Hall's Camaros were allowed to race unhindered, but not on that day. The race was rained out, so the cars would compete with the spoilers on May 9, 1970, at Lime Rock Park, in Lakeville, Connecticut.

Fixing the Front: Another Spoiler

Penske and Hall, being seasoned race veterans, both realized another design flaw with the second-generation Camaro was its front spoiler. Hall

It wasn't just the rear that had a traction problem. The front also needed some improved aero. The remedy was to install a lower spoiler made of clear Lexan, which was held in place with quick-release screws. Cutouts at the corners fed ducts that sent fresh air to the brakes.

The race car's lower spoiler was a modified production piece made of black plastic, and it became standard equipment on the Z28, sans the brake-cooling ducts. It was a vast improvement over the stock spoiler of the time.

race cars. The last engineering revision of it was signed off on May 5, 1970.

The back spoiler was manufactured from April until the beginning of May, while the front spoiler was installed on cars starting in late May, running through early June 1970. As such, there's a four-week period of COPO cars that were created that only had the rear spoiler. The front spoiler was never installed at the factory but rather shipped in the cars' back seats for installation at the dealerships. If installed, it wouldn't clear the ramps for loading onto the transporter trucks.

Winning at Watkins Glen

The Chaparral cars wouldn't see a major victory until the 10th round of racing at Watkins Glen in August. Surprisingly, it wasn't Hall behind the wheel. Team captain, Jim Hall, decided he wasn't driving the Camaro to its full limit and bowed out, turning the reins over to 25-year-old Vic Elford of London, England. Elford was an accomplished long-distance Porsche racer in Europe and had only been on the team for two weeks.

wanted to add one but its advantages were far outweighed by the bigger concern with the rear spoiler. With the rear spoiler matter resolved, he and General Electric engineered a front spoiler made of clear Lexan. A production version in flat black was soon added to the COPO production vehicles, as well as the

A brief rainstorm blew through and, following the downpour, the Chaparral team used its strategy of mounting two dry tires on the outside wheels and two rain tires on the inside. The trick, and Elford's skill, paid off

A development car sits parked on GM's testing facility. Note how the Chaparral's front lower Lexan spoiler has now been turned into a smooth, flowing, matte black production piece. (Photo Courtesy the General Motors Heritage Center)

The 1970 Camaro Z28's rear spoiler is a unique part of the COPO story, as it is directly tied to a track-bred performance component. The piece certainly changed the look of the street version, giving it an enhanced visual presence. (Photo Courtesy the General Motors Heritage Center)

Final testing, tuning, and tweaking is performed underhood by GM engineers, but out back the rear COPO-sourced spoiler is mounted and ready for action. Note the lack of a center-mounted Z28 badge. (Photo Courtesy the General Motors Heritage Center)

Even with the compressed design and work schedule, the rear spoiler fit nicely, blending in quite well with the rear of the Camaro's fenders. (Photo Courtesy the General Motors Heritage Center)

as he roared in front of 30,000 spectators to first place, averaging a top speed of 103.80 mph. "Driving a Trans Am car in the rain is a bit like driving on ice . . . but actually the car does handle very well," said Elford. "The Trans Am cars twist a little bit sideways when they come out of the corners. They really don't handle like pure road racing cars."

As the rest of the season closed, the Chaparral and Chevrolet would finish in third place with 40 points, behind the champ, Ford with 72 points, and American Motors with 59 points. The track-oriented Camaros were sold and competed in other series.

Meanwhile, Chevrolet slowly backed away from SCCA racing after the close of the season but, having spent the time and resources to develop the special COPO 9796 spoiler, made the decision to not only offer it again on the street-going Z28 in 1971, but also made it an option (RPO D80) on any Camaro in the lineup. It would stay in production through the end of 1981.

Mechanix Illustrated July 1970

Tom McCahill reviewed the new 1970 Camaro Z28 for *Mechanix Illustrated*, and his tester was equipped with the three-piece COPO spoiler. Not only did he reference the delay of the 1970 Camaro, but he described the Z28 as being "built with the connoisseur in mind who wants a GT-type car. One that with a little juggling can race successfully in Trans Am events, of which the Camaro has been the champ for the last

This COPO Camaro was built in the fifth week of May 1970 and sold October 16, 1970, from Roller Chevrolet in Monterrey, California. The original owner paid $4,621 for it. Few Camaros can be documented as receiving the 9767 AA, and today there's less than 10 in the world that have the required paperwork to verify it.

two years." He references that while a front spoiler is not standard with the Z28, the rear spoiler is and comes in several sizes, calling the tester's the "king-size" model.

Trans Am Wrap-up

The COPO ordering process was used heavily throughout the 1960s to meet a need of some kind, and no clearer was that seen than with the 1970 Camaro. Through COPO 9796 the Chevrolet brand was able to, in a matter of weeks, amend a serious problem, hampering actively competing race cars. Vince Piggins showed ingenuity and quick thinking to get the job done. While he, Jim Hall, and the rest of Chevy enthusiasts would have preferred it contributing to a rousing victory in the Trans Am class, the spoiler did have another lasting effect.

After scrambling to get the part made and installed, its value was seen and it became standard on Camaros for years to come. This was one of the few times that a COPO order directly altered the state of regular options for production Chevrolet cars.

Chevrolet repurposed one of its marketing ads (right) to call attention to the Z28's "special spoiler" (left). The text, tagline, and layout remain the same, but to draw attention to the car equipped with the high-back spoiler, the design team chose an image of not just a static vehicle, but one peeling out. They further targeted the ad's audience, placing it in such (very appropriate) places as official race programs for NASCAR's Grand American race series. (Photo Courtesy of GM Archives)

In recent years, Tomy wheeled a modern Camaro in retro livery, mimicking his vintage factory Chaparral Camaro.

This certainly isn't the kind of traction problem the Chaparral race team was experiencing on the track, but it goes to show the 350-ci V-8 had no trouble breaking the tires loose when the driver wanted. The engine was rated at 360 hp. That's Carl Bolander, the car's owner, behind the wheel.

THE VEGA YENKO STINGER

"MUSCLE'S NOT DEAD, JUST BREATHING HARD . . ."

A s the 1970s dawned, car buying habits were shifting. Large, lumbering land yachts were slowly losing their luster as a crop of small, fuel-efficient rides burst onto the scene. New mini-models from overseas competitors were starting to show up in dealerships, making a dent in the Big Three's sales figures.

Don thought fast, moving from rumbling V-8 muscle machines back to sporty corner carvers. He knew he could blow off the competition by getting a COPO approved to have a factory-installed turbocharger. This 1972 example, owned by Dennis Albaugh, is one of 30 hatchbacks painted in Man-O-War Red that year.

Only three months into 1970, foreign cars captured a record 13 percent of new-car sales, up from 10.2 percent in 1969. Volkswagen, with its "Think small" advertising message accounted for nearly 7 percent of all new car business, passing Oldsmobile. The lone American minicar out on the roads competing against the Beetle was AMC's newly introduced Gremlin. It didn't stay that way for long: Ford and Chevrolet soon joined the fray with their own subcompact cars: the Pinto and the Vega.

Super Secret: The XP-887

The Vega, originally to be called the GMini, had been in the works as early as 1967, and it showed real promise. The little cruiser had sporty looks (some calling it a small Camaro), a low center of gravity, and, unlike Ford's Pinto, there were no leaf springs underneath it. Instead, it had a live rear axle on a four-link coil suspension, making for better road-holding abilities. During the design phase, the Vega project was called the XP-887 internally, and as soon as he heard about it, Don Yenko wanted to be a part of it.

Don's connections within General Motors helped him learn about the new car. On July 3, he wrote to Ed Cole, GM president, hoping to get Cole behind Yenko's involvement with the Vega. Wisely, Don led off with some of Yenko Sportscars' successes. "By the end of the year," Don wrote, "we will have sold 350-plus special units through our network of dealers . . . and, had we been able to get more cars, would have covered more of the nation." He went on, saying, "I wish you could see the enthusiasm and activity this program [Yenko Sportscars] creates in a Chevrolet dealership."

Don then transitioned to his main point, which was for his brand to move away from big cars packing big engines. Don wanted to return to his roots: lightweight, nimble race cars ripping around a twisting road course. He wrote: "I am still very much interested in promoting, manufacturing, and/or campaigning the new 887 car. I've already discussed such a possibility with [the] SCCA and they would be most interested in classifying a 'specialized' version in one of the Spitfire/Sprite production classes. As we are also recognized as a bona fide manufacturer/constructor by the FIA, we'd get one of the little fellows into GT classes also. We will need 500: 499 to sell and one prototype. Being under 500 allows us to build them without crash testing; SCCA will count the prototype in with the 500 to qualify in production and GT."

Cole reached out to Don on August 1, stating that he hoped the activities that Don had under way with the Yenko Sportscars would continue. Moving to the upcoming small car, Cole wrote: "I don't know how far Chevrolet is willing to go with the new XP-887, but the configuration would certainly lend itself to some 'Yenko-izing.' If there is anything further I can do to give this a push, please let me know."

On November 24, Don wrote another letter to Cole, reiterating that although he intended to continue the big car program for 1970, he'd really

Watching car shoppers' habits and seeing them gravitate toward economical commuters, Chevrolet debuted its contender: the Vega. For a while, it was referred to as the Vega 2300, matching the badge on the hood, before being shortened to just Vega. The 2300 was derived from its 140-ci engine, which converted to 2,300 cubic centimeters.

A Vega is parked inside the Yenko Chevrolet showroom. The model was a clear response to the wild success of Volkswagen's Beetle. Both were powered by 4-cylinders, but the VW made 57 hp while the Vega in stock form was capable of 90 or 110 hp. (Photo Courtesy the Barr Collection)

To entice shoppers, Chevrolet gave every buyer of a new Vega a 112-page do-it-yourself service manual. It explained with photos and simple language how an owner could perform 49 service items using mostly readily available hand tools. (Photo Courtesy the Barr Collection)

like to get back into the sports car field. Don wrote: "We feel sure that the XP-887 will be campaigned actively on the Sedan circuit but we'd like to extend its capabilities where the most discerning car buffs dwell—the sports car scene—establishing itself in Class G or Class F Production, or in whatever class the Sports Car Club of America designates." In all fairness, it's one thing to have a car raced successfully under the Sedan classification where rules permit virtual rebuilding. It's quite another thing for sports car people to see a practically stock production sports car with very little changes beating exotic marques on their own ground. "Porsche still hasn't gotten over the Stinger's [Corvair] win at Daytona."

Don went on to lay out his plan: "Therefore, Yenko Sportscars would like to take the XP-887 model best suited for the production sports car category, add a few COPOs, purchase the minimum number required for production status (500), and submit an application to SCCA for classification. Yenko Sportscars would modify and merchandise the product and finance a professional-type race team which would campaign the cars. I would be one of the drivers." Don stated he'd like to work closely with Vince Piggins, Vega design team leader Jim Musser, and 'if possible" with Mr. DeLorean's blessing." John DeLorean of Pontiac GTO fame had just become Chevrolet's vice president and oversaw the Vega model launch. Don finished with: "We can't help but feel this project should be a tremendous promotion and a great kick-off for the XP-887, plus a worthwhile financial venture for Yenko Sportscars."

Chevrolet released the Vega to the public on September 10, 1970, upstaging Ford, which released its Pinto on September 11, a day it heralded as "Small Car Day."

More Power!

While it had the makings to be a corner carver, the Vega fell short with what was underhood. The engine was an overhead single camshaft, 140-ci 2.3L 4-cylinder that featured an aluminum alloy block. The engine block was advertised as being lightweight, weighing around 35 pounds, but that wasn't the real reason for the material choice. Whereas aluminum had been used with the ZL1's engine for its rapid heat-dissipation and weight-saving properties, Chevy went with it in the Vega for an entirely different reason: it was cheap. The aluminum alloy die-cast process was simple and required a small labor force to create it. General Motors even toyed with automating the whole process in the years to come.

Besides the construction, the engineers felt their greatest breakthrough was with the elimination of the engine's cylinder liners. The pistons' travel would still wear the cylinder walls of the aluminum block but the engineers felt they had a winning solution. What they ended up doing was filling the alloy with microscopic particles of silicon (about 17 percent) then etching away the aluminum around the particles. That way the pistons would slide up and down on zillions of bits of tiny, hard silicon. Silicon makes for a tough surface and in theory, resistant to wear. The whole thing sounded

Chevrolet advertised that "more research, more engineering, and manufacturing know-how, and more technology went into the development of this [Vega] engine than into any other Chevrolet production engine in history." The industry-first engine was unveiled at the 1970 New York Auto Show in April before the car was officially named a few weeks later.

Don saw the light with the current market trends, and his Stinger, by all accounts, should have been a homerun for shoppers who wanted something small but sporty. (Photo Courtesy the Barr Collection)

1970, production had ramped up by December to 100 final vehicles an hour or almost 1.5 every minute. All of this was with the same two-shift workforce as in years prior. By comparison, output for the Chevy Nova was at 65 completed cars an hour.

It's Turbo Time!

There was lots of excitement surrounding the launch of the model, but Don and Chevrolet both knew the first step in whipping the Vega into a serious sportster was to get more power. One route that other speed shops and dealers were opting for was to install a small-block V-8. Don initially picked a different route, and one that would still allow him to run in stock race classes. In the fall of 1970, his team had begun work on a 4-barrel carburetor, but then they looked to go bigger. Much bigger.

Turbocharging was a new and fast-growing phenomenon. Up until then, turbos were used mostly in high-end race motors, airplanes, and trucks. They had shown up in sporadic racing applications, first in May 1952 at the Indianapolis 500 when one was paired to

exotic and high-tech but presented a real problem down the road: mechanics wouldn't be able to hone the cylinders over time. In the end, it was a case where the cheaper manufacturing cost beat out the cost of repair, with General Motors figuring the engine would be long-lasting, given its low compression and simple construction.

To help give strength to the whole assembly, the cylinder head was made of cast iron. Had it been a simpler part to construct, General Motors would have die-cast it out of aluminum, too, to save some bucks. The main caps and crankshaft were also cast iron. It was a novel idea, but one that had performance as a low priority, making output less than thrilling. Horsepower was rated at a ho-hum 90 for the single-barrel carburetor version and 110 for one with an optional 2-barrel carb (RPO L11).

It wasn't just engine construction where pennies were pinched; to keep pricing low, the whole car was built around the idea of cost-saving and streamlining. In preparation for Vega production, Chevrolet spent $300 million rebuilding its Tonawanda, New York, engine plant and the assembly line in Lordstown, Ohio, which had 85 percent gutted to make way for new tooling and a highly automated and computerized assembly line. Modular construction was used extensively, with many large body panels and sub-assemblies installed at once. This was an improvement over normal protocol in which many small parts were bolted on, adding time and inflating costs.

The Lordstown facility, which was billed as one of the most advanced production facilities in the world, had a final output at 40 more cars an hour than when it was used for other models. After building began on June 26,

After a multiyear hiatus, the Stinger name was resurrected for the new hopped-up Yenko hatchback. Always trying new things, now the Yenko text would appear above the car's side stripes, as opposed to in the stripe as found on earlier sYc vehicles.

a Cummins diesel-equipped race car. They charged back onto the scene in the mid-1960s when veteran mechanic Herb Porter brought a turbocharged Offenhauser engine in a roadster chassis to an Indy race. That paved the way for turbo-Offys and turbo-Ford engines, which were delivering more than 700 hp from just 159 ci of displacement

With the clamping down on big engines, turbo kits started popping up to boost performance on the new wave of US-built mini-compact cars. Everything from VW Beetles and Mercury Capris to Datsun 240-Zs and Ford Pintos were having kits designed for them. The bolt-on kits weren't cheap; most were priced around $500, but the performance gains spoke for themselves. Some cars saw as much as 3 seconds knocked off their quarter-mile times with the addition of a blower. The strong benefit of turbocharging was that normally there wasn't a need to dismantle the engine to install the kit.

Another plus was for the cost of the kits when compared to using conventional performance enhancers such as cams, pistons, intake manifold, and larger carbs. Add up the costs of those other components and it typically was more than a turbo. A third advantage was that a turbocharged engine could match the output of a larger displacement engine, thus putting out fewer emissions. No matter the engine size, the turbocharging process significantly lowered exhaust emissions under full-throttle operation. It achieved this by imposing back pressure on the exhaust system, which in turn brought about higher temps, which aided in the completion of the burning process in the exhaust manifold. One consideration (and in effect, downside) with turbocharging was the strain the setup added to the lower portion of the engine. With all the added air being crammed in and the subsequent power, the crankshaft, connecting rods, and bearings took a beating.

Chevrolet was aware of the advantages turbocharging brought and surely Don, being a performance enthusiast, liked the turbo idea. As early as September 3, he was working on what was being called the Yenko Stinger 2; the name was a nod to his successful Corvair Stinger from a few years earlier. But his approach was to request that General Motors bolt on the turbocharger, using the COPO process that had worked so well in years past. Chevy engineers had been busy working on this behind the scenes, but in the end, they weren't ready to make it happen.

As with previous COPO models, Don's ambition was to compete in production race classes with the car, which gave it the best chance of moving the most inventory at the Yenko dealership. The back and forth with General Motors stretched for months; in the meantime, Don went about making plans to have 500 built and laying the groundwork with suppliers to get his aftermarket parts ready. The 500 was in response to the new SCCA regulations requiring that many vehicles to be produced in order to be considered in the production classes. They granted him a provisional status to compete the Yenko Stinger MKII, a name the car would be called frequently early on, in class D production classes for the 1971 race season.

Showing Off at SEMA

Don and his team assembled a prototype and had it on display at the Speed Equipment Manufacturing Association (SEMA) show held that year in Anaheim, California, on January 26–28, 1971. By then, the creation was called the Yenko Turbo Stinger. Underhood, the 4-cylinder engine had been given alloy-plated forged pistons, as well as a turbocharger. Yenko press releases listed "impressive" performance from the combo, citing the quarter-mile standing start, with two passengers aboard and with the standard 3.36:1 axle, as coming in at 15.5 seconds at 90 mph. A non-turbocharged Vega did the same test at 19 seconds at 70 mph. The modified engine was rated at 155 hp with 9 pounds of boost. The show car had plenty of pizazz too, boasting fiberglass flares, a rear deck spoiler, a front Trans Am–type air dam, a special hood, customized louvers covering the rear side windows, and custom Yenko styling and striping. Many of those pieces would make it to production, being made available as options.

Race Exposure

Now that he had caught the public's attention, the next phase was showing off the Vega Stinger's track prowess. Don entered a blue tester in the B Sedan class of the grueling 24 Hours of Daytona, held on Saturday and Sunday, January 30–31, 1971, on the Daytona Speedway's 3.81-mile road course. It marked the country's first road racing Chevrolet Vega with Don's plan being to use it as a development test, as well as to get his racing options together.

As Don was racing the Stinger in stock classes, the car was not turbocharged. The unaided engine wasn't powerful enough to be competitive.

Just as with previous models, Don had taken advantage of a wonderful process using the COPO order and getting Chevrolet to bolt on parts that few others knew about or could get themselves. Unfortunately for him, those grand plans for the Yenko Turbo Stinger would grind to a halt. (Photo Courtesy the Barr Collection)

"We ran a few laps with the car at Nelson Ledges [Ohio]," said Don, just prior to the Daytona race. "It seemed to handle pretty well, but we didn't exactly get whiplash from the power. We've tried a number of cams and we've got the compression up to 12:1. We're using big V-8 valves—they almost touch each other—and we've designed new headers and flywheel. But we just haven't come up with the right combination yet. I guess we're having trouble because this is a new engine. We don't know much about it, and we don't know who to ask. If you hook a blower on it, it goes like stink, and we're planning to turbocharge a lot of these jobs and sell 'em on the market. But you can't do that for racing [in stock classes], of course."

When faced with the development issues, Don was asked why he would stay with the Vega. "Well, it might have something to do with the fact that I've got 500 of 'em ordered from Chevrolet," he said. "And we've had so much interest in the car it's unbelievable. We've been swamped with calls, everybody asking, 'When can we get one? When can we get one?' I don't know what people's racing plans are for the car. I think most people will be buying them because they want a peppy little street machine that'll out-run dad's V-8." Aiding Don's efforts were test engines that had come from Chevrolet under the guise that Yenko Sportscars would campaign and build the car. ". . . The trick . . . is to stay out of the pits," said Don, ". . . and stay out of trouble. We'll probably use a red line of about 6,000 or so—although we're pretty sure the engine has a lot more than that in it if we need it."

In early January, Don was saying he would drive the Vega, but that plan changed and the drivers became Donna Mae Mimms, Bob Johnson, Kirt Wetzel, and Bob Nagel. While a class win would've been preferred and a big boost to the program it didn't happen. In the days leading up to the race, the engine developed problems and the car was never entered. Not that it mattered. An unfamiliar rule stated that no car with higher than 130 percent of the top qualifying lap time would be allowed to start. Many drivers found out Friday night that they would not be allowed to compete, including the Vega Stinger team. In total, the field was cut from 65 to 45. Had Don and his team been successful, it would have marked the first time one of the new economy cars had been raced in an international event.

SCCA Trans AM Under 2.5 Class

Another option was competing in the SCCA's Trans Am race series, which had, in 1971, upped its 2.0L class to a new under-2.5L D Production class to encompass the Vega as well as Pinto, which would be going up against the AC Bristol, the Jaguar XK120, the Triumph TR4, as well as Corvair Stingers.

When Don was asked by *Sports Car Graphic* in March about competing, he replied: "We'll have to find out if we're competitive first, and we'll learn that at Daytona and Sebring. If we're not competitive, we won't run. And, unless Chevy becomes interested in Vega, the amateur will have to stay home. Everything we've done is nickels in horsepower. In order to be competitive, we'll have to have at least 180 hp. We've got some developments we're trying out on the dyno now [January 1971], which we hope will give us the power we need. The engine is a good engine for the highway, no question about that, but we'll just have to wait and see if we can make it good for the track as well. It's harder to make a sedan race because it just wasn't made for racing. It takes a lot of hard work. And since the factory is not putting money into the car for racing, it makes it that much harder. We'll have some parts available for competition, but our major effort with the Vega will be what we call Stinger II, a turbocharged Vega for street use. With a turbocharger, we can get 160 easy horsepower from the engine, and meet the pollution requirements as well."

By spring of 1971, things weren't looking good for the class; no compacts had been entered. Don was quoted as saying the rules precluded the possibility of Vega being competitive because it has an overhead cam engine and a 2,300-cc engine. According to the rules, the car had to weigh at least 1.1 pounds for each cc of displacement; meaning 2,530 pounds. But when the Vegas rolled off the assembly line, they weighed 2,100 pounds. Furthermore, the Vegas' cheaply built engine didn't fare so well with the "more sophisticated double overhead cam engines of the Alfa Romeo, the top contenders in the class." Alfa, the 1970 winner, had a 1,750-cc engine making 230 hp. Instead of Vega, it was teams from BMW and a new entrant, Datsun, that Alfa was focused on. Don wouldn't compete, no doubt frustrated that his only hopes of being competitive were in getting a factory turbocharger approved, and even then that would be a long shot. Concerns lingered that even if that went through, the car would still be outclassed.

COPO 9734

The racing woes were troublesome but didn't keep Don down. He moved forward with finalizing the details needed to sell the Stinger. By now it became clear Chevy wasn't going to install the turbocharger, but they did offer an alternative. As part of "COPO 9C2AA2 Special Vega Engine," which was shown on the invoice, they would install a set of forged alloy plated pistons, replacing the cast stock pieces.

Knowing Don was going to install a turbocharger, the GM engineers felt the pistons would handle the internal pressure much better. Don and Hugh McGinnis, chief engineer at Rajay (the turbocharger supplier), felt otherwise, saying the stock cast pistons wouldn't give any issues. In the end, they took the engineers' advice and had them installed under COPO 9C2AA2. As with all Vegas from the factory, the engine block deck was stamped on the passenger's side with an engine assembly identification number. The suffix for this COPO for 1971 and 1972 was unique.

On March 18, 1971, Don released the first price list for the new model. The car would start off as the Vega GT hatchback, equipped with a Ride

Up front, the Stingers' headlight bezels would be blacked out and a lower spoiler installed. It was common for the factory Chevrolet badge to be swapped out for a Yenko crest, but not all received it.

This Stinger has been test fitted with many of the aftermarket components Don planned to offer. It has the wheelwell flares, rear spoiler, rear window louvers, and Minilite Wheels but no front spoiler. Yenko teamed up with BORT Performance Products of Detroit, Michigan, to get the parts created. (Photo Courtesy the Barr Collection)

Ken Halvorsen owns this 1971 Yenko Stinger after purchasing it from his dad, Kent. Kent was no stranger to the Yenko brand, having bought a brand-new Deuce on March 1, 1971, from H&H Chevrolet in Omaha, Nebraska. He still owns it today. This Vega was sold new at Joseph Chevrolet in Cincinnati, Ohio.

Stingers rode on the factory GT 13x6 wheels, wrapped in A70 white-lettered tires. Don offered a 90-day/4,000-mile warranty on the styling elements added to the car. This Stinger was sold new at DeNooyer Chevrolet in Albany, New York.

and Handling Package (RPO Z29), which included 13x6 wheels wrapped in A70 white-lettered tires and a torsion bar rear suspension. The engine received a turbocharger, supplied by Rajay, based in Long Beach, California, whose most popular automotive kit at that point was one for the VW Beetle. The Stinger would also get a custom-tailored exhaust, boost gauge, a 4-speed transmission, and a sport steering wheel and full instrumentation as part of RPO Z29.

With its hatchback design, the Vega packed plenty of practicality. With the back seat folded down, the flat load floor was nearly 5.5 feet long and 3.5 feet wide, totaling 18.9 cubic feet. There was even a small concealed storage compartment underneath to keep valuables out of sight.

An AM radio was optional for $61.15. Exterior dress-up consisted of side striping and Stinger emblems with optional rear spoiler ($100), fender flares ($35), front air dam ($45), and rear side window louvers ($24). Surprisingly, the vehicles received a full factory warranty, including the engine as well a Yenko Sportscars 90-day/4,000-mile warranty on the Turbo and the styling elements.

Beside the pricing, Don also released his list of nearly 70 Yenko Sportscars dealers who would be distributing the Stingers. It was also announced that Holman & Moody Inc. in Charlotte, North Carolina; Johnny Londoff Chevrolet in Florissant, Missouri; and Vic Hickey Enterprises in Ventura, California, would help in building the vehicles to facilitate quicker and less-costly delivery. As of April 1971, Don was claiming the cars would be available in the middle of May and that they would, in fact, comply with the Federal Smog Emission requirements, smartly stating, "Yes [they do comply], or else we would not be able to sell the car." His claim that turbocharged cars would be available right from the factory was in fact not true.

Clean Air Act of 1970

As 1970 drew to a close, the federal government began to take steps to clean up air pollution, setting its sights on the auto industry. In December, air pollution control was turned over from the Department of Health, Education, and Welfare to the newly created Environmental Protection Agency. In addition, a US Senate-House conference committee passed the Clean Air Act of 1970 that assured a "virtually pollution-free" car by 1976. If automakers weren't going to comply they must "supposedly" stop producing cars. The bill went on to state that no manufacturer, dealer, or parts seller can modify the fuel intake or exhaust system of any automobile sold in the

Tech Insight: Rajay to Schwitzer Turbo Switch

Up until May, the Stinger prototypes had been using Rajay turbochargers. The particular turbocharger's primary application was in light aircraft engines and, by design, would "suck more than it would 'blow.'" In aircraft, it would be mounted at the rear of the engine, close to the cockpit, and pull air through the air intake and push it back forward and down into the engine. Adapting it to automobiles was doable but a little tricky. It required a special intake manifold to allow the turbo to be installed between the carb and the manifold, thus sucking the fuel charge into the engine, just like it would on planes. The setup didn't require an auxiliary fuel pump. Don had originally designed the Stinger to accommodate the setup but then switched to a different company, Switzer, citing he needed an emission-content–approved setup and Rajay hadn't run a certification check on the Vega installation.

The Schwitzer unit was essentially the same as what was used on trucks and tractors but traditional in the sense that it mounted ahead of the carb and thus would shove fresh, pressurized air through the intake, carb, manifold, and finally into the engine. The carburetor would have to be pressurized, which meant running a line from the turbo to the carb base plate, piped in below the throttle butterflies. This allowed the pressure within the manifold to be equalized and prevented the high-pressure fuel mix from escaping before it reached the manifold. The unit could also run less boost than the Rajay to deliver similar horsepower ratings. Whereas the Rajay needed to be at around 13 pounds, the Schwitzer's maximum was close to 10 pounds. A Holley variable pressure fuel pump was added to provide gas flow at 3 psi more than blower boost and was hooked up so that the ignition resistor was bypassed when the engine was putting out full boost. The turbo had no waste gate and, for the 1972 models, Don had plans to install a green light on the dash that would light up when the blower began boosting, around 2,800 to 3,000 rpm. The setup all fit on the left side of the 140-ci 4-cylinder, allowing the cars to be equipped with an air conditioner. Schwitzer tasked Sid Brong to be the Project Engineer of adapting the turbo to the Vega.

While driving, the turbo wouldn't kick in under 3 psi of boost and so for the most part, would remain unnoticed during around-town cruising. That docile nature would change once you dropped your right foot. The turbo spooled up and would kick in but, according to a 1971 *Car and Driver* review, "not with a bang but with extraordinary smoothness. Suddenly you are moving at an incredible speed, with a kind of quantum increase in power as the velocity escalates. The beautiful part of the entire experience is the subtlety: There is no moaning or whining from the blower, no growling exhaust—simply power." On stock tires, Don claimed quarter-mile times in the 15.3 second region at around 91 mph and a top speed of 120 mph. He also reported that a recent run over local roads and highway in a Stinger came back with 24 mpg, roughly the same as the non-turbo Vega.

The plan was to use the Rajay company as the supplier for the Vega's turbocharger, but Don eventually switched to Schwitzer, which was based in Indianapolis, Indiana. Its turbocharger produced 10 pounds of boost.

United States without first receiving full certification that it conforms with government exhaust emissions standards.

Seeing as the Stinger had a modified induction exhaust system, the EPA mandated that it must clear a 50,000-mile durability test and rumors lingered of crash testing too. It probably took a couple months to get all the details fleshed out, given that through the spring of 1971, Don was planning on selling the modified Stinger and he more than likely did think that he could get it distributed, perhaps thinking he wouldn't be affected or could dodge the new legislation. Don and Hugh McGinnis of Rajay were quietly confident that the Stinger's system would pass the emission laws without trouble.

With the tail panel blacked out and the rear spoiler added, the Stinger had a distinct look from behind. Don was really hoping this would be the only view competitors would see on the tracks.

Don tried multiple times to satisfy the EPA's requirements, which would have allowed him to have a turbocharger installed as part of the Stinger package instead of as an aftermarket component. Here's some testing in process. (Photo Courtesy the Barr Collection)

The Vega body style used for testing was a sedan. Note the crest placement on the trunklid. The sticker below the Chevrolet Vega 2300 badge advertises Schwitzer. (Photo Courtesy the Barr Collection)

A Vega GT (note the squared-off Sport striping on the hood) undergoes testing on a dynometer. As hard as he tried, Don couldn't appease the EPA. (Photo Courtesy the Barr Collection)

In stock form, the most you could get from Vega's 4-cylinder with 2-barrel carb was 110 hp and 138 ft-lbs of torque. Here's a photo from when Don's team was perfecting the Schwitzer turbocharger installation. Note that while this engine has the turbo, it still retains the stock and very plain valve cover. (Photo Courtesy the Barr Collection)

Another nod to the behind-the-scenes support, their confidence stemmed from the Chevrolet engineering team as well as Oldsmobile, who both had been working on factory turbocharging. Don felt confident, even saying that "turbocharging may become a Vega option right from the factory in 1972."

Media Drives

Don started inviting media to drive his prototype, and the test drivers came away rather impressed with the little car's performance. During an

A Stinger's engine has been fitted with a Schwitzer turbocharger and reassembled and it is ready for action. Note the sticker on the air cleaner. During the preliminary testing, Schwitzer added several around the car but the final Stingers didn't have any. (Photo Courtesy the Barr Collection)

April road test session with the prototype, *Car Craft* noted that because of the close spacing of first and second gears, the turbocharger doesn't have any real opportunity to build much boost. But once they shifted into third and fourth gears, the performance really changed, citing the little 4 suddenly became a big 6-cylinder. Overall the magazine liked the look of the Stinger, saying the "conservative sportiness seethe(s) with an animal sensuousness."

In May 1971, *Hot Rod* got its hands on a Stinger and conducted a proper thrashing. Rajay had difficulties in getting a 110-hp version to modify and had to turbocharge the 90-hp version of the Vega. Based on Yenko's estimated output, the tester would have made 120 to 125 hp. The 110-hp engine had a higher lift and longer-duration cam than the 90-hp version and would be a better pairing with the boost from the turbo. The Rayjay turbocharger had a 3-inch-diameter wheel and ran at 10 pounds of boost. It was paired to a Carter YH single-barrel carb mounted ahead of the turbo, meaning it didn't have to be pressurized and used the same stock fuel pump.

Despite all that, *Hot Rod* reported it still performed well during testing at the Orange County International Raceway, running the quarter mile in

Ads for the Stinger ran, proclaiming, "Who would do such a thing to an innocent little? Don Yenko would—and did!" The Vega was designed to be a simple commuter, and even in GT form, didn't pack overwhelming pep. The Stinger set out to change that image.

15.72 seconds at 87.46 mph. Rajay told *Hot Rod* the proper, final version of the turbocharged 110-hp Stinger would have 25 to 30 more horsepower. *Hot Rod*'s feature also stated, "Unlike a number of dealer-special cars, the Yenko machine is fully factory-warranted, which means it also passes established emission standards."

Motor Trend was present for the Chevrolet Long Lead Press Preview and detailed its experience in an October 1971 feature. Appropriately, the writer acknowledged that in the current economic climate, "muscle cars aren't dead, they're just having trouble breathing," finding that the turbocharged Vega would "destroy any of the old 'classic' performance cars in a

A trainload of newly converted Yenko Stingers is getting shipped out to waiting dealers. This load includes both hatchbacks and Kammbacks. (Photo Courtesy the Barr Collection)

quarter mile." *Motor Trend* testers found that behind the wheel of a Stinger they could get 0–60 mph times in the high 9-second range (9.9 seconds to be exact) while the quarter mile ticked off in mid-16 seconds (16.5 at 78.5 mph).

They came away impressed since stock 110-hp Vegas were about 3 seconds slower. In spite of this, when they informed Vega project engineer Chuck Hughes of their triumph, he thought something must be wrong, saying the car had previously dipped into the low 15 second range. *Motor Trend* chalked it up to many hours of heavy testing (their example showed 6,000 miles) and reported that, just like other outlets had, the turbo didn't kick in until after 3,000 rpm and then "you just seem to magically find yourself going one heck of a lot faster than in the stock version. Start by banging home the clutch at about 3,500 rpm and it's another thing altogether, the [turbo] 'charger's 13 pounds of boost making the Vega a mini Z28."

200 Cars: June 1971

Despite the positive reception, by the end of May and into June, the writing was on the wall: due to the heavy EPA testing requirements, Don wouldn't be able to have a turbocharger installed on the Vegas at the Chevrolet factory. A June 21 revised Yenko pricing sheet now listed the turbocharger as a $575 option instead of standard equipment. Still believing there was a market, Don put in the COPO with Chevrolet, requesting an initial run of 200 vehicles. They were built in the second week of June 1971 at the Lordstown, Ohio, plant. Five exterior colors (Yellow Jacket, Man-O-War Red, Wasp Blue, Scorpion White, and Hornet Green) were selected, and each color came in a batch of 40 vehicles. All interiors came in standard black (RPO 860) except for cars painted green; they got dark green interiors and white exterior striping.

Images like this, showing nearly two dozen vehicles, make you think that Yenko Vega Stingers would be readily found at car shows and cruise nights; instead, they're nowhere to be found. Seeing just one today is a rare sight to behold. (Photo Courtesy the Barr Collection)

A two-position adjustable driver's seat back was included in the GT package, which also brought wood accents and the passenger-side assist handle mounted in the dash. All Vegas had foam-filled front bucket seats and European-style control knobs.

GT Vegas got this four-spoke sport steering wheel and a revised dash, providing a separate pod for such things a tachometer, ammeter, temperature gauge, and an electric clock.

To ensure a spirited driving experience, Don requested all 400 of the COPO Vegas be equipped with an M20 4-speed manual transmission. Three other transmissions were offered in the Vega: a 3-speed manual, Torque-Drive, and Powerglide.

This Stinger had the iconic red, white, and blue Yenko crest mounted to the front fenders. This would later be changed to a black and silver one and mounted behind the front wheels. This angle also shows off the front spoiler that Don's team installed. (Photo Courtesy the Barr Collection)

All of the vehicles were hatchback coupes and came equipped with the following options per the GT equipment package (RPO Z29): tachometer, ammeter, temperature gauge, electric clock, a passenger grab handle on the dash, four-spoke sport steering wheel with center GT emblem, two-position adjustable driver's seat back, woodgrain accents on the door panels and instrument cluster, black-finished grille and lower body sills, bright grille outline and lower body side moldings, parking lights with clear and amber bulbs, and a Special Ride and Handling package that included front and rear stabilizer bars, A70x13 bias belted ply white-lettered tires and special 13x6 wheels. The vehicles came with a 4-speed transmission (M20), Positraction rear end (G80) with 3.36:1 ratio, and an AM radio with windshield antenna (U63). On the front fenders, the cars had a GT emblem, and on the hood, the GT's optional Sport striping of a wide white or black stripe on the hood was left off.

Stinger Package: What You Got

Once the Vegas left the GM factory and arrived in Canonsburg, they received further modifications to be transformed into Stingers. At one point in the fall of 1970, Don's plan was to rework the Vega and restyle it along the lines of the Ferrari Dino sports car. He talked of modifying the roofline, replacing the hatchback with a panel similar in appearance to that of the Corvette, and making the car appear more like a two-seater.

Somewhere along the line, this plan was scrapped. Instead, per a June 21, 1971, price list, the cars received much needed anti-hop traction bars, Trans Am–type rear spoiler and front air dam, a custom aluminum Yenko Vega valve cover (cast by the Atlas Foundry, the same group that also made the copied American Racing wheels), custom side striping, and Yenko

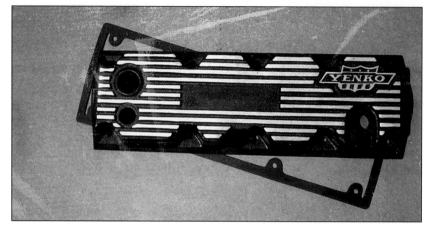

This is the photo Don used to market the custom-created valve cover. It was advertised as having heat-resistant crinkle paint. It costs $35. For another $2, customers could have a reusable neoprene valve cover gasket. (Photo Courtesy the Barr Collection)

A Fly-Eye air cleaner, like this one, was offered through the Stinger catalog of speed parts. This engine also includes the Offenhauser 4-barrel intake and Holley carburetor.

From a branding standpoint, the valve cover was Don's most ambitious project under the hood. He had used stickers in the engine compartment and created badges for the exterior of his vehicles but never anything like this. It did push the Atlas Foundry's abilities, becoming backordered due to slow production.

The Yenko side stripe ran the full length of the vehicle at the beltline. This Wasp Blue example sports American Racing Libre Wheels, which Don offered through the Move 'N Groove catalog.

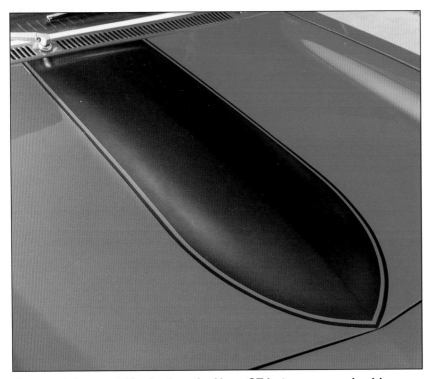

Sport striping could be had on the Vega GT but was a much wider stripe that ran down the center of the hood, squaring off on the front fascia. Don devised a variation on it, going with a much narrower spear design.

The rear of the Stingers was blacked out and, even though the spoilers could be painted body color, many owners chose to leave them black. The center Chevrolet Vega 2300 badge was removed and replaced with a black and silver Yenko Crest. Anti-hop traction bars were included in the package too, but these are heavier duty aftermarket examples.

Donna Mae took these pictures outside of her apartment complex. No doubt her neighbors were used to the sports car enthusiast bringing home unusual and interesting stuff. (Photo Courtesy the Barr Collection)

Don and Donna Mae said all the parts installed on the Stinger and those available through the catalog had been developed back in the "laboratory" in the Competition Department and they "knew they would work." (Photo Courtesy the Barr Collection)

emblems. The fender GT badging was removed and Yenko crests were applied with double-sided tape. Technicians didn't bother to cover or fill the holes left behind by the GT badges. A black and silver crest was also applied right in the center of the rear tail panel below the trunk keyhole. To mimic the look of the other Yenko Supercars, a few original owners went back and painted in the red, white, and blue on their Vega's crest. On some of the early prototypes, Don experimented with locating a colored crest ahead of the front wheels under the tip of the side stripe and also at the front above the grille, swapping out the factory "Chevrolet Vega 2300" badge. Always tinkering, he also tried the Yenko lettering on the rear quarter panel as outline lettering but eventually went with solid black script. The Stingers also had their headlamp bezels, taillight panel, and the raised power bulge on the hood painted in shadow styling flat black.

Don retailed the cars for $3,077.80, but additional optional equipment was available, including an AM radio ($61.15), Positraction ($40.75), and the dealer-installed Yenko turbocharger ($575).

Move 'N Groove Catalog

Sensing that the hot compact craze was catching on fast, Don, just one day after sending out the price sheet, announced the release of a mail-order catalog, called the Move 'N Groove Stinger Parts Catalog. It was full of aftermarket ways to make plain Vegas way hotter. A price sheet, proclaiming "Stingerize your Vega!" was sent out, saying the components on it were the dealership's "really HOT Vega parts," proven in their "laboratory" that had been working with a blue race Vega by testing it on the dyno with all kinds of combinations of carbs, manifolds, cams, and pistons.

With its traction bars and front and rear spoilers, Don knew his Stinger was capable of way more than just zipping through residential streets. He wanted it to be as successful on the track as his first Stinger had been. (Photo Courtesy the Barr Collection)

In his letter to Chevy enthusiasts announcing the Stinger, he said, "Now, happily, Chevrolet has placed on the market a fine new small grand-touring car. The Vega has already won countless awards for its prodigious engineering and customer acceptability has been understandably spectacular. It's the car we at Yenko Sportscars have been waiting for. Already 200 specially trimmed Vegas with bolt-on appearance and handling goodies are available through our Yenko Sportscars dealers. Soon, a turbocharged version will be available and eventually we hope to obtain GT classification to again scorch the road racing circuits. The name? What else? The Yenko Stinger."

Under the section titled "Yenko's Stingerized Go-Pac," buyers could select a whole slew of speed parts. The list included such items as an aluminum Offy manifold with 4-barrel dual ports ($89.95), a Carter 4-barrel carb ($67.95), a lightweight flywheel ($49.95), forged alloy plated pistons ($24.95), Quik steering unit ($39.95), and a finned aluminum 7-quart oil pan ($33.75). The pièce de résistance was the Yenko Vega Indy-Type Turbocharger, advertised as such since the turbo was an "exact scaled-down version of the turbochargers which were on the first place Indy 500 cars in 1970, 1968, and 1968." Schwitzer was based in Indianapolis and did quite a lot of work with the competing cars. Yenko advertised it could be installed on either the 90- or 110-hp Vegas, with or without air-conditioning, and was good for 155-plus hp. It costs $575 and included the necessary variable electric fuel pump.

Don stated it would fit any Vega engine, saying it "is as clean, smog-wise, as your brand-new Chevrolet," citing an independent lab-testing report that showed emission above the Federal government requirements. Suspension upgrades could be made with heavy-duty springs. The front pair ($43) dropped the car 1 inch while the rear pair ($44) dropped it 2 inches from stock ride height. Heavy-duty brakes came by way of front discs ($21) and rear drums ($22). Anti-hop Trac-bars cost $32.95 and KONI shocks were $24.50 each.

The "Stinger Clinger" car cover wasn't much to look at but certainly did the job. Here it's fitted on a Stinger in the back lot of Yenko Chevrolet. It listed for $49.95 and could only be had for the hatchback and sedan. (Photo Courtesy the Barr Collection)

A rear spoiler is mounted on a Vega before the back panel was painted black or the side stripe applied. Vega hatchbacks had a center-mounted Chevrolet Vega 2300 badge, which matched the one on the hood. Here, a Yenko crest is mounted underneath it but later cars would have the crest swapped out for it. (Photo Courtesy the Barr Collection)

Donna Mae recruited one of her friends to model the Stinger shirts she had made to sell through the Move 'N Groove catalog. While similar to the logo of the Corvair Stinger, the design was updated slightly to give the hornet a more graphic appearance. (Photo Courtesy the Barr Collection)

There was a section titled "Yenko's Stingerized Show-Pac," which listed the available parts to make ordinary Vegas look like Stingers or spiff up existing ones. Buyers could choose components such as the finned aluminum valve cover coated in a black crinkle finish for heat dissipation ($37, another $2 for a reusable neoprene gasket), a rear spoiler ($39.95), a front Trans Am–type air dam ($31.95), rear window louvers ($26.20), fender flares ($35), and Rally Stripes with "2.3 liter" lettering in black, white, or aluminum for the rocker panels ($12.95).

Stinger Clinger car covers for both hatchbacks and sedans were available ($44.95) as well as "Yenko Tuned" and "Yenko Stinger" decals, various shirts, and Yenko crests. All of the parts were made available through Yenko's dealer network. Don stated there wouldn't be any insurance issues getting the Stinger covered, saying for instance if a driver was older than 25 and had a clean record, the premium for one year's insurance would be about $30 more than the standard Vega hatchback coupe.

As with the Corvair Stinger, it was entirely possible that a customer could order all the parts to make his or her Vega a Stinger, but don't be fooled. The car would be classified as a Stinger but not a COPO, as it lacked the factory-installed alloy plated forged pistons.

EPA Woes

As the summer wore on, it became painstakingly clear that the EPA would not budge on its stance. Don considered the turbocharger cleaner, stating emissions could be 2 percent cleaner, but the EPA still wanted to see its thorough and exhaustive durability test performed. Don pushed back, saying that it's entirely possible to run the whole test without the turbo kicking in at all, explaining it's the nature of turbochargers to be inactive at low speed when the throttle is only open partially. Because of that, he reasoned, it was more than possible that the Stinger would behave just like a non-turboed Vega while driving around town. The EPA didn't buy it. "The whole thing is unreal," said Don. "I can't believe it. All we are trying to do is put a simple turbocharger unit on a Vega—and we know that the emissions are reduced with the unit, that the car runs cleaner with the turbocharger than without, but I've run smack into the government because I want to change the induction system and that causes all kinds of problems according to the law."

Unable to skirt the 50,000-mile test, Don set about trying to make it happen in the fall. Initially, the EPA told Don the test could be run on public

Don stands in front of one of the Turbo Stingers during testing at the Phoenix Dragway. Note how the stripe design blends up into the rear spoiler, which on this tester, was painted body color. The final design would be different, running straight underneath. (Photo Courtesy the Barr Collection)

The Turbo Stinger tester boasted the blacked-out panel surrounded by an exterior stripe. More than likely to streamline the conversion process, this stripe wasn't added to the rest of the Stingers. (Photo Courtesy the Barr Collection)

roads around the dealership in Canonsburg. Don measured out a course on public roads, including a short section on interstate highway, where drivers could hit 70 mph, which was required in part of the test. But he gave up because the stringent EPA cycle required some interstate portions to be run at 20 mph. Don didn't want to create a traffic hazard or put his drivers at risk for fatigue. The EPA then agreed to let Don perform it on a satisfactory test track or proving ground, but none were in his area. The closest facility was the half-mile oval Heidelberg Speedway near Pittsburgh. To pass and complete the full test, the Stinger would have to run 100,000 times around the track, which Don estimated would cost him $40,000. Besides the enormous costs, Don was concerned about his drivers trying to take the tight turns at 70 mph.

Overall, Don wasn't happy. "Fifty-thousand goddam miles. Do you realize how long that will take? According to the government requirements that I average 32 miles per hour, the whole thing will take me three months if I start right now," said Don. "I'd never get my money back in a million years. Maybe I ought to fly up there to Detroit and see those guys once more. You know, talk to them, sort of face to face. They're good guys, not really bad—except none of them will admit who's in charge. . . ." In the end, he did just that, flying to the Division of Motor Vehicles Pollution's office in Detroit and attempting to reason with them. He offered running a full-throttle test for 5,000 miles, using the turbo all the time as opposed to the 50,000 miles of cruising. He was turned down. The reason cited was that the EPA had no way of duplicating the results from 50,000 miles of actual tests.

"You know, if I was just going to be an automobile dealer for the rest of my life I'd go nuts. Who the hell could face the prospect of that kind of boredom? That's why the Stinger thing means so much to me. It's my chance to inject some of my own thinking into automobiles, to make my personal statement about cars. If we can just get this thing cleared up with the government, we can introduce an entire line of high-performance parts for the Vega. In fact, Donna Mae has the whole thing worked out . . . but the cornerstone of the deal is the turbocharger. And according to the law, I, as a dealer, cannot sell a turbocharger, either installed on a car or as a kit, until it has passed this 50,000-mile test. It's got me nuts."

Don Seeks Sponsorships

In an effort to offset the ballooning costs, in August 1971 Don personally reached out to the public relations director at Clayton Manufacturing Company in El Fonte, California. Yenko Sportscars purchased a used CT-400 Clayton Dynometer in late 1966 and was using it for performance tuning. For the Vega project, it was to be used for the EPA test. Don had already lined up Gulf Research to conduct and perform the also required 4,000-mile emission tests. He appealed to Clayton, saying "it would seem natural that Clayton would wish to participate." Since this was the first of its kind, Don was confident that the tests would "definitely be highly publicized" and then asked if Clayton would consider paying "something like 5 cents per mile for advertising rights." There's no evidence of Clayton biting on the proposal.

An unnamed tester checks some instruments before blasting off another straight-line pass at the Phoenix Dragway. (Photo Courtesy the Barr Collection)

Changes are made under the hood during the testing of the Yenko Turbo Stinger. (Photo Courtesy the Barr Collection)

A manual was created to help Vega owners install the Schwitzer turbo-charger themselves. It included step-by-step instructions and detailed pictures.

At the same time, Don also reached out to the STP Corporation, writing a letter to one of its execs. He filled him in on the 50,000-mile durability test and touted that since his company was "the only American manufacturer except the Big Three to ever make this test," it was attracting lots of media attention, with the press "swamping" them with inquirers. "It would seem natural, for advertising purpose, that we use STP products in the crankcase," wrote Don. He went on to pitch advertising rights. Again, there's no clear indication if the deal went through.

While Don had plans for his next batch of COPO'd Vegas to be run through the EPA test and be considered factory cars, he came to the conclusion this wasn't meant to be. He still followed through, ordering another 200 vehicles with the Chevy engine COPO for the 1972 model year. "We thought we had a breakthrough with the Vegas, but the EPA shut us down," said Don. "We had performance with mileage and the exhaust emissions were actually down. If you want to build a new engine for just 10 cars, you can't do it until you run a 50,000-mile durability test. The test averages 32.5 mph, so to go 50,000 miles takes the better part of four months. You have to own a proving ground or a very sophisticated dynometer. The lowest bid we got to have somebody else run the test was $50,000."

While the logical conclusion would be to sell the turbo kits through the Yenko dealer network as an aftermarket accessory, that's not what Don wanted to do. "We want to sell cars, not kits," said Don. Still, as that was his only option, that's exactly what he did. The Schwitzer turbo could be purchased separately. An installation manual gave a detailed explanation and step-by-step instructions on how to properly install the unit for those that wanted to attempt it themselves. They recommended 10 to 14 hours total to install the kit.

Fall Media Drives

Hot Rod tested a Stinger again in October 1971 at the Pittsburgh International Dragway, posting a best quarter-mile time of 14.70 seconds at 89 mph. The crew found room for improvement, claiming low 14s would be possible with tweaking. They also tested it at the Nelson Ledges 2-mile road course in Warren, Ohio. The SCCA D/Production class record was 1 minute 20 seconds or 90 mph flat. With the test Vega, the Hot Rod team posted times of 1 minute 40 seconds or 72 mph. Donna Mae slid behind the wheel and shaved off a few seconds, posting a time of 1 minute 30 seconds.

1972 Stinger

In spring of 1972, Don ordered an additional 200 Stingers, which were shipped on April 18, 1972. Fifty were Vega Kammback station wagons, which, besides the hatchback, could be had in GT form from Chevrolet. The body style featured an enlarged rear hatch area and, like the hatchback, a folding rear seat, offering an abundance of interior cargo room. It didn't get a rear spoiler and there was not a Yenko crest anywhere on the rear panel or door. The Kammback was one of the four forms Vega could come in; it got its name from German doctor Wunibald Kamm, who pioneered theories on auto design and streamlining. For 1972, the Stinger Kammback cost $3,164.83, while the coupe rang up at $3,152.48.

A couple of new options were made available by Don, including a walnut brake handle sleeve ($5.95), a center console with padded lid ($25), splash guards ($2.50), a chrome exhaust extension ($1.95), and a vinyl top kit ($47). The heavy-duty radiator that was optional in 1971 was now included in the Stinger package. For 1972, Yellow Jacket was dropped and replaced with Stinger Silver. The other colors remained the same: Hornet Green, Man-O-War Red, Scorpion White, and Wasp Blue. And the cars still carried a full factory warranty through Yenko Sportscars. The coupes came in 30 vehicles per color while the wagons had 10 made per color.

Don took hauling to a whole new level, rolling out the Stinger package to the Kammback variant of the Vega in 1972. This one is owned by Mark Pieloch, a passionate Yenko collector.

Very little was changed on the inside for the 1972 model year. The biggest addition was a glove box. Chevy ads stated, "We don't know why we left it out last year, but if you were busy designing a little car that outshines all others, you'd probably overlook a few things too."

With no decklid, the rear spoiler was left off the Kammbacks. This Hornet Green example was sold at Galles Chevrolet in Albuquerque, New Mexico. It's one of 10 wagons painted green.

While the Vega hatchback wasn't short on cargo space, the Kammback offered even more interior room. Flip the back seat down and the squared-off wagon boasts 50.2 cubic feet of load space.

The tiny Vega rode on a 97-inch wheelbase and could turn around in 33 feet. Don wanted them to turn on a track, not in a cul-de-sac. (Photo Courtesy the Barr Collection)

There were four flavors of Vega offered in 1971 and 1972, but Don passed on the sedan and truck versions because they didn't come in GT form. The Kammbacks' little louvers on the side are functional, allowing for flow-through ventilation.

A Stinger Kammback and hatchback are parked side by side for a promotional photoshoot. Besides the wagon's unique rear end, it would get a center stripe and Yenko text instead of being painted black. No Yenko crest was installed either. (Photo Courtesy the Barr Collection)

This picture was part of the set Don used to market the Stinger. In his ads, he claimed to be the "leading US producer of high-performance Chevrolet-based vehicles." By the sheer volume of go-fast cars he and his team created, he probably wasn't wrong. (Photo Courtesy the Barr Collection)

By this time, the cat was out of the bag in terms of knowing how Don got these built. An April Stinger test by *Super Street Cars* magazine filled in readers, saying, "He [Don] placed a special COPO with Chevy to get these cars [Vegas] fitted with special pistons to make sure the blower [turbo] would not shorten engine life. A COPO is a Central Office Production Option. It means Chevy will build a special custom package for the firm that places the order. If you order enough, Chevy will build it. No one dealer has enough volume to get a COPO car built, but Yenko was able to set up a network of dealers." Clearly the fog had lifted on any lingering mystique surrounding how the COPO-built vehicles came about.

Besides explaining the COPO process, the magazine did a road test on a dealer's Stinger, borrowing one from Hory Chevrolet in Larchmont, New York. The tester had the optional Koni shocks, anti-hop suspension bars, and a massive Yenko shield graphic on the door that was also optional and perhaps a dealer-specific treatment they offered. The testers found that when running the engine above "3,500 rpm the car screams," and it would run 15.2 seconds in complete street trim with a full tank of gas and with "juggling the tire pressures." Don told them that the car would dip in to the 14s with more tire pressure juggling, less gas in the tank, and no spare tire. They also explained that customers could order a Yenko Turbo Stinger but the parts came in the trunk, and after you paid for the car and the parts, they could install it for you. According to the article, the turbo was maintenance free and worked very well. Summing up their time with the Stinger, they stated "The Vega with the turbo charger will run rings around 99% of the so-called sports cars that are imported into this country."

No doubt from Atlas's inexperience in creating auto parts, the special finned valve cover was backordered for some of the 1971 Stingers. Don still wanted to get them out to buyers to dress up their engine bays. In September 1972, he sent letters to his network of dealers asking for the addresses of Stinger owners so he could send them one.

In 1973, the Group 7 Filters company offered a sweepstakes, with the grand prize being a 1973 Yenko Turbo Stinger. This ad was run in Car Craft. Note how it's listed as coming with a "Yenko turbocharger." It was supposed to also come with window louvers, which were never installed. (Photo Courtesy Brian Henderson)

Vega Stingers' Survival

The Vega Stinger was Don's return to his ultimate dream, which was keeping Chevrolet products competitive in racing. It was an uphill battle given the current economic climate with ever-growing pressure. Insurance companies were still keeping a tight watch on performance-oriented vehicles, and the EPA didn't help, keeping Don on his toes working overtime in making his dream a reality. The hard work paid off as, with 400 units sold, the Stinger was the highest-selling vehicle of the Yenko Sportscar program.

Despite the plethora of Stingers buzzing around, over time they faded from the collector and enthusiast scene. Several reasons contributed to this. All the cost-cutting measures taken on the Vega (which was intended to be inexpensive) came back to haunt the model's short- and long-term reliability. Problems were present underhood too. Despite its aluminum construction, the engine was prone to overheating, attributed to a too small radiator. The problem was addressed in the 1972 model year, with many dealers ordering the heavy-duty radiator option be equipped on new orders. Don did the same on his order of 1972 Stingers, adding it to the COPO.

In a December 1971 six-car comparison of "super coupes," *Car and Driver* found that if the shootout winner was selected purely on looks, the Vega (non-Stinger) would win without "a wheel ever being turned." However, back in November, it wrote about its long-term test comparing a Pinto and a stock Vega and it wasn't glowing. The Vega was equipped with the optional 110-hp engine and 4-speed transmission and after thousands of miles logged, while the test car wasn't a Stinger, its findings weren't positive:

Donna Mae congratulates the winners of the Group 7 sweepstakes and hands over the keys to their brand-new 1973 Yenko Turbo Stinger. (Photo Courtesy the Barr Collection)

While it is obvious that Chevrolet engineers have made a heavy commitment toward occupant comfort in the Vega, the effect of their work has been very nearly canceled out by the car's one colossal esthetic failure—the engine. Never mind all the talk about the marvelous technology involved in the liner-less aluminum block: From a noise and vibration standpoint, the Vega's four is unfit for passenger car use. At high speeds, where wind noise is the dominant sound, there is very little to choose from between the two cars, but in traffic, when accelerating up through the gears, the Vega's clattering engine and fruity sounding exhaust are genuinely unpleasant."

In addition, the second order engine shake, characteristic of all in-line 4-cylinder engines, is particularly strenuous in the Vega. It's pretty much confined to two periods with peaks at about 2,200 and 4,100 rpm. A tuned mass damper attached to the rear of the transmission effectively absorbs the high-speed disturbance but the low-speed one still tingles your toes and buzzes the shift lever as you pass

through—when we need a Magic Fingers massage we'll pay our quarter, thanks. This, combined with the noise and the rubbery, balky shifter, takes the fun out of low speed and sporting driving.

Based on that review, it's no wonder that many owners hammered on their Vegas and then quickly moved on to something else. Many Vegas rusted out and that's true for Stinger Vegas too. Yenko or not, there was little thought given for preserving them, and given their relatively cheap price point, they were used and then discarded.

The greatest reason why these special Stingers have faded into the automotive annuals of time is that no master list of serial numbers has ever surfaced. This would have allowed real Yenko Vega Stingers to be documented, accounted for, and saved. In the same way, there would be far fewer 1969 Camaro ZL1s if their identities had not been published in a magazine in the 1980s, allowing enthusiasts' hands to get to work tracking them down and preserving them. Slowly but surely, the story of the Vega Stinger is growing in attention, and enthusiasts are diligently restoring the scant few that remain to their former glory.

The EPA's unswerving stance certainly was irritating, but it didn't throw cold water on Don's plans to craft the Vega into a sporty little cruiser. While the COPO for a factory-installed turbocharger would have been a big boost to sales, making lemonade from lemons, clever Don pivoted and offered it and other speed parts to customers through his special catalog.

EPILOGUE
THE RESURGENCE OF COPO

Launching with one Stinger and closing with another, with loads of unique stuff in-between, the COPO method of ordering higher powered and performing Chevrolet vehicles story arc was complete. As the 1970s waned on, General Motors relaxed its stance and slowly but surely the brand began to re-enter the racing scene, this time officially. With it, the covert work-around to build special vehicles through the Central Office had shown it had run its course and was no longer required. In 1970, Chevrolet debuted a massive 454-ci V-8 for its Chevelle with plans to equip the latest Camaro with it too. It was clear that big motors such as the L72 427-ci V-8 were no longer the key to pump up Chevy's performance image.

COPO cars haven't lost their luster in the eyes of automotive enthusiasts. Today, they are regarded as prized crown jewels in collections. Part of their strong draw is the mystique surrounding their surreptitious creation.

Not that it mattered much, as the timing was all wrong. Going fast in a big bruiser wasn't in vogue anymore. The newly created Environmental Protection Agency (EPA) was hot and heavy in making sure automobiles were running cleaner and burning fewer emissions. Automakers scrambled to catch up and meet the demands, devoting tons of resources to develop ways to build vehicles that could comply and attract shoppers. Compression came screaming way down on engines of all makes, models, and sizes. Before long, the rumbling performance car scene had faded away, replaced by mass interest in catchy commuters and intriguing imports and a return to sensible transportation.

Awareness in the COPO-created vehicles themselves almost faded away too. Many original owners didn't know the full ins and outs of their special rides, with many making the hard decision to sell their well-loved (but extremely thirsty) muscle machines, when faced with skyrocketing gas prices. Most didn't hear the words "COPO" and "Central Office" until the 1980s if not 1990s, for years only considering their cars "427s" or "Yenkos."

True to his nature, Don Yenko endured in this new time, persistently working to develop cars that could go faster. He never failed to adapt, going even smaller than his Vega, creating his Yenko Mini Stinger, which was a hopped-up version of Honda's Civic, before moving to his Camaro Yenko Turbo Z. Neither met his expectations nor had any substantial market penetration. The Chevy dealership moved to a new location and his store at 575 West Pike became Don Yenko Imports, selling Subarus. Don Yenko was killed on March 5, 1987, when his plane crashed in Charleston, West Virginia. He was 60 years old.

Up in LaHarpe, Illinois, Fred Gibb stayed with his dealership until the early 1980s. He and his team never again attempted the kind of herculean feat they had accomplished, helping to move 50 performance-oriented Novas and 50 ZL1 Camaros and putting a flag in the sand to say that Chevrolet could compete and win. Fred passed away in 1994.

Vince Piggins remained with the Chevrolet brand until his retirement in 1983. Besides the COPO cars, he was a major force in creating the Z28 Camaro and

The Yenko Chevrolet building still stands today in Canonsburg, Pennsylvania. In 1972, Frank and Don Yenko broke ground and built a new building in nearby McMurray, relocating the dealership. The new space featured 20 shop lifts, a 12-car showroom, and more than 10,000 square feet of floor space for the parts department. Today, it's Sun Chevrolet.

It's easy to forget that the Yenko COPO cars craved by collectors all came from a humble and unassuming beginning. Rewind the clock several decades and this dusty, gravelly back lot would have been a flurry of activity with high-performance cars coming and going. The farthest back section of the building (closest to the tree line) was the dealership's paint and body area.

Imagine the heyday of the 1960s and the cool Chevy iron that would have rolled through this bay door. Before it appears too glamorous, keep in mind that former technicians, such as Warren Dernoshek, attest it was tough work, with the engine conversions happening just behind this wall, taking place in an area without a vehicle lift and a single chain hoist for pulling motors.

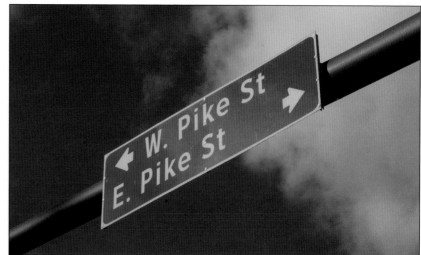

You could find Yenko Chevrolet by heading to 575 West Pike Street, not far from the quaint downtown of Canonsburg, Pennsylvania.

stayed committed to Chevy's participation in racing. He passed away in Livonia, Michigan, on October 17, 1985.

The ingenuity and hard work put in by Don Yenko, Fred Gibb, and Vince Piggins came close to being lost in the shifting sands of time. A devoted group of diehard enthusiasts worked hard to preserve their names, their memories, and the matchless cars they each helped assemble. Besides loving the vehicles, motoring enthusiasts make regular pilgrimages to the surviving buildings that housed both the Yenko and Gibb dealerships to see firsthand where it all started.

2012–2019 COPO Camaro

Recognizing the staying power and loyal following the Central Office Production program developed, in 2011 Chevy revived the name at the most fitting of locations, choosing the Specialty Equipment Market Association (SEMA). The annual show in Las Vegas is a hotbed of automotive customizing, with all kinds of dazzling creations being shown. Increasingly it's becoming the place for automakers to debut teases of performance-oriented models and concepts of their own, and for 2011, Chevrolet rolled out one wild machine, calling it the COPO Camaro. Unlike its predecessors that had some sort of streetability to them, there was no guise with this one. Just like its four-wheeled ancestors, it was meant to do one thing: drag race. The vehicle was set up specifically for the specifications of the NHRA Stock Eliminator classes.

"The COPO Camaro is a proof of concept for what a Chevrolet Stock Eliminator entry could look like," said Jim Campbell, GM US vice president of Performance Vehicles and Motorsports. "And it is a clear indication that Chevrolet intends to homologate the Camaro for sportsman drag racing."

To cement its image of being a serious competitor, the concept featured such components as a full chrome-moly roll cage, a solid rear axle, a fuel cell, a window net, and a driveshaft loop. Manual brakes and steering were also included. The car on the show floor featured a supercharged 5.3L V-8 but, in a nod to its forefathers, was built to accommodate a LSX-based 427. Many doubted that such a car would see life beyond concept phase, and best estimates were that enthusiasts could get some of the parts through GM Performance parts. But due to the overwhelming excitement and support, General Motors moved forward with it and announced a limited, special-edition run for the 2012 model year. Chevy has continued that trend ever since, choosing to build a mere 69 of the race-specced Camaros each year with that quantity nodding to the special group of 1969 ZL1s from decades ago. Each year, interested buyers register in advance and then an independent third party randomly selects purchasers from the pool of interested customers.

The cars are hand built in a special facility to top specifications and all in a matter of weeks. The cars arrive as bare bodies and then have any unwanted sheet metal removed before the chrome-moly roll cage is installed. More than 150 parts are custom fabricated for the COPO Camaro. It is also fitted with a racing chassis and suspension components, including a unique solid rear axle system in place of a regular-production Camaro's independent rear axle. Engine options include a 302-ci racing engine, a supercharged 350-ci V-8, and a naturally aspirated 427-ci V-8. All the COPO Camaro engines are backed by an SFI-approved ATI TH400 3-speed automatic transmission. The supercharged 350 enables mid-8-second quarter-mile times at

A fleet of newly created COPOs sit awaiting final inspection and customer delivery. Note the front fender badging that calls out the Camaros' unique origin. While customers can opt for different engines, you'll usually find out what's under the hood by looking at the car's hood scoop.

From the exterior to the interior, every aspect of these purpose-built track terrors is gone over in the sake of getting it faster. Note the emblazoning of COPO on the center plate, right above the toggle switches. That was something you'd never see on the COPOs of old, but now it's a bold mark of honor and heritage.

nearly 160 mph, averaging about a gallon of fuel a pass. Keeping with its dragstrip DNA, lightweight manual brakes are still installed.

Whereas during the 1960s and 1970s, "COPO" only showed up on paperwork, Chevy has now brought it back as an official badge of honor. The script shows up stamped on several parts underhood and is emblazoned on the center stack in the dashboard. Since the fuel tank has been relocated to a fuel cell inside the trunk, the standard fuel door hides a release for the trunk.

With the return of COPO and the growing awareness of the clandestine program and the cars that resulted, there's been mounting interest in the collector car circles. Information is coming to light, helping to further fan the flames and ignite the passion and desire in the hearts of enthusiasts around the globe. The vehicles command big dollars and big attention, and rightfully so. People young and old love a good story and especially one as rich as the narrative of these muscle-oriented vehicles and the colorful characters behind them.

The COPOs were born out of a desire to win, first on the track, then in the showroom, and all while under the scrutinizing eye of the US

Each year, Chevrolet Performance keeps raising the bar on what these COPO Camaros can do. With their wheelie bars, parachute, and drag slicks, there's no mistaking these for anything else but the biggest and baddest bowtie bruisers.

One Shared Part

While this new COPO Camaro is all about using the latest and greatest advances in technology, the team of engineers behind it found a fun and functional way to connect it to the model's storied lineage. The car is a thoroughly modern machine, but there's a single component with retro roots. When it came time to mount the brake lines to the underside of the vehicle, it was decided to use the same brake line retaining clips that were and can be installed on a 1969 COPO Camaro. They function as good as any new part created or available. It's a neat little throwback and subtle reminder that even though the two vehicles span decades of time and technology, they're tied together in spirit and purpose.

Tucked up on the underside of the Camaros are high-performance brake lines held in place by several clips. All that chassis and suspension bracing is necessary to keep the car planted during hard launches.

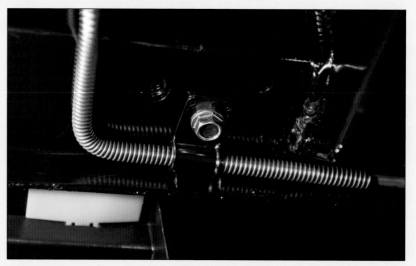

It's a simple little component, but the brake line clip was chosen specifically to harken back to the brand-new COPO Camaros' 1960s roots. It's easy to spot the brilliant blue pieces on the underside of the vehicle.

government. Shrouded in mystery, the vehicles developed a motoring mystique as they were gobbled up by leadfoots who wasted no time putting them to use, cooking tires and slamming gears, showing to all that Chevrolet still had the gusto to build a proper factory hot rod.

As fast as they came, they eerily disappeared, but today they're back in a big way, regarded as being in the upper echelons of collecting. The highly sought after, iconic COPO cars of all years are revered, esteemed, and, quite simply, the stuff of four-wheeled folklore and all-out legend.

Diehard enthusiasts gather regularly to celebrate these ultra-cool cars at such events as the Muscle Car and Corvette Nationals, held in Chicago, Illinois, and the Super Car Reunion, pictured here. Another special opportunity to get up close and personal with COPO vehicles is the Solid Lifter Showroom in Carlisle, Pennsylvania, as part of the Chevrolet Nationals. The showcase is presented by renown restorer, Super Car Workshop.

Mark Pieloch has amassed an impressive collection of COPO and Yenko vehicles in his beautiful American Muscle Car Museum. Seeing just one 1968 Yenko Camaro is a rare sight, so three parked together is an over-the-top experience.

World-class collections, like this one belonging to Dennis Albaugh, are the closest we'll come to experiencing the thrill of walking into a Chevrolet dealer showroom and being greeted by a full lineup of high-performance Yenko Camaros.

APPENDIX 1

COPO MUSCLE CARS: All 69 1969 ZL1 Camaros

COPO 9560 High-Performance Package included:

Chevrolet required power front disc brakes and limited transmission choice to 4-speed manual Muncie or Heavy-Duty Turbo-Hydramatic 400 automatic. All cars had standard black interiors.

VIN: 124379N66 x x x x	
1	Chevrolet Division
24	Camaro, 8-cylinder
37	Two-door sport coupe
9	1969 model year
N	Norwood, Ohio, assembly plant
66 x x x x	Sequence number

RPO ZL1: 427-ci V-8 aluminum engine [Factory rated: 430 hp]
- *Aluminum intake, cylinder heads, block with cast-iron sleeves*
- *NOTE: The Muncie's transmission case, bellhousing, and Turbo 400 case were aluminum too*
RPO ZL2: Special steel ducted hood assembly with underhood insulation
RPO V01: Heavy-duty 4-core radiator (NOTE: Several late build 4-speed cars had straight neck outlets)
RPO K66: Electronic transistor ignition system
RPO F41: Heavy-duty suspension (12-bolt Positraction differential [heat treated ring and pinion gears, service Posi case], five-leaf springs, special springs and shocks)

	VIN	COLOR	ORDERED BY	SOLD BY	FACTORY OPTIONS	
1	9N569358	5923 51-55 Dusk Blue	Gibb Chevrolet La Harpe, Illinois	Gibb Chevrolet La Harpe, Illinois	5J52 Power disc brakes 5M40 Turbo-Hydramatic automatic transmission (column shift) 5PL5 F70x14 white lettered tires 5711 Black vinyl trim 9560 High-performance unit	
2	9N569359	5923 51-51 Dusk Blue	Gibb Chevrolet La Harpe, Illinois	Gibb Chevrolet La Harpe, Illinois	5J52 Power disc brakes 5M40 Turbo-Hydramatic automatic transmission (column shift) 5PL5 F70x14 white lettered tires 5711 Black vinyl trim 9560 High-performance unit	
3	9N608193 2D: 4th week of February 1969	5926 76-76 Daytona Yellow	Berger Chevrolet Grand Rapids, Michigan	Berger Chevrolet Grand Rapids, Michigan	5B37 Floor mats (two front and two rear) 5D80 Air spoiler equipment 5J52 Power disc brakes 5M22 Special 4-speed transmission 5U62 AM pushbutton radio VE3 Special front bumper 5Z21 Style trim group	5711 Black vinyl trim 9560 High-performance unit 9737 Sports car conversion E70x15 R WL tires Rally wheels 13/16-inch stabilizer bar 140-mph speedometer
4	9N608214	5912 69-69 Cortez Silver	Gibb Chevrolet La Harpe, Illinois	Hauser Chevrolet Bethlehem, Pennsylvania	5J52 Power disc brakes 5M40 Turbo-Hydramatic automatic transmission (column shift) 5PL5 F70x14 white lettered tires 5711 Black vinyl trim 9560 High-performance unit	

	VIN	COLOR	ORDERED BY	SOLD BY	FACTORY OPTIONS
5	9N608381	5923 51-51 Dusk Blue	Gibb Chevrolet La Harpe, Illinois	Gibb Chevrolet La Harpe, Illinois	5J52 Power disc brakes 5M40 Turbo-Hydramatic automatic transmission (column shift) 5PL5 F70x14 white lettered tires 5711 Black vinyl trim 9560 High-performance unit
6	9N608536	5912 69-69 Cortez Silver	Gibb Chevrolet La Harpe, Illinois	Holley Chevrolet Brownwood, Texas	5J52 Power disc brakes 5M40 Turbo-Hydramatic automatic transmission (column shift) 5PL5 F70x14 white lettered tires 5711 Black vinyl trim 9560 High-performance unit
7	9N608613	5927 72-72 Hugger Orange	Gibb Chevrolet La Harpe, Illinois	Bill Dale Chevrolet Waukesha, Wisconsin	5J52 Power disc brakes 5M40 Turbo-Hydramatic automatic transmission (column shift) 5PL5 F70x14 white lettered tires 5711 Black vinyl trim 9560 High-performance unit
8	9N608761	5912 69-69 Cortez Silver	Gibb Chevrolet La Harpe, Illinois	Rosenthal Chevrolet Arlington, Virginia	5J52 Power disc brakes 5M40 Turbo-Hydramatic automatic transmission (column shift) 5PL5 F70x14 white lettered tires 5711 Black vinyl trim 9560 High-performance unit
9	9N608879	5912 69-69 Cortez Silver	Gibb Chevrolet La Harpe, Illinois	Gibb Chevrolet La Harpe, Illinois	5J52 Power disc brakes 5M40 Turbo-Hydramatic automatic transmission (column shift) 5PL5 F70x14 white lettered tires 5711 Black vinyl trim 9560 High-performance unit
10	9N608969	5923 51-51 Dusk Blue	Gibb Chevrolet La Harpe, Illinois	Van T. Chevrolet Topeka, Kansas	5J52 Power disc brakes 5M40 Turbo-Hydramatic automatic transmission (column shift) 5PL5 F70x14 white lettered tires 5711 Black vinyl trim 9560 High-performance unit
11	9N609016	5912 69-69 Cortez Silver	Gibb Chevrolet La Harpe, Illinois	Merollis Chevrolet Detroit, Michigan	5J52 Power disc brakes 5M21 4-speed close ratio transmission 5PL5 F70x14 white lettered tires 5711 Black vinyl trim 9560 High-performance unit
12	9N609149	5923 51-51 Dusk Blue	Gibb Chevrolet La Harpe, Illinois	Stauffer Chevrolet Scranton, Pennsylvania	5J52 Power disc brakes 5M21 4-speed close ratio transmission 5PL5 F70x14 white lettered tires 5711 Black vinyl trim 9560 High-performance unit
13	9N609171	5912 69-69 Cortez Silver	Gibb Chevrolet La Harpe, Illinois	Jack Coyle Chevrolet San Bernadino, California	5J52 Power disc brakes 5M21 4-speed close ratio transmission 5PL5 F70x14 white lettered tires 5711 Black vinyl trim 9560 High-performance unit

	VIN	COLOR	ORDERED BY	SOLD BY	FACTORY OPTIONS
14	9N609238	5924 71-71 Lemans Blue	Gibb Chevrolet La Harpe, Illinois	Ammon R. Smith York, Pennsylvania	5J52 Power disc brakes 5M21 4-speed close ratio transmission 5PL5 F70x14 white lettered tires 5711 Black vinyl trim 9560 High-performance unit
15	9N609372	5912 69-69 Cortez Silver	Gibb Chevrolet La Harpe, Illinois	Gibb Chevrolet La Harpe, Illinois	5J52 Power disc brakes 5M21 4-speed close ratio transmission 5PL5 F70x14 white lettered tires 5711 Black vinyl trim 9560 High-performance unit
16	9N609395	5927 72-72 Hugger Orange	Gibb Chevrolet La Harpe, Illinois	Gibb Chevrolet La Harpe, Illinois	5J52 Power disc brakes 5M21 4-speed close ratio transmission 5PL5 F70x14 white lettered tires 5711 Black vinyl trim 9560 High-performance unit
17	9N609462	5912 69-69 Cortez Silver	Gibb Chevrolet La Harpe, Illinois	Roger Penske Chevrolet Philadelphia, Pennsylvania	5J52 Power disc brakes 5M21 4-speed close ratio transmission 5PL5 F70x14 white lettered tires 5711 Black vinyl trim 9560 High-performance unit
18	9N609510	5923 51-51 Dusk Blue	Gibb Chevrolet La Harpe, Illinois	Tamson Chevrolet Danville, Virginia	5J52 Power disc brakes 5M21 4-speed close ratio transmission 5PL5 F70x14 white lettered tires 5711 Black vinyl trim 9560 High-performance unit
19	9N609530	5923 51-51 Dusk Blue	Gibb Chevrolet La Harpe, Illinois	Gibb Chevrolet La Harpe, Illinois	5J52 Power disc brakes 5M21 4-speed close ratio transmission 5PL5 F70x14 white lettered tires 5711 Black vinyl trim 9560 High-performance unit
20	9N609599	5912 69-69 Cortez Silver	Gibb Chevrolet La Harpe, Illinois	Ammon R. Smith York, Pennsylvania	5J52 Power disc brakes 5M21 4-speed close ratio transmission 5PL5 F70x14 white lettered tires 5711 Black vinyl trim 9560 High-performance unit
21	9N609651	5923 51-51 Dusk Blue	Gibb Chevrolet La Harpe, Illinois	Gibb Chevrolet La Harpe, Illinois	5J52 Power disc brakes 5M21 4-speed close ratio transmission 5PL5 F70x14 white lettered tires 5711 Black vinyl trim 9560 High-performance unit
22	9N609690	5912 69-69 Cortez Silver	Gibb Chevrolet La Harpe, Illinois	Macs Chevrolet-Olds Crete, Nebraska	5J52 Power disc brakes 5M21 4-speed close ratio transmission 5PL5 F70x14 white lettered tires 5711 Black vinyl trim 9560 High-performance unit

	VIN	COLOR	ORDERED BY	SOLD BY	FACTORY OPTIONS
23	9N609747	5923 51-51 Dusk Blue	Gibb Chevrolet La Harpe, Illinois	Lafferty Chevrolet Warminster, Pennsylvania	5J52 Power disc brakes 5M21 4-speed close ratio transmission 5PL5 F70x14 white lettered tires 5711 Black vinyl trim 9560 High-performance unit
24	9N609838	5923 51-51 Dusk Blue	Gibb Chevrolet La Harpe, Illinois	Merollis Chevrolet Detroit, Michigan	5J52 Power disc brakes 5M21 4-speed close ratio transmission 5PL5 F70x14 white lettered tires 5711 Black vinyl trim 9560 High-performance unit
25	9N609856	5927 72-72 Hugger Orange	Gibb Chevrolet La Harpe, Illinois	Roger Penske Chevrolet Philadelphia, Pennsylvania	5J52 Power disc brakes 5M40 Turbo-Hydramatic automatic transmission (column shift) 5PL5 F70x14 white lettered tires 5711 Black vinyl trim 9560 High-performance unit
26	9N609880	5927 72-72 Hugger Orange	Gibb Chevrolet La Harpe, Illinois	Nankivel Chevrolet Indianapolis, Indiana	5J52 Power disc brakes 5M21 4-speed close ratio transmission 5PL5 F70x14 white lettered tires 5711 Black vinyl trim 9560 High-performance unit
27	9N609965	5920 57-57 Fathom Green	Gibb Chevrolet La Harpe, Illinois	Alan Green Chevrolet Seattle, Washington	5J52 Power disc brakes 5M40 Turbo-Hydramatic automatic transmission (column shift) 5PL5 F70x14 white lettered tires 5711 Black vinyl trim 9560 High-performance unit
28	9N610014	5927 72-72 Hugger Orange	Gibb Chevrolet La Harpe, Illinois	Gibb Chevrolet La Harpe, Illinois	5J52 Power disc brakes 5M21 4-speed close ratio transmission 5PL5 F70x14 white lettered tires 5711 Black vinyl trim 9560 High-performance unit
29	9N610123	5927 72-72 Hugger Orange	Gibb Chevrolet La Harpe, Illinois	Bill McKay Chevrolet Fort Worth, Te x as	5J52 Power disc brakes 5M21 4-speed close ratio transmission 5PL5 F70x14 white lettered tires 5711 Black vinyl trim 9560 High-performance unit
30	9N610168	5927 72-72 Hugger Orange	Gibb Chevrolet La Harpe, Illinois	Gibb Chevrolet La Harpe, Illinois	5J52 Power disc brakes 5M21 4-speed close ratio transmission 5PL5 F70x14 white lettered tires 5711 Black vinyl trim 9560 High-performance unit
31	9N610413	5927 72-72 Hugger Orange	Gibb Chevrolet La Harpe, Illinois	Dan Streakley Chevrolet Temple, Te x as	5J52 Power disc brakes 5M40 Turbo-Hydramatic automatic transmission (column shift) 5PL5 F70x14 white lettered tires 5711 Black vinyl trim 9560 High-performance unit

	VIN	COLOR	ORDERED BY	SOLD BY	FACTORY OPTIONS
32	9N610515	5927 72-72 Hugger Orange	Gibb Chevrolet La Harpe, Illinois	Merollis Chevrolet Detroit, Michigan	5J52 Power disc brakes 5M40 Turbo-Hydramatic automatic transmission (column shift) 5PL5 F70x14 white lettered tires 5711 Black vinyl trim 9560 High-performance unit
33	9N610732	5927 72-72 Hugger Orange	Gibb Chevrolet La Harpe, Illinois	Jim Rathman Chevrolet Melbourne, Florida	5J52 Power disc brakes 5M21 4-speed close ratio transmission 5PL5 F70x14 white lettered tires 5711 Black vinyl trim 9560 High-performance unit
34	9N610899	5920 57-57 Fathom Green	Gibb Chevrolet La Harpe, Illinois	Govans Chevrolet Baltimore, Maryland	5J52 Power disc brakes 5M21 4-speed close ratio transmission 5PL5 F70x14 white lettered tires 5711 Black vinyl trim 9560 High-performance unit
35	9N612763	5920 57-57 Fathom Green	Gibb Chevrolet La Harpe, Illinois	Sutliff Chevrolet Harrisburg, Pennsylvania	5J52 Power disc brakes 5M21 4-speed close ratio transmission 5PL5 F70x14 white lettered tires 5711 Black vinyl trim 9560 High-performance unit
36	9N612913	5920 57-57 Fathom Green	Gibb Chevrolet La Harpe, Illinois	Gibb Chevrolet La Harpe, Illinois	5J52 Power disc brakes 5M21 4-speed close ratio transmission 5PL5 F70x14 white lettered tires 5711 Black vinyl trim 9560 High-performance unit
37	9N612963	5920 57-57 Fathom Green	Gibb Chevrolet La Harpe, Illinois	Merollis Chevrolet Detroit, Michigan	5J52 Power disc brakes 5M21 4-speed close ratio transmission 5PL5 F70x14 white lettered tires 5711 Black vinyl trim 9560 High-performance unit
38	9N613633	5920 57-57 Fathom Green	Gibb Chevrolet La Harpe, Illinois	Nankivel Chevrolet Indianapolis, Indiana	5J52 Power disc brakes 5M40 Turbo-Hydramatic automatic transmission (column shift) 5PL5 F70x14 white lettered tires 5711 Black vinyl trim 9560 High-performance unit
39	9N613787	5920 57-57 Fathom Green	Gibb Chevrolet La Harpe, Illinois	Jack Head Chevrolet Alhambra, California	5J52 Power disc brakes 5M40 Turbo-Hydramatic automatic transmission (column shift) 5PL5 F70x14 white lettered tires 5711 Black vinyl trim 9560 High-performance unit
40	9N615198	5920 57-57 Fathom Green	Gibb Chevrolet La Harpe, Illinois	Lustine Chevrolet Hyattsville, Maryland	5J52 Power disc brakes 5M21 4-speed close ratio transmission 5PL5 F70x14 white lettered tires 5711 Black vinyl trim 9560 High-performance unit

	VIN	COLOR	ORDERED BY	SOLD BY	FACTORY OPTIONS
41	9N615229	5924 71-71 Lemans Blue	Gibb Chevrolet La Harpe, Illinois	Sport Chevrolet Silver Spring, Maryland	5J52 Power disc brakes 5M21 4-speed close ratio transmission 5PL5 F70x14 white lettered tires 5711 Black vinyl trim 9560 High-performance unit
42	9N615242	5924 71-71 Lemans Blue	Gibb Chevrolet La Harpe, Illinois	Lustine Chevrolet Hyattsville, Maryland	5J52 Power disc brakes 5M21 4-speed close ratio transmission 5PL5 F70x14 white lettered tires 5711 Black vinyl trim 9560 High-performance unit
43	9N615362	5924 71-71 Lemans Blue	Gibb Chevrolet La Harpe, Illinois	Hauser Chevrolet Bethlehem, Pennsylvania	5J52 Power disc brakes 5M21 4-speed close ratio transmission 5PL5 F70x14 white lettered tires 5711 Black vinyl trim 9560 High-performance unit
44	9N618396	5920 57-57 Fathom Green	Gibb Chevrolet La Harpe, Illinois	Roger Penske Chevrolet Philadelphia, Pennsylvania	5J52 Power disc brakes 5M21 4-speed close ratio transmission 5PL5 F70x14 white lettered tires 5711 Black vinyl trim 9560 High-performance unit
45	9N618522	5920 57-57 Fathom Green	Gibb Chevrolet La Harpe, Illinois	Gibb Chevrolet La Harpe, Illinois	5J52 Power disc brakes 5M40 Turbo-Hydramatic automatic transmission (column shift) 5PL5 F70x14 white lettered tires 5711 Black vinyl trim 9560 High-performance unit
46	9N618562	5924 71-71 Lemans Blue	Gibb Chevrolet La Harpe, Illinois	Sutliff Chevrolet Harrisburg, Pennsylvania	5J52 Power disc brakes 5M21 4-speed close ratio transmission 5PL5 F70x14 white lettered tires 5711 Black vinyl trim 9560 High-performance unit
47	9N618713	5924 71-71 Lemans Blue	Gibb Chevrolet La Harpe, Illinois	Martin Chevrolet Virginia, Minnesota	5J52 Power disc brakes 5M40 Turbo-Hydramatic automatic transmission (column shift) 5PL5 F70x14 white lettered tires 5711 Black vinyl trim 9560 High-performance unit
48	9N618902	5924 71-71 Lemans Blue	Gibb Chevrolet La Harpe, Illinois	Gibb Chevrolet La Harpe, Illinois	5J52 Power disc brakes 5M21 4-speed close ratio transmission 5PL5 F70x14 white lettered tires 5711 Black vinyl trim 9560 High-performance unit
49	9N619976	5924 71-71 Lemans Blue	Gibb Chevrolet La Harpe, Illinois	Bill Dale Chevrolet Waukesha, Wisconsin (possibly)	5J52 Power disc brakes 5M40 Turbo-Hydramatic automatic transmission (column shift) 5PL5 F70x14 white lettered tires 5711 Black vinyl trim 9560 High-performance unit

	VIN	COLOR	ORDERED BY	SOLD BY	FACTORY OPTIONS	
50	9N620498	5924 71-71 Lemans Blue	Gibb Chevrolet La Harpe, Illinois	Merollis Chevrolet Detroit, Michigan	5J52 Power disc brakes 5M40 Turbo-Hydramatic automatic transmission (column shift) 5PL5 F70x14 white lettered tires 5711 Black vinyl trim 9560 High-performance unit	
51	9N620923	5911 50-50 Dover White	Brooks Chevrolet Mullen, Georgia	Brooks Chevrolet Mullen, Georgia	5A01 Soft-Ray tinted glass 5D80 Air spoiler equipment 5J52 Power disc brakes 5M21 4-speed close ratio transmission	5Z21 Style trim group 5Z23 Special interior group 5715 Dark blue vinyl trim 9560 High-performance unit
52	9N620934	5924 71-71 Lemans Blue	Gibb Chevrolet La Harpe, Illinois	Jim Rathman Chevrolet Melbourne, Florida	5J52 Power disc brakes 5M40 Turbo-Hydramatic automatic transmission (column shift) 5PL5 F70x14 white lettered tires 5711 Black vinyl trim 9560 High-performance unit	
53	9N634918	5911 50-50 Dover White	Robert Lyle Chevrolet Cuyahoga, Ohio	Robert Lyle Chevrolet Cuyahoga, Ohio	5D80 Air spoiler equipment 5J52 Power disc brakes 5M22 Special 4-speed transmission 5PL5 F70x14 white lettered tires	5U63 AM pushbutton radio 5ZJ7 Rally wheels 5711 Black vinyl trim 9560 High-performance unit
54	9N635720	5924 71-71 Lemans Blue	Stedelbauer Chevrolet Edmonton, Alberta, Canada	Cliff Bristow Motors Three Hills, Alberta, Canada	5C08 Vinyl top 5D55 Center console 5D80 Air spoiler equipment 5J52 Power disc brakes 5M40 Turbo-Hydramatic automatic transmission (column shift) 5N40 Power steering 5PL5 F70x14 white lettered tires 5729 Ivory/Houndstooth trim 9560 High-performance unit 5T60 Heavy-duty battery 5U17 Special instrumentation	5VE3 Special front bumper 5Z87 Custom interior *Additional Canadian codes:* 5V48 Increased engine coolant 5W84 Additional gas ZK8 Tire pressure decal ZN1 COPO axle 4.10 Posi ZP1 COPO F70x14 RWL tires ZQ7 Canadian warranty booklets ZV9 Special order processing
55	9N641266	5924 71-71 Lemans Blue	Whit Chevrolet Fayetteville, Arkansas	Whit Chevrolet Fayetteville, Arkansas	5A01 Soft-Ray tinted glass 5C08 Vinyl top 5D55 Center console 5D80 Air spoiler equipment 5J52 Power disc brakes 5M21 4-speed close ratio transmission 5N40 Power steering 5PL5 F70x14 white lettered tires	5727 White vinyl trim 9560 High-performance unit 5U17 Special instrumentation 5U63 AM pushbutton radio 5U80 Rear seat speaker 5Z22 Rally sport equipment 5Z23 Special interior group
56	9N641310	5911 50-50 Dover White	Lowe Chevrolet Upper Marlboro, Maryland	Sport Chevrolet Silver Spring, Maryland	5D80 Air spoiler equipment 5J52 Power disc brakes 5M21 4-speed close ratio transmission 5Z21 Style trim group	5VE3 Special front bumper 5711 Black vinyl trim 9560 High-performance unit
57	9N642468	5926 76-76 Daytona Yellow	Brewers Chevrolet Campton, Kentucky	Brewers Chevrolet Campton, Kentucky	5D80 Air spoiler equipment 5J52 Power disc brakes 5M21 Special 4-speed transmission 5PL5 F70x14 white lettered tires	5U63 AM pushbutton radio 5711 Black vinyl trim 9560 High-performance unit

	VIN	COLOR	ORDERED BY	SOLD BY	FACTORY OPTIONS	
58	9N642835	5913 52-52 Garnet Red	Indian River Chevrolet Cocoa, Florida	Indian River Chevrolet Cocoa, Florida	5A01 Soft-Ray tinted glass 5D80 Air spoiler equipment 5J52 Power disc brakes 5M22 Special 4-speed transmission 5N34 Sport-styled steering wheel	5VE3 Special front bumper 5ZJ7 Rally wheels 5711 Black vinyl trim 9560 High-performance unit
59	9N642876	5927 72-72 Hugger Orange	Hechler Chevrolet Richmond, Virginia	Courtesy Chevrolet Fredericksburg, Virginia	5J52 Power disc brakes 5M22 Special 4-speed transmission 5NC8 Chambered dual exhaust 5PL5 F70x14 white lettered tires 5U63 AM pushbutton radio	5Z21 Style trim group 5ZJ7 Rally wheels 5711 Black vinyl trim 9560 High-performance unit
60	9N642903	5920 57-57 Fathom Green	Scuncio Chevrolet Inc. Greenville, Rhode Island	Scuncio Chevrolet Inc. Greenville, Rhode Island	5D80 Air spoiler equipment 5J52 Power disc brakes 5M22 Special 4-speed transmission 5PL5 F70x14 white lettered tires	5U63 AM pushbutton radio 5711 Black vinyl trim 9560 High-performance unit
61	9N642927	5920 57-57 Fathom Green	Seltzer Chevrolet Yukon, Oklahoma	Seltzer Chevrolet Yukon, Oklahoma	5J52 Power disc brakes 5M21 4-speed close ratio transmission 5711 Black vinyl trim 9560 High-performance unit	
62	9N642934	5913 52-52 Garnet Red	Seltzer Chevrolet Yukon, Oklahoma	Colonial Chevrolet Norfolk, Virginia	5J52 Power disc brakes 5M22 Special 4-speed transmission 5PL5 F70x14 white lettered tires 5U63 AM pushbutton radio	5Z23 Special interior group 5Z18 Red vinyl trim 5Z21 Style trim group 9560 High-performance unit
63	9N643047	5927 72-72 Hugger Orange	Burt Chevrolet Englewood, Colorado	Burt Chevrolet Englewood, Colorado	5D55 Center console 5D80 Air spoiler equipment 5J52 Power disc brakes 5M22 Special 4-speed transmission 5PL5 F70x14 white lettered tires 5N34 Sport-styled steering wheel	5U63 AM pushbutton radio 5Z23 Special interior group 5Z21 Style trim group 5U17 Special instrumentation 5711 Black vinyl trim 9560 High-performance unit
64	9N643171	5927 72-72 Hugger Orange	Indian River Chevrolet Cocoa, Florida	Indian River Chevrolet Cocoa, Florida	5A01 Soft-Ray tinted glass 5D80 Air spoiler equipment 5J52 Power disc brakes 5M40 Turbo-Hydramatic automatic transmission (column shift) 5U63 AM pushbutton radio	5VE3 Special front bumper 5N34 Sport-styled steering wheel 5ZJ7 Rally wheels 5711 Black vinyl trim 9560 High-performance unit
65	9N643779	5920 57-57 Fathom Green	Lavery Chevrolet Alliance, Ohio	Lavery Chevrolet Alliance, Ohio	5J52 Power disc brakes 5M21 4-speed close ratio transmission 5PL5 F70x14 white lettered tires 5711 Black vinyl trim 9560 High-performance unit	9737 Sports car conversion - E70x15 RWL tires - Rally wheels - 13/16-inch stabilizer bar - 140-mph speedometer
66	9N644311	5912 69-69 Cortez Silver	Huffmans Chevrolet Farmington, Illinois	Huffmans Chevrolet Farmington, Illinois	5D80 Air spoiler equipment 5J52 Power disc brakes 5M22 Special 4-speed transmission 5VE3 Special front bumper	5ZJ7 Rally wheels 5711 Black vinyl trim 9560 High-performance unit

	VIN	COLOR	ORDERED BY	SOLD BY	FACTORY OPTIONS	
67	9N644314	5927 72-72 Hugger Orange	Huffmans Chevrolet Farmington, Illinois	Huffmans Chevrolet Farmington, Illinois	5D80 Air spoiler equipment 5J52 Power disc brakes 5M21 4-speed close ratio transmission 5PL5 F70x14 white lettered tires	5VE3 Special front bumper 5U63 AM pushbutton radio 5711 Black vinyl trim 9560 High-performance unit
68	9N650643	5912 69-69 Cortez Silver	Tom Harris Chevrolet Zionsville, Indiana	Geyer Chevrolet-Olds Winchester, Indiana	5DX1 Front accent striping 5D55 Center console 5D80 Air spoiler equipment 5J52 Power disc brakes 5M22 Special 4-speed transmission 5N44 Special steering equipment 5PL4 F70x14 FG belted white lettered tires 5U63 AM pushbutton radio	5U17 Special instrumentation 5VE3 Special front bumper 5ZJ7 Rally wheels 5Z22 Rally Sport equipment 5Z23 Special interior group 5Z11 Black vinyl trim 9560 High-performance unit
69	9N650977	5927 72-72 Hugger Orange	Huebner Chevrolet Carrollton, Ohio	Huebner Chevrolet Carrollton, Ohio	5D80 Air spoiler equipment 5J52 Power disc brakes 5M22 Special 4-speed transmission 5U63 AM pushbutton radio	5Z21 Style trim group 5711 Black vinyl trim 9560 High-performance unit

Paint Color Distribution

1969 ZL1 CAMARO PRODUCTION			GIBB'S 50 CARS		OTHER 19 CARS	
PAINT COLOR	QTY.	Percent	M40	MANUAL	M40	MANUAL
HUGGER ORANGE	15	22	4	6	1	4
CORTEZ SILVER	12	17	4	6	--	2
FATHOM GREEN	12	17	4	6	--	2
Lemans BLUE	12	17	4	6	1	1
DUSK BLUE	10	15	4	6	--	--
DOVER WHITE	4	6	--	--	--	4
DAYTONA YELLOW	2	3	--	--	--	2
GARNET RED	2	3	--	--	--	2
TOTAL	69	100	20	30	2	17

APPENDIX 2

1968 Gibb Novas

Digit 1: GM Division: 1 = Chevrolet
Digit 2 and 3: Model Series: 14 = Chevy II Nova, V-8
Digits 4 and 5: Body style: 69 = Four-door sedan

Digit 6: Model Year: 8 = 1968
Digits 7: Assembly Plant: W = Willow Run, Michigan
Digits 8-13: Production Sequence

	VIN Number	Color Code	Color Description	Trans
1	114278W369422	KK	Tripoli Turquoise	A/T
2	114278W369560	KK	Tripoli Turquoise	A/T
3	114278W369560	KK	Tripoli Turquoise	A/T
4	114278W369657	KK	Tripoli Turquoise	A/T
5	114278W369684	HH	Grecian Green	A/T
6	114278W369724	HH	Grecian Green	A/T
7	114278W369775	HH	Grecian Green	A/T
8	114278W369802	KK	Tripoli Turquoise	A/T
9	114278W369826	KK	Tripoli Turquoise	A/T
10	114278W369853	HH	Grecian Green	A/T
11	114278W369877	HH	Grecian Green	A/T
12	114278W369904	HH	Grecian Green	A/T
13	114278W369928	RR	Matador Red	A/T
14	114278W369954	KK	Tripoli Turquoise	A/T
15	114278W369979	HH	Grecian Green	A/T
16	114278W370006	HH	Grecian Green	A/T
17	114278W370037	KK	Tripoli Turquoise	A/T
18	114278W370060	RR	Matador Red	A/T
19	114278W370097	HH	Grecian Green	A/T
20	114278W370118	KK	Tripoli Turquoise	A/T
21	114278W370138	HH	Grecian Green	A/T
22	114278W370191	KK	Tripoli Turquoise	A/T
23	114278W370254	RR	Matador Red	A/T
24	114278W370275	RR	Matador Red	A/T
25	114278W370293	RR	Matador Red	A/T

	VIN Number	Color Code	Color Description	Trans
26	114278W370324	RR	Matador Red	A/T
27	114278W370677	RR	Matador Red	A/T
28	114278W370804	RR	Matador Red	A/T
29	114278W370905	RR	Matador Red	A/T
30	114278W371036	RR	Matador Red	A/T
31	114278W372684	EE	Fathom Blue	A/T
32	114278W372827	EE	Fathom Blue	A/T
33	114278W372841	EE	Fathom Blue	A/T
34	114278W372858	EE	Fathom Blue	A/T
35	114278W372910	EE	Fathom Blue	A/T
36	114278W372933	EE	Fathom Blue	A/T
37	114278W372950	EE	Fathom Blue	A/T
38	114278W372997	EE	Fathom Blue	A/T
39	114278W373034	EE	Fathom Blue	A/T
40	114278W373043	EE	Fathom Blue	A/T
41	114278W373063	EE	Fathom Blue	A/T
42	114278W373148	EE	Fathom Blue	A/T
43	114278W373165	EE	Fathom Blue	A/T
44	114278W373175	EE	Fathom Blue	A/T
45	114278W373216	EE	Fathom Blue	A/T
46	114278W373233	EE	Fathom Blue	A/T
47	114278W373318	EE	Fathom Blue	A/T
48	114278W373335	EE	Fathom Blue	A/T
49	114278W373441	EE	Fathom Blue	A/T
50	114278W373518	EE	Fathom Blue	A/T

INDEX

Additional books that may interest you...

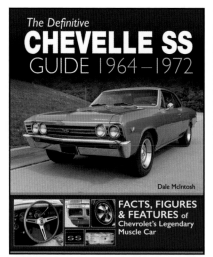

THE DEFINITIVE CHEVELLE SS GUIDE 1964–1972 *by Dale McIntosh* Beginning in 1969, the Chevelle SS was no longer its own model and relegated to being an option package. Hence, it can become difficult to determine if a 1969–1972 model was ordered from the factory with Super Sport equipment. Author and noted Chevelle expert Dale McIntosh discusses each model in a year-by-year format providing correct information on what was and wasn't part of the Malibu SS, SS396, and SS-optioned Chevelle. Softbound, 8.5 x 11, 192 pages, 450 photos. *Item # CT604*

CHEVY BIG-BLOCK ENGINE PARTS INTERCHANGE: The Ultimate Guide to Sourcing & Selecting Compatible Factory Parts *by John Baechtel* Hundreds of factory part numbers, RPOs, and detailed color photos covering all generations of the Chevy big-block engine are included. Every component is detailed, from crankshafts and rods to cylinder heads and intakes. You learn what works, what doesn't, and how to swap components among different engine displacements and generations. Author John Baechtel shares his experience of more than 34 years of engine and vehicle testing to answer your tough interchange questions. He also offers tips for tracking down rare parts. Softbound, 8.5 x 11 inches, 144 pages, 350 color photos. *Item # SA254*

SELLING THE AMERICAN MUSCLE CAR: Marketing Detroit Iron in the 60s and 70s *by Diego Rosenberg* Manufacturers poured millions into racing programs, operating under the principle of "Win on Sunday, Sell on Monday." Cars were given catchy nicknames, such as The GTO Judge, Plymouth Roadrunner, Cobra, and Dodge Super Bee. Entire manufacturer lines were given catchy marketing campaigns, such as Dodge's Scat Pack, AMC's Go Package, and Ford's Total Performance. Selling the American Muscle Car: Marketing Detroit Iron in the 60s and 70s takes you back to an era when options were plentiful and performance was cheap. You will relive or be introduced to some of the cleverest marketing campaigns created during a time when America was changing every day. Hardbound, 10 x 10 inches, 192 pages, 290 color and 145 b/w photos. *Item # CT542*

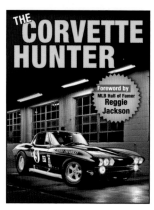

THE CORVETTE HUNTER: Kevin Mackay's Greatest Corvette Finds *by Tyler Greenblatt* Kevin Mackay tells story after story of finding and restoring valuable Corvettes such as the 1960 Briggs Cunningham Le Mans racer that took 1st in class. He also tells stories of Steve McQueen's 1966 Corvette, the 1967 Bounty Hunter racer, 1968 Sunray DX #2 and #3, and chassis #003 from 1953. If you like L88 Corvettes, no one has bought and restored more of them than Kevin Mackay! Few authorities in the hobby could be counted on to provide this much entertainment in a single volume. Hardbound, 6 x 9 inches, 240 pages, 110 photos. *Item # CT599*